ACADEMIC CAPITALISM

Sheila Slaughter
and
Larry L. Leslie

ACADEMIC CAPITALISM

Politics, Policies,
and the
Entrepreneurial
University

The Johns Hopkins University Press
BALTIMORE AND LONDON

© 1997 THE JOHNS HOPKINS UNIVERSITY PRESS
All rights reserved. Published 1997
Printed in the United States of America on acid-free recycled paper

Johns Hopkins Paperbacks edition, 1999
9 8 7 6 5 4 3 2 1

THE JOHNS HOPKINS UNIVERSITY PRESS
2715 North Charles Street
Baltimore, Maryland 21218-4363
www.press.jhu.edu

Library of Congress Cataloging-in-Publication Data will be
found at the end of this book. A catalog record for this book is
available from the British Library.

ISBN 0-8018-6258-2 (pbk.)

To Gary Rhoades, who generously filled in for us when we were in Australia and who carried on with us a sustained dialogue that contributed greatly to the final manuscript; to Doug Woodard, who always reminded us that education at public research universities is for undergraduate students; to John Levin, last but not least, who checked our American analyses with Canadian sensibilities

CONTENTS

TABLES

ACKNOWLEDGMENTS

We wish to thank the Fulbright Foundation for funding our initial research in Australia, as well as the many Australians who helped us find our way in a strange land: Jan Currie, Don Smart, Grant Harmon, Kay Harmon, Ross Harrold, Roy Laurens, Simon Marginson, Brian Martin, and the many faculty and administrators who were willing to be interviewed and share with us their views on the entrepreneurial university and the changing nature of academic labor. We also want to thank the many people who read and commented on various versions of this manuscript: Philip Altbach, Robert Berdahl, Jan Currie, Ross Harrold, John Levin, Gary Rhoades, Michael Skolnik, and Gareth Williams. We are grateful to the Ethics and Values Studies Program, now expanded to the Societal Dimensions of Engineering, Science, and Technology Program of the National Science Foundation, for funding that supported our research on academic science and technology policy.

ACADEMIC CAPITALISM

1

ACADEMIC CAPITALISM

In this book we examine ongoing changes in the nature of academic labor between 1970 and 1995, with an emphasis on the 1980s and 1990s. We argue that the changes taking place currently are as great as the changes in academic labor which occurred during the last quarter of the nineteenth century. As the industrial revolution at the end of the nineteenth century created the wealth that provided the base for postsecondary education and attendant professionalization, so the globalization of the political economy at the end of the twentieth century is destabilizing patterns of university professional work developed over the past hundred years. Globalization is creating new structures, incentives, and rewards for some aspects of academic careers and is simultaneously instituting constraints and disincentives for other aspects of careers.

The Scope of Change

We are not the only ones to argue that higher education as an institution and faculty as its labor force face change unprecedented in this century. David Breneman (1993b) deploys financial data persuasively, making the case that state and federal funds are diminishing as part of the higher education resource mix. He does not see these financial changes as an aberration in historical funding patterns, but as a new reality to which higher education will have to accommodate. James Fairweather (1988) studies how colleges and universities try to compensate for diminished government revenues through liaisons with business and industry, through partnerships focused on innovative product development, and through the marketing of educational and business services. Patricia Gumport and Brian Pusser (1995) examine the power accrued by state system administrative offices to shape programs and curricula and to standardize and routinize faculty work while costs are transferred to students. William Massy and Robert Zemsky (1990, 1994) speak to changing patterns of academic work, driven by an academic ratcheting process that encourages ever more research and is accompanied by a complex "administrative lattice" to

1

manage it, especially the growth of research on the perimeter of the university, where entrepreneurial centers and institutes bring in increasing amounts of external funds. Gary Rhoades (1997) writes about the legal and economic changes that promote increased management prerogatives to shape academic work and the concomitant loss of power on the part of unionized faculty. His analysis of union contracts reveals the erosion of faculty ability to set work loads, to establish staffing parameters, and to set broad curricular directions. Henry Etzkowitz and Loet Leydesdorff (1997) document the place of universities in the global knowledge economy.

Scholars of other countries address similar changes in higher education. Burton Clark (1993) writes about innovative European universities that are characterized by increased entrepreneurship; conflicting faculty and administrative values, especially around governance issues; and greater diversification of institutional funding. He points to a shift of cutting-edge institutional action from the liberal arts core to an entrepreneurial periphery. In the United Kingdom, Gareth Williams (1992, 1995) describes broad patterns of financial change which reduced government funding for universities and encouraged faculty to bring in increased external money for their units to survive. Michael Gibbons et al. (1994) study how changes in funding work to bring the university and its faculty in line with economic production and the managerial revolution taking place as a global economy develops. Although they emphasize the changes in science, engineering, and professional schools, which they now see as the center of the university, they also note that segments of all fields, including the social sciences and the humanities, are aligning themselves with the market. In Australia, John Smyth's (1995) edited volume *Academic Work* chronicles changes that, in broad outline, parallel those that have occurred in the United Kingdom. Simon Marginson (1993, 1995) elaborates on the "marketization" or increased market and marketlike behavior in which Australian institutions and faculty engage. In Canada, Howard Buchbinder and Janice Newson (1990), Buchbinder and Rajagopal (1993, 1995), and Newson (1994), too, describe diminished government funding and the beginning of marketization.

Our book draws heavily on the work of these scholars, using it to paint a broad picture of the changes faced by faculty and institutions of higher education, in particular, public research universities. Our work differs from that of these scholars in that we bring together topics that are usually treated separately, notably undergraduate and graduate education, teaching and research, student aid policies and federal research policies. Rather than looking at undergraduate education and the issues related to it (student aid policy, tuition costs, faculty productivity) as separate from graduate education, and at the issues that surround graduate education (national science and technology policy, including government research priorities, federal research funding, business and industry research funding), we bring these together so we can better grasp the degree of change taking place and begin to understand the forces driving it. We try to analyze change using a variety of theories and data sets, depending on our level of analysis: macro-political economic theory and national higher education policies to understand the global reach of change and how it plays out in higher education and research policies; resource dependence theory and data on national higher education financial trends to help us grasp the degree of postsecondary education change which has occurred at the level of the nation state; process theories of professionalization and case studies of institutions where faculty and administrators engage in entrepreneurial activities that are the spearhead of change; sociology of knowledge and case studies of faculty engaged in technology transfer which allow us to glimpse how faculty create new epistemologies in a changing world.

We divided our book informally into two parts and a conclusion. The first three chapters provide an introduction and overview. Chapter One introduces the key concepts and theories. In Chapter Two we examine global political economic change and then look at how Australia, Canada, the United Kingdom, and the United States developed national higher education and research policies that responded to the emergence of global markets. In Chapter Three we present data on higher education finance patterns for these four countries over a twenty-year period. These data show how the countries' postsecondary systems were shaped by the emergence of a global economy and resultant national higher education and research policy changes.

In the second part of the book, Chapters Four through Six, we present case studies of various institutions. The case studies concentrate on faculty and administrators engaged in the sorts of entrepreneurial activity so characteristic of academe's response to the macro-level changes presented in the first three chapters. In Chapter Four we examine how successful academic entrepreneurs assess the advantages and disadvantages of their work. We interviewed all faculty who generated external revenues above a certain cutoff point; the units they represented ranged from engineering centers to physical education. In Chapter Five we present case studies of faculty who were involved with a particular form of entrepreneurial activity, technology transfer, which is the movement of products and processes from the university to the market. In Chapter Six we focus again on faculty who transferred technology to the market, looking closely at how their work shapes their epistemology. We explore changing faculty values, norms, and beliefs. *base?*

In the conclusion, Chapter Seven, we sum up our findings and spell out the consequences for faculty and administrators in terms of academic life at the unit level (center and department), at the college level, and with regard to central administration. We also suggest likely impacts that increased faculty and institutional interaction with the market might have on different segments of the university, analyzing them in terms of closeness to or distance from the market.

During the industrial revolution, faculty in various nation states were able to position themselves between capital and labor, protecting themselves from the harsh discipline of the market (Abbott 1988; Perkin 1989). Professionals negotiated a tacit social contract with the community at large, in which they received monopolies of practice in return for disinterestedly serving the public good (Furner 1975; Bledstein 1976; Haskell 1977). The very concept of a professional[1] turned on the practitioner eschewing market rewards in return for a monopoly of practice. Professionals made the case that they were guided by ideals of service and altruism. They did not seek to maximize profits; they claimed to put the interests of client and community first.

Although numerous scholars have questioned the degree to which profes-

1. All want to define themselves as professionals because professionalism is associated with status and prestige. In modern parlance the term is often used loosely to describe any occupation other than manual labor or blue collar work. In medieval times professionals were usually organized in guilds, were learned, and frequently possessed higher degrees, most often in theology, medicine, and law. In the nineteenth and twentieth centuries as specialization occurred, more occupations were classified as professions. Those included usually called for advanced learning and were often protected by state licensure from the pressures of the market, as was the case with medicine and law. University professors were not licensed by the state but were examined extensively by members of their specialties in the course of obtaining advanced degrees. From the 1950s through the 1970s sociologists of the professions frequently made the case that professionals were characterized by command of a body of specialized knowledge informed by theory, had sufficient autonomy to use that knowledge effectively, were licensed or accredited, and had a code of ethics and a tradition of service to society, in return for which they were exempted from market competition but received adequate compensation. Before the 1970s professionals were often, but certainly not always, self-employed. Professionals who met these criteria but were inadequately compensated were often referred to as members of the semiprofessions, which were often heavily dominated by women, for example, teachers, nurses, social workers, and librarians. In the 1970s and 1980s process theorists of professionalization challenged the earlier view, arguing that professionals were defined as much by their organizational ability and political power as by their expertise; they were deemed professionals when they were able to win jurisdictional wars and create monopolies of practice which ensured them prestige, power, and high salaries. In other words, the definition of a profession has always been hotly contested. Scholars agree that doctors, lawyers, and university professors are professionals, but these are only a very few of those who lay claim to being professionals. Professions are not fixed and static but always in the process of being socially constructed. For a more detailed review of the sociology of professions, see Chapters Five and Six as well as Larson (1977), Collins (1979), Abbott (1988), and Brint (1994).

sionals realized these ideals, for the most part professionals in the first half of
the twentieth century did not participate directly in the market (Larson 1977;
Starr 1982). Their interaction with the market was mediated by professional associations and by the law. Professionals did not advertise; they served clients,
not customers; they often charged standardized fees that would have been considered price fixing on the open market. Persons not professionally certified
were legally prevented from offering a wide variety of professional services
(Brint 1994).

Faculty are a subset of professionals, although in some ways they are the
paramount professionals because they have monopolies on advanced degrees
and train and credential all other professionals. In this, their professional status
is almost unique. In many ways, faculty historically have been more insulated
from the market than have other professionals. Because they have worked for
institutions that were nonprofit and often state funded, they have not become
fee-for-service practitioners, whether solo or in group practice. Moreover, colleges and universities have had a tradition of autonomy from the market and
the state (American Association of University Professors 1915; Berdahl, Levin,
and Ziegenhagen 1978).

During the second half of the twentieth century, professors, like other professionals, gradually became more involved in the market (Slaughter and
Rhoades 1990; Brint 1994). In the 1980s globalization accelerated the movement of faculty and universities toward the market in ways we will describe below. We think the 1980s were a turning point, when faculty and universities
were incorporated into the market to the point where professional work began
to be patterned differently, *in kind* rather than in degree. Participation in the
market began to undercut the tacit contract between professors and society because the market put as much emphasis on the bottom line as on client welfare.
The *raison d'être* for special treatment for universities, the training ground of
professionals, as well as for professional privilege, was undermined, increasing
the likelihood that universities, in the future, will be treated more like other
organizations and professionals more like other workers.

The changes surrounding faculty and universities as they move into the market are complex and are seen most clearly at the increasingly permeable boundaries between the research university and its work force and the world outside
the academy. Although these changes have far-reaching consequences for all of
postsecondary education, we concentrate on public research universities
because the changes in the nature of faculty patterns of work are most dramatic
at these sites. Because these changes are impelled as much by organizations,
institutions, and social forces outside higher education as inside, we use

theories and concepts that are not an integral part of the higher education literature to explain them. To deal with the complexity of the change we use different theories, data sets, and methods. At the international level, we use political economic theories, data on global economic change, and data on various higher education and research policies. At the national level, we use higher education finance data from Australia, Canada, the United Kingdom, and the United States, and we connect these data to resource dependence theory. At the institutional level, we use process theories of professionalization and sociology of science to help us interpret data from our case studies. In the course of this book we try to explain terms, to define what may be unfamiliar concepts, to provide an understanding of the several theories, and to clarify the way the theories articulate with each other at the several levels. We ask our readers to have patience and bear with us as we put forward our lines of argument, which at times are complex; we hope the material we present will repay close attention.

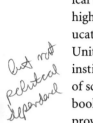
but not political dependent

The political economic changes we examine are global and structural; they are not likely to disappear, allowing us to return to business as usual. In the 1970s and 1980s markets became global, in considerable part because of increased economic competition from Pacific Rim countries. Multinational conglomerates (large corporations manufacturing unrelated products) began to dominate the world economy. Established industrialized countries, such as the United Kingdom and the United States, lost shares of world markets to the Pacific Rim countries. Multinational corporations in established industrialized countries responded to the loss of market share by investing in new technologies so they would remain competitive in global markets. These corporations turned increasingly to research universities for science-based products and processes to market in a global economy.

The biological sciences exemplify the growing involvement of science and technology (or perhaps science *as* technology [Forman 1994]) in the marketplace. Before the 1980s, biology was a basic science whose faculty were concerned primarily with performing research for the National Science Foundation and authoring papers for scholarly conferences and journals. As corporations became more aggressive in their search for products for highly competitive global markets, they began to invest in molecular biology, the key to biotechnology. By the mid 1980s, most full professors of molecular biology held equity positions (they were given stock in return for their expertise) in spinoff companies (small corporations based on products developed in university or government laboratories) that sold products to large corporations and were on the national advisory boards of corporations with biotechnology products (Kenney 1986; Krimsky 1991). Corporations supplied 45 percent of the funding for academic biotechnology (U.S. Congress, Office of Technology Assessment 1991). When biology departments were restructured to feature molecular biology, many faculty became entrepreneurs.

Biology was not the only basic science that became entrepreneurial and whose faculty lost their relative insulation from the market. In the 1980s a variety of interdisciplinary centers and departments developed—materials science, optical science, cognitive science—which became involved increasingly in market activity. The shift occurred because the corporate quest for new products converged with faculty and institutional searches for increased funding.

As the economy globalized, the business or corporate sector in industrialized countries pushed the state to devote more resources to the enhancement and management of innovation so that corporations and the nations in which they were headquartered could compete more successfully in world markets (Jessop 1993). Business leaders wanted government to sponsor commercial research and development in research universities and in government laboratories. In the United States, the National Science Foundation, once regarded as the bastion of basic research, developed industry-university cooperative research centers in the 1980s and, under President Clinton, a national science and technology policy exemplified by the Advanced Technology Programs housed in the Department of Commerce (Slaughter and Rhoades 1996). In the United Kingdom, interdisciplinary research centers involving academic-industry-government funding emerged in the 1980s. Australia modeled its Cooperative Research Centers, founded in the 1990s, on the models provided by the United Kingdom and the United States (Hill 1993). Under Prime Minister Mulroney, Canada attempted to develop university-industry-government partnerships by tying increases in university research funding to corporate contributions for university research or for national research councils (Julien 1989). In all four countries, corporate CEOs worked with university leaders and government officials to develop partnerships aimed at bringing new products and processes to market (Slaughter 1990; Slaughter and Rhoades 1996). Faculty and research universities were willing to consider partnerships with business and government based on commercial innovation because government spending on higher education was slowing down.

The flow of public money to higher education was receding, in part because of increasing claims on government funds. In the 1970s the emergence of global financial markets made possible the financing of ever larger debts in western industrialized countries. These moneys were used primarily for entitlement programs (federally funded programs to which every citizen has a claim, e.g., primary and secondary education, health care, and Social Security), for debt service, and in the United States, for military expansion. As borrowing increased, federal shares of funding for postsecondary education programs, particularly research and development, decreased (Slaughter and Rhoades 1996).

In public research universities in the United States, the federal government is the primary funding agent for student aid and for research grants and contracts, but the several states[2] generally pay faculty salaries and institutional operating expenses. As the share of federal funds for higher education decreased, the states picked up some of the burden, but not all, because the states, too, were spending the bulk of their moneys on entitlement or mandated programs such as health care and prisons. After 1983, states periodically experienced fiscal crisis (state income failed to match state expenditures) that precipitated restructuring in higher education. In 1993–94 the several states, for the first time, experienced an absolute decline in the amount of money expended on higher education rather than a decline in the share of resources provided or in inflation-adjusted expenditures per student. Restructuring often put increased resources at the disposal of units and departments close to the market, that is, those relatively able to generate external grants and contracts or other sources of revenue. At the state and federal levels, then, conditions of financial uncertainty encouraged faculty and institutions to direct their efforts toward programs and research that intersected with the market.

To maintain or expand resources, faculty had to compete increasingly for external dollars that were tied to market-related research, which was referred to variously as applied, commercial, strategic, and targeted research, whether these moneys were in the form of research grants and contracts, service contracts, partnerships with industry and government, technology transfer, or the recruitment of more and higher fee-paying students. We call institutional and professorial market or marketlike efforts to secure external moneys *academic capitalism*.[3]

We had numerous and lengthy discussions with our colleagues about the term *academic capitalism*. Although some thought the term appropriate, others thought that it too strongly connoted a Faustian bargain with the "business class" (heads of large corporations who have regular face-to-face meetings on

---

2. When we use the term *state*, we mean the executive branch and administrative arm of government at the federal or national level. For the United States and Canada we will specify states or provinces or use the terms *the several states* or *the provincial governments*.

3. We are not the first to use the term *academic capitalism*. Edward J. Hackett (1990) uses the term to summarize important structural changes in academic science and notes that Max Weber described medicine and natural science as state capitalist enterprises sixty-five years earlier.

a series of boards and forums and are concerned with national policy formation [Useem 1984]). Especially in Australia, our somewhat social democratic
colleagues saw *academic capitalism* as conjuring up stronger images of exploitation of the academic labor force than were warranted by current practices
in colleges and universities. Others in Australia thought the term slighted the
state, especially given that the state in most cases provided the great bulk of external moneys for universities and colleges, whether these were for basic or applied research, for university-industry partnerships, or for for-profit ventures
handled through arm's-length corporations (corporations that are related to
universities in terms of personnel and goals but are chartered legally as separate
entities). Generally these (sometimes heated) discussions revealed the inade-
quacy of extant language to address changes that blur the customary boundaries between private and public sectors. The same kinds of language limitations make problematic descriptions of the increasing numbers of hybrid
organizations emerging in a period of privatization and deregulation. In the
end, because no one was able to formulate a more precise term, we decided to
employ *academic capitalism* in part because alternatives—*academic entrepreneurism* or *entrepreneurial activity*—seemed to be euphemisms for *academic
capitalism* which failed to capture fully the encroachment of the profit motive
into the academy.

Of course, the word *capitalism* connotes private ownership of the factors of
production—land, labor, and capital—and considering employees of public
research universities to be capitalists at first glance seems a blatant contradiction. However, *capitalism* also is defined as an economic system in which allocation decisions are driven by market forces. Our play on words is purposeful.
By using *academic capitalism* as our central concept, we define the reality of the
nascent environment of public research universities, an environment full of
contradictions, in which faculty and professional staff expend their human
capital stocks increasingly in competitive situations. In these situations, university employees are employed simultaneously by the public sector and are increasingly autonomous from it. They are academics who act as capitalists from
within the public sector; they are state-subsidized entrepreneurs.[4]

Although faculty and administrators at research-intensive universities may

---

4. We use the term *academic* to cover college and university employees who are professionals or
quasi-professionals. In other words, we include tenure-track faculty, academic professionals, and
administrators in the term *academic*, since academic capitalism is a phenomenon that encompasses
the professorate, academic support staff, and administrators. We use the term *faculty* interchangeably with *professors* and mean by it tenure-track personnel. When we discuss a particular rank we
will specify it, for example, *full professor*.

be state-subsidized entrepreneurs, their position in many ways is analogous to that of industrial researchers and entrepreneurs in primary sector industries (large, oligopolistic industries that produce critical goods and services and employ large numbers of persons, many of whom are unionized and receive a social benefits package as part of their wages and salaries [O'Connor 1973; Braverman 1975]). Many of these industries—for example, aerospace, computers, electronics, and nuclear industries, as well as pharmaceutical, chemical, and agriculture industries—are cushioned from the market by state support from a variety of federal agencies—for example, the Department of Defense, the Department of Energy, the National Aeronautics and Space Agency, the Department of Agriculture, and the National Institutes of Health. These industries are supported by the federal government because they are perceived to be critical to a number of national missions—primarily defense, food supply, and health. So important are these missions that the industries contributing to them are partially subsidized by the state rather than left to the vagaries of the market. Many of the science-based commodities and processes produced by these industries rely on the same technologies for which academic capitalists receive public and private support. In other words, academic capitalists are subsidized primarily from the same sources and for many of the same reasons as are industrial capitalists. The market, the state, and the academy (public universities are, of course, technically arms of the several states) are related in complex and sometimes contradictory ways. (For a fuller account of the relation among state-subsidized primary sector industry, universities engaged in basic research, and the emergence of market-oriented research, see Slaughter and Rhoades 1996.)

Another way to approach the idea of academic capitalism is through the widely accepted notion of *human capital*. What we mean by this is as follows. Almost everyone, today, is aware that the knowledge and skills possessed by workers contribute to economic growth. Conceptually, these worker capabilities make their contribution by adding to the *quality* of labor, which of course is one of the three factors of production, land and capital being the other two. Empirical demonstration of the importance of labor quality traces back at least to the work of Edward Denison (1962), who built national growth-accounting models. (Leslie and Brinkman [1988] update and synthesize the results of this long line of research up through the mid 1980s.) For production work, the quality of labor is built largely through formal education and on-the-job training. This brings us to the role of university academics in contributing to economic growth. Universities are the repositories of much of the most scarce and valuable human capital that nations possess, capital that is valuable because it is essential to the development of the high technology and technoscience necessary for competing successfully in the global economy. The human capital possessed by universities, of course, is vested in their academic staffs. Thus the specific commodity is *academic* capital, which is no more than the particular human capital possessed by academics. This final step in the logic is to say that when faculty implement their academic capital through engagement in production, they are engaging in *academic capitalism*. Their scarce and specialized knowledge and skills are being applied to productive work that yields a benefit to the individual academic, to the public university they serve, to the corporations with which they work, and to the larger society. It is indeed academic capitalism that is involved, both technically and practically.

Academic capitalism deals with market and marketlike behaviors on the part of universities and faculty. *Marketlike behaviors* refer to institutional and faculty competition for moneys, whether these are from external grants and contracts, endowment funds, university-industry partnerships, institutional investment in professors' spinoff companies, or student tuition and fees. What makes these activities marketlike is that they involve competition for funds from external resource providers. If institutions and faculty are not successful, there is no bureaucratic recourse; they do without. *Market behaviors* refer to for-profit activity on the part of institutions, activity such as patenting and subsequent royalty and licensing agreements, spinoff companies, arm's-length corporations, and university-industry partnerships, when these have a profit component. *Market behavior* also covers more mundane endeavors, such as the sale of products and services from educational endeavors (e.g., logos and sports paraphernalia), profit sharing with food services and bookstores, and the like. When we talk about restructuring of higher education, we mean substantive organizational change and associated changes in internal resource allocations (reduction or closure of departments, expansion or creation of other departments, establishment of interdisciplinary units); substantive change in the division of academic labor with regard to research and teaching; the establishment of new organizational forms (such as arm's-length companies and research parks); and the organization of new administrative structures or the streamlining or redesign of old ones.

In this book we explore the emergence of academic capitalism by tracing the growth of global markets, the development of national policies that target faculty-applied research, the decline of the block grant (undesignated funds that accrue to universities, often according to formulas) as a vehicle for state support for higher education, and the concomitant increase in faculty engagement with the market. We argue from our data that a quiet revolution has already taken place. Analysis of financial data shows a shift from state block grants to grants and contracts that are targeted on commercial endeavor. Within public research universities, fewer and fewer funds are devoted to instruction and more and more to research and other endeavors that increase institutional ability to win external funds. Faculty face a Catch-22 situation. Even when they are asked to focus on undergraduate teaching, most rewards are attached to bringing in external funds, funds that require them to perform research that may keep them from the classroom.

We concentrate our examination of changes in professional labor on four large English-speaking countries: Australia, Canada, the United Kingdom, and the United States, emphasizing Australia and the United States. We chose the major English-speaking countries because our research design and methods called for examination of documents and financial data and in-depth interviews and observations of faculty; and we are both essentially monolingual. Although we confined our study to English-speaking countries, we noted from various Organization for Economic Cooperation and Development publications that the public universities of *most* Western industrialized countries were moving toward academic capitalism, pushed and pulled by the same global forces at work in the English-speaking countries.

We did not consider private institutions because three of the four countries (Australia, Canada and the United Kingdom) have very little in the way of an independent (private) sector. The United States has a developed private sector but it serves only 20 percent of all students and only a relatively small number of private universities are heavily involved in the research enterprise. Although American exceptionalism figured in our decision not to study private research universities, the main factor in our decision not to include them was that private universities in the United States do not receive much in the way of government block grants; thus, the major factor we see as driving university destabilization did not affect private universities. Private universities in the United States have been involved in a variety of markets for a number of years and in some ways are prototypes of postindustrial universities, a concept we explore in the book's final chapter.

Movement toward academic capitalism is far from uniform; indeed, it is characterized by unevenness. Even within the English-speaking countries, there exists a continuum on this dimension, with Canadian academics probably least involved with the market and U.S. academics perhaps most involved. U.S. higher education institutions have always participated to some degree in commercial activity although we think the intensification in the last fifteen years has greatly exceeded past involvement and, as we said earlier, represents a difference *in kind* rather than in degree. In contrast, higher education in the United Kingdom and Australia has moved rapidly toward the market, the United Kingdom in the mid 1980s, Australia in the late 1980s.

We emphasized two of these countries, the United States because of our familiarity with it, and Australia because in 1991 we received Fulbright research grants to investigate the changing nature of academic labor there and the costs and benefits of commercial science and technology. Although the decision to emphasize the United States and Australia was to some extent happenstance, the two countries captured the political economic variation we sought to examine: incremental change and abrupt change, the United States under a Republican president, Australia under a Labor prime minister. Despite the great political differences between the United States and Australia in the relative power of the state, in the power of private capital, and in the rates of change in postsecondary education, both systems of higher education were moving toward what we called academic capitalism, providing an ideal situation for looking at the underlying forces moving the systems in the same direction.

We turn now to the plan of the book, providing a brief overview of the research questions that drive the several sections and separate chapters, a description of the data we use, and the theories that guide our interpretations of the data. The theories, the data, and the methods vary by level of analysis (global, national, institutional, individual), so in this section we concentrate on explaining the linkages among these. A more complete account of theory, data, and methods, as well as more detailed citations, is presented later in the book.

International Changes That Shape Higher Education

In Chapter Two we examine the growth of a global political economy and the development of Australian, Canadian, British, and American national higher education policies that seek to enhance national competitiveness by linking postsecondary education to business innovation. This linking is an effort to create national wealth by increasing global market shares through the discovery of new products and processes in order to increase the number of high paying, high technology jobs.

Two research questions inform Chapter Two. What forces are driving the restructuring of higher education? How are these forces manifested in national policy in the four countries? The data for the chapter are national policy documents, white papers, and legislation from the four countries which pertain to higher education. The method is comparative analysis of documents.

To answer the first question—what forces are driving the restructuring of higher education—we look at political economic explanations of the emergence of global markets and explore the implications of global markets for research universities. Given that the changes occur across the four countries, we look to theories that deal with social forces shaping global change. We review three political economic interpretations of globalization: neoliberal political economics, as manifested in the Chicago school (Friedman 1981, 1991; Friedman and Leube 1987); liberal or post-Keynesian interpretations (Thurow 1985; Kuttner 1991; Reich 1991); and radical or post-Marxist ones (Jessop 1993; Barnet and Cavanagh 1994; Chomsky 1994). Although these theorists disagree markedly with regard to agency—be it market, capital mobility, or business class—all see the emergence, in traditional industrialized nations in the 1980s, of a global market creating conditions that mean less money for social welfare and education functions and more money for building corporate competitiveness. This trend has powerful implications for postsecondary education. National policy makers in advanced industrialized countries are moving discretionary research and training moneys into programs focused on the production aspects of higher education, programs that complement areas of innovation in multinational corporations, such as high technology manufacturing, development of intellectual property, and producer services (non–life insurance and reinsurance, accounting, advertising, legal services, tax consultation, information services, international commodity exchanges, international monetary exchanges, and international securities dealing [Thrift 1987; Sassen 1991]) and are reducing moneys that are targeted for programs for education and social welfare functions of the state. With regard to postsecondary education, some departments, colleges, and curricular areas gain revenue shares (e.g., some areas of the physical and biological sciences and engineering, business, and law), whereas areas such as the humanities, some physical sciences (e.g., physics), and most social sciences lose shares, as do fields such as education, social work, home economics, or family studies. In other words, policy makers at the level of the nation state, whether responding to pressures from the market, international capital mobility, or the business class, are concentrating state moneys on higher education units that aid in managing or enhancing economic innovation and thereby, competitiveness.

If changes in the global economy were causing national policy makers to shift resources to technology innovation, intellectual property, and producer services fields, we see changes in national legislation and in administrative directives to that effect in Australia, Canada, the United States, and the United Kingdom. Very generally, we found that all four countries developed national policies that promoted a shift from basic or curiosity-driven research to targeted or commercial or strategic research. We were particularly concerned with the ways in which national policies dealt with access to higher education, curricula, research, and autonomy for the postsecondary sector. In all four countries, policies that affected higher education were instituted, using a rhetoric about maintaining global market shares, creating national wealth, increasing the number of high paying jobs, and building prosperity. With regard to access, higher education policies encouraged greater student participation, but at a lower national cost. Most countries increased tuition, and most systems switched the balance from student grants to loans. In terms of curricula, national policies exhibited a strong preference for departments and colleges close to the market. The several countries, with the possible exception of Canada, were moving away from basic research toward entrepreneurial research. All of the countries, with one exception, started integrating higher education into broad government planning processes, processes that focused primarily on economic development. In short, national policies in three of the four countries moved decisively toward academic capitalism. At the same time, a variety of national policies pushed for greater higher education economy and efficiency, which turned universities toward restructuring and other adjustments.

In Chapter Three we look at the financing of postsecondary education in the four countries to see whether changes in national policy which foster market and marketlike behaviors have had an impact on colleges and universities. Specifically, we ask whether the changes in national policy described in Chapter Two have had concrete, measurable effects on spending patterns in the four countries. At the national level, we found resource dependence theory (Pfeffer and Salancik 1978) more useful than global political economic theory. At this level of analysis, we were no longer concerned with what caused changes in policy and how the new policies took shape. Instead, we wanted to analyze the national patterns of higher education revenue changes which these policies produced. Resource dependence theory suggested that public universities and colleges would focus on maintaining and expanding revenues, especially those most critical to the organization. We expected public research universities to respond to national policy directives and move toward marketlike behaviors because these organizations were heavily dependent on the state for funding, especially for research moneys.

Although there was some variation by country and postsecondary sector (research universities, polytechnics, community colleges), in general the results were in the expected direction. The percentage of gross national product devoted to postsecondary education did not always decline absolutely, but the rate of growth did decline. Further, revenue shifts were away from block grant funding sources to those that reflected a "competition" or "market" base. Overall, general public funds for higher education were down, particularly when considered in constant dollars per enrolled students. However, revenue shares from other sources such as sales and services increased, as did shares from tuition. Private gifts, grants and contracts, and sales and services also were up. Expenditure patterns reflected the changes in the revenue environment. With regard to institutional expenditures, measured in shares of all expenditures, instructional funds declined, whereas research, public service, and administration expenditures increased. Relatively discretionary funding categories, such as operations and maintenance of plant and libraries, experienced large decreases, whereas student aid increased sharply. Very generally then, universities and colleges in all four countries seemed to be changing their revenue-generating patterns, moving from funding by general public means toward higher tuition and grants and contracts, private gifts, and other competitive sources of moneys.

Our analysis of financial patterns in the four countries demonstrated that all postsecondary institutions were receiving increasing revenues from market and marketlike activities, suggesting that academic capitalism may go far beyond research universities. Our case studies at public research universities indicate that academic capitalism is not confined to science and engineering and that faculty across a wide array of units engage in academic capitalism. Faculty seem to take for granted resources provided automatically by the state or several states—salary, space, some equipment—and actively seek those resources that go beyond standard institutional issue. In other words, money at the margins alters faculty behavior. If this pattern prevails throughout postsecondary education, academic capitalism will become the watchword of academic behavior.

Faculty and Institutional Response to Political Economic Change and Resource Dependence: Australian Cases

In Chapters Four through Six we look at the ways in which changes described in Chapters Two and Three play out in the daily lives of administrators, department heads, and faculty, using data from Australian research universities as our base. We pose two research questions: How do administrators and faculty describe the advantages and disadvantages of academic capitalism? How do individual academics respond to the rise of academic capitalism? We used qualitative analysis to deal with interview data from the several cases, although some interview data were quantified and used in cost-benefit taxonomies. In

other instances institutional statistics were used to compare patterns of external income generation by departments at various institutions.

Resource dependence theory guides Chapter Four. Oversimplified, resource
dependence theory suggests that organizations deprived of critical revenues
will seek new resources. In the late 1980s Australian national higher education
policies changed higher education financing so that faculty had to compete for
government research funds rather than receive them as a prerogative of holding a university position. (A detailed account of these policy changes is presented in Chapter Two.) These government research funds were targeted increasingly on national priorities that were often concerned with Australian
economic development. The federal government began to monitor institutions
through a quality assurance scheme, rewarding universities that met agreed-
upon goals and objectives. At the same time, the government share of funds for
higher education decreased, and professors and institutions were encouraged
to raise money from outside the government. Faculty and institutions began
to recruit full–fee-paying overseas students, develop partnerships with industry for research and training, and create products and processes suitable for
the market.

In other words, universities and faculty had to compete—engage in market
and marketlike behavior—for critical resources. Research money is a critical
resource for universities not only because most research money is raised competitively, but also because universities are prestige maximizers. Since most
faculty teach, and many faculty perform public service, but fewer win competitive research funds from government or industry, research is the activity that
differentiates among and within universities. Resource dependence theory suggests that faculty will turn to academic capitalism to maintain research (and
other) resources and to maximize prestige. Put another way, if faculty were offered more resources to teach more students, it is not clear that they would
compete for these moneys with the same zeal with which they compete for external research dollars. Further, faculty are selective in their pursuit of external
research money. They go after basic or fundamental research funds with the
same vigor as always, but increasingly they look for commercial research funding for frontier science and engineering projects that are tied to national policy initiatives and are partnered by prestigious firms, usually those that are national or multinational in scope.

Chapter Four uses two data sets. First, it examines the financial records of
two Australian research universities. These were used to identify internal units
that self-generated more than a few thousand dollars annually, regardless of the
source of external funds. The associated entrepreneurial activities encom-

passed a broad array of projects, ranging from applied social science research contracts to moneys secured by engineering departments for the development of intellectual property. Second, we interviewed representative project managers and staff from the units that had entrepreneurial agreements as well as unit members who were *not* a party to these agreements or related work. The first part of each interview was a subjective discussion of the advantages and disadvantages of academic capitalism for the unit and for the university. The second part employed a technique used in economics research to impute quantitative values to qualitative variables, permitting a rough means of assigning dollar values to the qualitative criteria and for the calculation of a cost-benefit ratio.

Based on the data presented in this chapter, we suggest that faculty are willing to invest a great deal of professional energy in winning financial awards so long as the resources secured allow them to maintain or even enhance their place in the status and prestige system and permit some degree of discretionary spending. Faculty are quite willing to compete for commercial moneys if these resources do not conflict directly with traditional status and prestige hierarchies and compensate with symbolic rewards such as media association of science and technology with national economic competitiveness. In other words, faculty behavior may not be as difficult to change as scholars of higher education have thought. If resources do not undermine faculty status and prestige systems, a relatively small amount of money at the margins can alter faculty activity substantially. In resource dependence theory this is known as the *Rule of 10 Percent.*

The research questions that guided Chapter Five asked how university managers, center heads, and individual faculty responded to changing markets and changing resource mixes. How did faculty perceive the impact of academic capitalism on their unit, their universities, and their careers? Were they developing new strategies to deal with political economic change and national higher education policy change? If new strategies were emerging, did they result in organizational change?

Chapter Five uses resource dependence theory and process theories of professionalization (Larson 1977; Starr 1982; Abbott 1988; Perkin 1989; Brint 1994). Resource dependence theory sets the stage by establishing the limited funding faced by faculty and the likely direction they will take to handle austerity. But resource dependence theory, like the political economic theories we discussed earlier, is a theory of constraint which addresses social and political economic structures and perhaps does not concentrate as much on individual and collective human agency. Professionalization theory, more strongly grounded in the daily practice of highly educated experts, helps us look at faculty as social actors in the drama of organizational change.

Process theories of professionalization view professionalization as a process for which knowledge, theory, expertise, and altruism are not enough; organizational, political, and economic skills are equally, if not more, important. Process theories of professionalization look at professionals' active agency, particularly at their intervention in the political economy, to gain a greater degree of control over their work lives and income streams, through, for example, state licensure laws. Because process theories of professionalization emphasize the ways that professionals act in moments of great change in the political economy—for example, the rise of industrialization (Bledstein 1976; Haskell 1977) and the formation of the welfare state (Finegold and Skocpol 1995)—they should help us understand how professors position themselves at the advent of global economy. Process theories of professionalization intersect political economic (Chapter Two) and resource dependence theories (Chapters Three and Four) in that the rise of a global economy exacerbates faculty and institutional resource dependence with regard to critical resources, especially those for research; faculty respond to these changes by attempting to develop new strategies to protect and enhance professional privileges at the level of the institution and the discipline.

The data for this chapter were interviews with forty-seven persons in eight units in three universities. We selected those units most deeply involved in technology transfer, which is the movement of products and processes from the university to the market. We selected faculty involved in technology transfer for close scrutiny because technology transfer is perhaps the most direct form of academic engagement with the market. Technology transfer often results in intellectual property, defined as patents and processes, trademarks or copyrights, and organized *consultancies* (an Australian term referring to faculty consulting activities that are channeled through the university and from which faculty receive one third of the profits, their college one third, and the university one third) aimed at the commercial market.

Generally, we found that faculty and institutional leaders were extremely sensitive to changes in the resource mix at the level of the institution and the field. In Australia, vice-chancellors encouraged faculty to act as entrepreneurs. Their hope was to develop products and services that would generate resources through for-profit activity such as licensing and royalties, direct sales, or shares of faculty consulting. The approaches administrators used to promote academic capitalism were various. Some administrators let faculty take the initiative. These administrators provided broad policy guidelines and offered incentives to encourage faculty to discover and develop products and processes for the market, but they did not otherwise participate. Other administrators targeted particular products and processes and regulated their development closely. Yet other administrators worked with the business community and government leaders to create a large resource pool to support the development of complex technologies. In the last case, faculty were encouraged to band together in interdisciplinary arrangements to act as partners in relatively stable, ongoing enterprises.

Heads of departments or heads of centers very often aggressively developed procedures for generating revenues from faculty activity, including income from technology transfer activities that provided intellectual property, and from faculty consulting. They used new organizational structures to create interdisciplinary knowledge that tapped fresh revenue flows. Their tactics looked more like business plans than professionalization strategies. Very often the new units called for the addition of large numbers of professional officers and nonacademic staff, who were fiercely loyal to center or institute heads, did not engage much with faculty, and were not very interested in teaching. They were much more a part of the commercial culture than the academic culture and tended to bring commercial values to their work, concentrating on making their centers operate more like small firms, expanding commercial activity, and generating increased amounts of profit.

Faculty were more varied in their response than were central administrators and center heads. All of the full professors, most of the associate professors, but fewer junior faculty, regarded positively the entrepreneurial activity and development of intellectual property. Faculty especially valued the improved relations with external bodies, heightened prestige of their units, closer linkage to the economy (consulting opportunities, student employment opportunities), and added monetary benefits. Given that the faculty were primarily applied scientists or were from professional schools, they saw their entrepreneurial work as an extension of the research in which they were traditionally engaged, or, in the case of intellectual property, as a justifiable extension of that work. Junior faculty, postdoctoral fellows, and graduate students were less favorable in their views of academic capitalism. They felt that performance expectations had doubled because they were now supposed to demonstrate excellence in two research venues, fundamental *and* commercial.

For Chapter Six, we asked whether academic conceptions of the nature of knowledge were changing. Did the faculty still value fundamental or basic theoretical knowledge above all else, or were market pressures and resource dependence changing academic epistemology? How did professors deal with the professional norm of altruism when they pursued the discovery and development of profit-making products and processes? If change was occurring, was it across all fields, or was it confined, in research universities, to fields that were close to the market? The complexity of the environment faculty faced pushed us to cross disciplinary boundaries, drawing on a variety of theories as we tried to understand the emerging epistemology of academic capitalism. As in Chapter Five, resource dependence theory set the stage for behavioral change on the part of faculty. Again, as in Chapter Five, we drew on professionalization theory to understand changes in faculty norms, values, and beliefs and the way the faculty, as organizational actors, manifested them. We pay particular attention to professionalization theory that examines faculty interactions with markets (Brint 1994). Because the majority of faculty we studied were scientists or engineers, we used sociology of science as well as science innovation theories to look at the intersection of science and markets (Gummett 1991; Etzkowitz 1994; Gibbons et al. 1994). We expected that faculty engaged in academic capitalism would begin to reconceptualize knowledge so that entrepreneurial research would be valued highly, especially entrepreneurial research on the frontiers of science and technology, research that involved discovery of innovative products and processes for global markets.

The data were from interviews with a subgroup of the sample in Chapter Five, the thirty tenure-track faculty located in units engaged heavily in academic capitalism. At the unit level—the interdisciplinary center or department—and in some fields or subfields, conceptions of knowledge were changing markedly. With regard to altruism, professors engaged in academic capitalism were ambivalent. Although they still hoped their research would benefit humankind, they began to speak about research paying its own way. If they were able to support their research with funds aimed at commercial targets, they saw no reason why other researchers could not. The same pattern held true in terms of basic versus applied research. They still considered basic research the bedrock of science, but they saw entrepreneurial research as folded into that stratum, forming a new composite. Merit was no longer defined as being acquired primarily through publication; rather it encompassed at least in part success with market and marketlike activities. Faculty were changing their conceptions of knowledge more rapidly than were administrators. For faculty in high technology fields close to the market, knowledge was valued as much for its commercial potential and resource-generating capability as for the power of discovery.

In our concluding chapter we explore the implications for the restructuring of postsecondary education, for patterns of professional work, and for emerging epistomologies of science. Although we draw on the data presented in our cases, we also speak broadly to postsecondary education changes currently taking place in the United States. Finally, we present some alternatives for faculty and institutional leaders to consider as they respond to political economic and policy changes.

We conclude that a better understanding of academic capitalism will help faculty and staff make better sense of their daily lives; that successful academic capitalists will gain personal power within universities, both individually and collectively; that personal stress will increase for all organizational actors; that central administrators, too, will gain in the redistribution of power, whereas middle managers may become less important to organizational life; and that the concept of university-shared governance may suffer. In this we see a loss to the concept of the university as a community, where the individual members are oriented primarily toward the greater good of the organization. A major vehicle for redistributing power to the operating units of the university will be budget devolution, granting to the individual units both responsibility for raising revenues and the authority for spending it. We see governments that provide block grant funding and students whose tuitions cover only a relatively small share of instructional costs as possessing only limited power in effecting university response to their desires; this is in contrast with university responsiveness to those who provide money for specific purposes and mandate the accomplishment of those ends.

Perhaps our most keenly felt desire in writing this book was that the state and the electorate would become aware that the decline in undergraduate education perceived to exist in public research universities is a natural, almost unavoidable outcome of the decline in the share of revenues provided by government in block grant form. Reversing this trend will require greater state support, some way of inducing greater university responsiveness to the desires of the state, or some combination of the two. Although we believe that ultimately, in a competitive market environment, proportional shares of state block grant support and tuition revenues must follow students to the units that enroll them, we are not sanguine about this eventuality in the short or intermediate term. We hold that governments must create incentives for universities to allocate their resources along the general lines for which the state intends that they be spent.

2

ACADEMIC SCIENCE AND TECHNOLOGY IN THE GLOBAL MARKETPLACE

To PROVIDE A THEORETICAL grounding for our examination of higher education policies in Australia, Canada, the United Kingdom, and the United States, we begin this chapter by examining the differences between industrial and postindustrial political economies. Specifically, we look at which countries are winners and losers in the global marketplace, paying special attention to the four countries with which we are concerned, and especially to the United States, given its previous dominance of global markets. Next, we review briefly theories of globalization which purport to explain why particular nations are successful in the global economy. Then we link changes in the global economy to higher education by outlining the ways in which globalization theory explains the increased centrality of higher education systems to national strategies for securing shares of global markets. Finally, we examine changes in national higher education policies in the 1980s and 1990s in the four countries under consideration.[1] We are particularly concerned with the ways in which national policies deal with access to higher education, curricula, research, and autonomy for the postsecondary sector.

This chapter is informed by two research questions: What forces drove the restructuring of higher education and research in the 1980s and 1990s? How were these forces manifested in national policy in the several countries? The

We thank Philip Altbach, Robert Berdahl, Jan Currie, Ross Harrold, John Levin, Gary Rhoades, and Michael Skolnik for careful reading and helpful comments on this chapter.

1. Despite the recently created Department of Education, the United States does not have a national ministry of education equivalent to those of Australia and the United Kingdom. Like Canada, U.S. higher education is decentralized. Nonetheless, the United States makes national higher education policy through federal student aid policies as well through a wide array of research and develop agencies, ranging from mission agencies to the National Science Foundation to, most recently, the Department of Commerce. Policy directions established at the national level are often complemented by the several states, as with supplemental educational opportunity grants and university-industry-state government commercial development projects.

first question is important because it lets us gauge whether the changes we see are likely to be long lasting or short term. Are they the products of worldwide structural adjustments and therefore changes to which higher education must somehow accommodate, or are these changes (relatively) short term shifts with which we can cope by waiting for a return to business as usual? We argue that the changes stemming from globalization are of such magnitude that higher education systems will be strongly affected. The answer to the second question—how were these global forces of change manifested in national higher education policy—suggests the direction that change may take. Generally, we see three of the four countries moving toward academic capitalism, which emphasizes the utility of higher education to national economic activity and the preference for market and marketlike activity on the part of faculty and institutions. With regard to access, higher education policies encourage greater student participation but at a lower national cost. Rather than financing student participation, all countries are raising tuition, and most systems are switching from grants to loans. In terms of curricula, national policies exhibit a strong preference for departments and colleges close to the market. The several countries, with the partial exception of Canada, are moving away from basic research toward academic capitalism, and three of the countries have started integrating higher education into broad government planning processes that focus primarily on economic development.

Although we make the case that national higher education policies are converging in some very important areas, we do *not* see Australia, Canada, the United Kingdom, and the United States as necessarily responding to globalization in the same ways. As we point out in our treatment of the higher education policies in each of the several countries, the nations take very divergent paths to policies that support and strengthen academic capitalism. For example, higher education policies that promoted academic capitalism were initiated under conservative governments in the United Kingdom and the United States but under a Labor (liberal) government in Australia. In the United States and Canada the several states and provinces often pioneered partnerships that involved universities in academic capitalism, whereas in the United Kingdom and Australia centralized higher education ministries guided these processes. In contrast, in the United States, at the national level, Congress rather than the executive branch actively developed legislation that fostered academic capitalism. In other words, globalization is a systemwide force to which countries, the several states, and provinces develop unique responses, but the system effects are so powerful that higher education polices in some areas—access, curricula, research, autonomy for faculty and institutions—converge.

We identified these changes in national policy by looking at white papers, legislation, and policy directives from administrative agencies concerned with higher education. We also read numerous secondary sources on policy changes in the four countries. The method we used was comparative analysis of policy documents.

Industrial and Postindustrial Economies

What is the scope of economic change that characterizes the last quarter of the twentieth century, and how does it affect higher education? We have moved from an industrial to a postindustrial society, and higher education is more important to the latter. Postindustrial societies depend on higher education for training and research and development (R&D) to a greater degree than do industrial societies. Paradoxically, postindustrial economies may require fewer workers, regardless of their level of education, than industrial societies, and postindustrial society may not need these workers' skills for a lifetime, rendering obsolete the traditional concepts of career.

Many political economists see modern society in the throes of change as great as that which characterized the industrial revolution. They believe that current changes in the organization of work and the displacement of workers will be of the same or greater magnitude as was the shift from agricultural society to urban factory production. (For classic treatments of the dimensions of the shift from agricultural to industrial society, see Durkheim 1951; Weber 1958; Marx 1975.) Because we are enmeshed in the early processes of change, the outline of the future is not clear, and scholars are engaged in retheorizing macro–political economics and rethinking empirical indicators of change, fueling heated debates that offer widely different explanations for the causes of change and very different visions of the future. Although political economics is rife with controversy, a descriptive model of the differences between past and future is emerging.

Scholars address these differences through a variety of competing dichotomies: industrial versus postindustrial (Bell 1973), Fordist versus post-Fordist (Jessop 1993), mass production versus flexible production (Cohen 1993), manufacturing versus service industries (Thrift 1987; Sassen 1991), low technology versus high technology (Reich 1991; Tyson 1992), and industrial versus informational economies (Castells 1993). Within each of these dichotomies there is intense controversy (i.e., Bonefeld 1993 versus Jessop 1993; Reich 1991 versus Tyson 1992; World Bank 1993 versus Sakakibara 1993). We will refer to the differences between past and possible future as differences between industrial and postindustrial political economies, not because we think that conventional industrial economies necessarily are disappearing or because we think industry and manufacturing are unimportant, but because the word *post* seems to characterize the nature of scholarly work on a number of fronts at this time—as in postmodernism, poststructuralism, post-Marxism—and captures our inability to name the present, let alone the future.

The industrial revolution was made possible by new sources of energy (steam, electricity, oil) which triggered mechanical invention in transportation (railroads, automobiles, airplanes), in agriculture (reapers, harvesters, processors), and in factory production (textiles, housing, food storage and processing), all of which served to move centers of population from rural to urban areas. The technological revolution that is sweeping the world today is powered less by harnessing new sources of energy and mechanical invention and more by advances in applied science and engineering, particularly in areas that deal with or make possible information generation, processing, and storage (Castells 1993). Among these new technologies are "advanced materials, advanced semiconductor devices and processes, digital imaging technology, high density data storage and optoelectronics . . . artificial intelligence, biotechnology, flexible computer-integrated manufacturing, medical . . . diagnostics and sensor technology" (Cohen 1993, 135). As important as the products derived from these processes are producer services—telecommunications packages, financial instruments, and legal tools that are as much product as service in that they can be sold and traded rather than immediately consumed—which make possible global trade and marketing of high technology goods and services (Thrift 1987; Sassen 1991).[2]

2. Producer services are tied to the rise of commercial capital, which has played an important role in globalization of the political economy. Producer services consist of non–life insurance and reinsurance, accounting, advertising, legal services, tax consultancies, information services, international commodity exchanges, international monetary exchanges, and international securities dealing. Business schools and law schools participate in the development of producer services and train graduates to use them (Thrift 1987; Sassen 1991). Castells (1993) argues that the change from an industrial to an information economy is more important than the change from manufacturing to services because the service sector encompasses so many diverse activities that it has become a residual category, ranging from producer services to janitorial services. He also points out, as do Thrift (1987), Cohen and Zysman (1987), and Sassen (1991), that there is "systemic linkage between manufacturing and the service sectors" so that many such activities are in fact "an integral part of the industrial production process." In other words, categories such as *manufacturing* versus *services* are less meaningful in a postindustrial economy, and scholars are attempting to develop new categories that break down old dichotomies and provide greater analytic leverage.

As many inventions of the industrial revolution were made by nonschooled amateurs and inventors as by trained scientists (Ben-David 1965; Noble 1976); most of the discoveries of the current technological revolution were made by persons with advanced degrees. The postindustrial technological revolution depends on universities.[3] Universities provide the training necessary for the increasing numbers of professionals employed by corporations to invent, maintain, and innovate with regard to sophisticated technologies and products. In an increasing number of cases universities are the sites where new technologies and products are developed, often in partnerships with business, through funding provided in part by the state.

The industrial revolution organized production through the assembly line, a mode of production often referred to as *Fordism* by non-American academics. As the term *Fordism* suggests, mass production was highly standardized, typified by the assembly line and *Taylorism* (scientific management, exemplified by supervisory control over workers' most minute movements on the assembly line), and usually occurred in vertically integrated, large-scale organizations. The system was fairly inflexible; products were not altered easily. It depended on massive accumulations of capital, top-down planning, and very long production runs. Tasks were repetitive and were supervised closely. In contrast, the organization of production in the dawning postindustrial era, exemplified by Japanese industry, is *flexible volume production*, which uses fewer workers, less space, and takes "half the investment in tools and machinery, half the engineering hours to develop a new product, and half the time to develop a new product. It also requires less than half the needed inventory on site, turns out products with far fewer defects, and yields a greater and growing variety of products" (Cohen 1993, 106).

Flexible volume production is a complex organizational strategy and is not a technological solution that could be imposed easily on manufacturing problems. Although the strategy can be learned, it is alien to Fordist organization of production and is correspondingly difficult for Fordist corporations to assimilate. Even though a number of Fordist corporations have attempted Japanese style management aimed at incorporating production workers into organizational decision making with regard to manufacturing, these efforts, often

---

3. As always, there are notable exceptions to generalizations such as the notion that the science and technology discoveries of the postindustrial revolution were made by college graduates. For example, Steven Jobs, of Apple Computer, and Bill Gates, of Microsoft, both dropped out of college but were nonetheless inventor-entrepreneurs of two of the most successful high technology corporations formed in the United States in the last quarter of the twentieth century.

labeled *total quality management*,[4] are not notably successful, in large part because Fordist management and workers seem unable to abandon their historic adversarial relationships.

Globally successful systems of flexible production are usually embedded in multinational corporations. As the trust was to the national economies of the twentieth century, so the multinational conglomerate is to the emerging global economy of the twenty-first century (Fligstein 1990). Multinational corporations are at the cutting edge of the market in most industrialized countries. From 1975 to 1990, U.S. multinationals' annual sales grew substantially faster than the U.S. economy as a whole: "the sales of the fifty largest industrial multinationals were 28 percent of U.S. GNP [gross national product] in 1975 and 39 percent of U.S. GNP in 1989" (Carnoy 1993, 49). Multinational services, particularly financial services, grew rapidly. The world's fifty largest banks more than doubled their assets between 1980 and 1990 (Carnoy 1993, 51, Figure 3.2; see also Sassen 1991; Cohen 1993).

The significance of multinational corporations to the world economy was enhanced in the 1980s when computers, harnessed to new telecommunications infrastructures, created a global market. For industrial corporations this meant managers were able to supervise far-flung business empires electronically, "so that the national economy now works as a unit at the world level in real time. In this sense we are not only seeing a process of the internationalization of the economy, but a process of globalization—that is, the interpenetration of economic activities and national economies at a global level" (Castells 1993, 19). With regard to financial services, advances in telecommunications in the 1980s made possible for the first time global trade in equities, bonds, and currency as well as more speculative financial instruments (Sassen 1991). Multinationals, then, were key organizational vehicles of globalization.[5] The infrastructure of

4. Total quality management focuses on the customer and the point of production rather than on management. Customer feedback is very important as is worker input. Workers committed to the corporation should be able to criticize constructively and improve the production process, creating more satisfied customers. Total quality management depends on shared commitment by management and workers to company goals as well as on a commitment on the part of management to workers and vice versa (Peters and Peters 1991). Under total quality management, managers would be unlikely to fire large numbers of workers during restructuring because that would create distrust, resistance, and undermine efforts to increase productivity. Given the adversarial relationships that often characterize Fordist manufacturing, the requisite level of trust is difficult to achieve, especially during periods of downsizing.

5. As a number of scholars note, the nationality of a corporation is sometimes very difficult to determine. For example, joint ventures allow U.S. automakers to market under their company names popular Japanese cars, as in the case of Mazda Navajo, which is a Ford Explorer made in Kentucky, and Geo Prism, which is a Toyota Corolla made in California. Conversely, Jaguars are

the global economy—computers, telecommunications, producer services—depends on university-trained personnel for continued innovation and for maintenance.

In the industrial era, labor was divided into craft and unskilled workers, with highly skilled craft unions gradually disappearing as increased emphasis was placed on mass production, a process that called for less skill on the part of labor (Braverman 1975). Mass production relied on large numbers of interchangeable blue collar workers in oligopolistic sector industries such as steel and auto and food processing, which were heavily unionized. The work was often boring, physically demanding, and dirty. These workers were full time, relatively highly paid, and had many fringe benefits—health, pension, vacation, time-and-a-half for overtime (O'Connor 1973). Assembly-line production was usually marked by hierarchy, with dramatic social and cultural distance between workers and managers, differences perhaps best captured by variations in education. Generally, assembly-line production required workers to have little education, often not asking for more than rudimentary reading and writing skills; not even completion of high school was necessary. In contrast, managers usually had some college (Jencks and Riesman 1968).

Under the postindustrial organization of production, labor looks very different, especially in Japan and the newly industrializing countries. Flexible volume production does away with the assembly line, taking instead a team approach. The distance between supervisor and worker is somewhat ambiguous, given that all employees are team members. Moreover, the team approach requires all workers to have a substantial grasp of design, engineering, and production processes. Sometimes production workers are even encouraged to participate in discussions about the organization of work and to introduce product and process changes. Workers who engage in the new organization of production—particularly in Japan, Sweden, and Germany—are well paid and receive a substantial array of benefits.

However, much of the work in established industrial countries has not shifted to flexible volume production, or it has adopted some features of the new organization of production and not others. Generally, redesign of work in

---

made in England by a wholly owned Ford subsidiary. The United States insists that foreign companies manufacturing in the United States have a large local content. The Japanese government takes the position that "more than 60 percent of 931 Japanese-owned companies in the United States obtain at least 'two thirds of their materials in America,' but many of these 'American' suppliers are Japanese owned." Increasingly, multinationals, regardless of country of origin, use their "overseas subsidiaries, joint ventures, licensing agreements, and strategic alliances to assume foreign identities when it suits their purposes" (Barnet and Cavanagh 1994, 279, 280).

traditional industries in established industrial countries means that labor costs are reduced by forcing down wages while reducing expenditures on working conditions and social benefits, so that, all else equal, profit ratios increase proportionately (Henderson and Castells 1987). Productivity and profitability are also increased by elimination of redundancies, reduction of work time, introduction of technical innovations, and speedup (Henderson and Castells 1987; Harrison and Bluestone 1990). In their home countries multinationals in traditional industries employed declining numbers of workers who labored longer hours for less pay and substantially reduced benefits.

As part of the process of making production "lean," automation increased, and jobs were relocated to less costly production sites; the use of part-time labor grew, and unemployment increased. In Europe, unemployment has been about 12 percent since the late 1980s. In the United States, "if part time employment was calculated as partial unemployment, if the military was excluded from the employed (as it had been until the Reagan Bureau of Labor Statistics revised the basis for computing the number of job holders), and if discouraged workers—those who had stopped looking for work—were factored into the jobless figure" (Aronowitz and DiFazio 1994, 2), the percentage of U.S. unemployed would be about the same for Europe—12 percent.

In sum, industrial political economies were fueled by new sources of energy and invention which moved production from agricultural to urban areas. Postindustrial political economies are fueled by new advances in science-based knowledge and are powered by computers and telecommunications. Industrial political economies were organized along Fordist or assembly-line models of production, whereas postindustrial political economies use flexible volume or just-in-time production. The central organizational unit of the industrial economy was the trust or oligopolistic corporation, operating at the level of the nation state. The central organization unit of the postindustrial economy is the multinational corporation, which retains strong oligopolistic tendencies, operating globally. Under industrial economies, workers were not educated, and their jobs were often dull and repetitive. In postindustrial political economies the jobs of workers organized for flexible volume production are often varied and interesting and call for substantial knowledge and decision making. However, the numbers of flexible volume production jobs are not great. Product innovation almost always depends on university-educated personnel, often persons with advanced degrees. Managerial positions too are almost always filled by college-educated persons, many of whom now have advanced degrees.

Although we posit a set of neat dichotomies to mark the differences between industrial and postindustrial political economies, reality is less tidy. Neither corporations nor countries adopt technologies and strategies for organization of production in a uniform manner. This unevenness is perhaps clearest with regard to the labor force. In established industrial countries some workers who are involved in flexible volume production have interesting and responsible, well-paid jobs with high benefits. But other workers, particularly in manufacturing jobs that still rely on many aspects of traditional industrial work organization, have had their jobs redesigned so that they work longer hours for less pay at repetitious jobs that have fewer and fewer benefits (Harrison and Bluestone 1990; Phillips 1993). And more and more workers are employed only part time or unemployed for significant segments of their careers.

Although the inventions that power postindustrial economies are likely to be made by scientists and engineers, MBAs and attorneys, computer and information scientists, the productivity gains embodied by these discoveries may reduce the demand for highly skilled professionals. A college degree no longer guarantees a good job. The percentage of net job growth for employees with some college or more in the low income stratum (less than $11,104 [in constant 1986 dollars]) increased by 12 percent from 1963–73 to 1979–86; the percentage of net job growth for employees in the middle income stratum ($11,104–44,412) decreased by 9.2 percent in the same period; the percentage of net job growth for the high income stratum ($44,413+) decreased by 7.8 percent (Harrison and Bluestone 1990, Table A.2) Postindustrial economies depend on personnel trained in colleges and universities and highly reward many, but they do not absorb all of the graduates these institutions produce, posing problems for higher education's claims to provide social mobility and adequate returns on students' investment in learning.

Winners and Losers: Theories of Globalization

Theories of globalization are those that purport to explain why some countries do better than others as political economies become more global. At first glance, globalization theories do not seem to speak directly to higher education. However, they do outline the magnitude of the political economic changes occurring across the four countries. These changes are putting pressure on national higher education policy makers to change the way tertiary education does business.

As the world makes the transition to postindustrial political economies, some countries do better than others. Overall, the rise of Japan and of a number of industrializing countries in Asia, often referred to as the Tiger Republics —Singapore, Malaysia, South Korea—as well as China, and now Vietnam, has destabilized the bipolar trade relations that dominated world trade for most of this century. Twentieth-century trade was dominated first by the United Kingdom and, after World War II, by the United States. Trade relations were bipolar in that most world trade flowed between the United States and Europe. In the 1970s as established industrialized countries lost some of the advantages conferred by early industrialization and empire and neocolonial trade relationships, world trade became multipolar (Carnoy 1993; Cohen 1993). Indeed, some argue that the center of global economic growth has moved to the Pacific Rim (Castells 1993).

If we look at national shares of world output, we see that Japan increased its share from 5.8 percent in 1967 to 7.7 percent in 1986, and the developing Asian countries increased from 10.8 to 17.4 percent. Japan and China raised output more rapidly than any other country in the world, and the developing Asian countries far outdistanced any others. The United States and the United Kingdom lost shares, Australia and New Zealand held steady, and Canada made a very slight gain. The United States declined from 25.8 percent in 1967 to 21.4 percent in 1986; the United Kingdom declined from 4.8 to 3.5 percent. Australia and New Zealand held steady a 1.2 percent share, and Canada grew from 2.1 to 2.2 percent (Castells 1993, 25, Table 2.1). If we look only at gains and losses in manufacturing exports, the sector of national economies usually seen as most important to global competition, the shift with regard to winners and losers is even more dramatic. Again, Japan and the newly industrializing countries of Asia made the greatest gains, whereas the United States and the United Kingdom suffered the greatest losses. Calculated in 1/1,000 parts of world trade, Japan increased its performance in manufacturing exports in the period 1967–73 by 15.6, in 1973–80 by 9.0, in 1980–86 by 10.4. For the same periods, the increases for the newly industrializing countries of Asia were 14.7, 17.0, and 9.4, respectively. In contrast, in 1967–73 the United States change was –22.9, in 1973–80, 1.5, and in 1980–86, –21.1. For the same periods, the figures for the United Kingdom were –17.8, 2.0, –13.1; for Canada, –5.4, –4.3, and –3.4; for Australia–New Zealand, 3.8, –4.2, –2.2 (Castells 1993, 26, Table 2.2). If we look at productivity in the period between 1960 and 1990, the story is essentially the same. In this period the United States increased productivity by 2.9 percent, Canada by 2.9 percent, and the United Kingdom by 3.7 percent, while Japan increased by 6.9 percent. Established industrial countries increased their productivity by about 1 percent per decade; Japan increased productivity at a much greater rate (Cohen 1993, 11).

As world output was redistributed, several of these countries increased their national debt. The U.S. net government debt as a percent of GNP/GDP (gross domestic product) increased from 19.2 percent in 1979 to 25.3 percent in 1984 to 31.2 percent in 1990. Canada's increased from 12.0 percent in 1979 to 26.1 percent in 1984 to 40.3 percent in 1990. The United Kingdom's debt decreased from 47.9 percent in 1979 to 47.4 percent in 1984 to 28.9 percent in 1990. Although the United Kingdom decreased its debt substantially, it still remained quite high, comparable to that of the United States, although not as high as Canada's. Only Australia brought its debt level close to that of Japan. Australia's debt was 27.7 percent in 1979, 25.1 percent in 1984, and 13.2 percent in 1990. Japan's net government debt was 14.9 percent in 1979, 27.0 percent in 1984, and 10.9 percent in 1990 (Oxley and Martin 1991, 148, Table 1).

At the same time, Australia, the United Kingdom, and the United States increased the inequality of income between the late 1970s and mid 1980s. "There was virtually no change in Canada. . . . Changes of around 1 percentage point in the Gini coefficient are observed in . . . Australia . . . [I]n the United Kingdom and the United States there was a more than 3 percentage point increase" (Atkinson, Rainwater, and Smeeding 1995, 49, Table 4.8).

Given that the United States dominated global markets from World War II through the 1970s, let us consider the U.S. case in somewhat greater detail. "Up to 1979, the United States had been the leading exporter of such [direct foreign] investments. By 1981, it had become the leading recipient, and had fallen to second place as an exporter of capital, behind the United Kingdom" (Sassen 1991, 37). In terms of balance of trade the United States was unable to uphold a "positive merchandise trade balance," falling from an indexed –2.3 in 1971 to –141.6 in 1985 (Cohen and Zysman 1987, 62, Table 5.1). The U.S. share of world exports fell "in value terms from 26 percent of world markets in 1960 to 18 percent in 1980—before the dollar aggravated matters" (Cohen and Zysman 1987, 64, Figure 5.1). Even the U.S. high technology position was weak, with the majority of high technology exports concentrated in military goods (Business–Higher Education Forum 1986a, 1986b; Cohen and Zysman 1987).

What loss of share in world output, loss in manufacturing output, declines in productivity and standards of living, and increases in national debt suggest is that the Fordist era of high wage, mass production, and mass consumption which characterized the established industrial countries from 1940 to 1970 is over. The rise of Japan and the other Asian countries destabilized the bipolar world trading patterns that had built prosperity within the established industrial countries. Political economists, together with politicians and business leaders, began to try to explain and correct the disturbing decline among the established industrial countries.

For the most part, the various political economic theories that explain patterns of winners and losers among countries are partial and incomplete, with visible lacunae, a situation not unexpected in a transitional period. The debates surrounding these theories are intense because the theories are at once explanations and proscriptions, the voice of research and attempts to influence the policies of nations. We present these theories in broad outline, hopefully not oversimplifying to the point of caricature, even though we gloss over the controversy among and within the various theoretical camps. In very rough terms, these theories can be characterized as neoliberal, liberal or post-Keynesian, and radical or post-Marxist.

The neoliberal or Chicago school perspective deemphasizes the polity, instead stressing the role of the market in national economic success. The neoliberal school sees market forces as impersonal, disembodied, and inexorable, as supplanting national economies with a global market. To compete successfully in the new global market, nations have to cut back, reducing social welfare and entitlement programs, freeing capital and corporations from taxation and regulation, allowing them to operate unfettered (Friedman 1981, 1991; Friedman and Leube 1987). In the neoliberal model the only acceptable role of the state is as global policeman and judge, patrolling the edges of the playing field to make sure it remains level, adjudicating trading infractions and transgressions. In this model the private sector is privileged as the engine of competition, and the state is no more than a drag on economic growth. A major problem for this explanation of losers and winners in global competition is that the most successful countries in the past twenty years are Japan and the newly industrializing Asian countries, all of which have well developed industrial policies, relying heavily on the state to coordinate their multinationals' global strategies. (For a dramatic instance of conflict over the Chicago model, see the Japanese objection to the World Bank [1993] report; for further elaboration, see Sakakibara [1993]). Indeed, the Asian countries seem not to employ the same rigid distinctions as do Western, English-speaking countries with regard to private and public, or, to speak somewhat more broadly, between civil society and the state, and instead see public and private as permeable and complementary.

Keynesian political economics were built at the level of the nation state. Federal control of the money supply was used to stimulate or slow national economies, thereby avoiding depression. As global markets emerged and national controls on international flows of capital were eased to take advantage of expanded opportunities, capital mobility increased. Greater international capital mobility made manipulation of the economy at the national level more difficult. At the same time, the warfare-welfare approach to the political economy characteristic of the United States and the United Kingdom became more difficult to sustain. The end of the Cold War, together with the growing critique of defense R&D as a tool for technology innovation, made stimulation of the economy through military expenditures problematic. Simultaneously, increased global competition made political and economic justification of the social wage or social safety net more difficult (Thurow 1980; Melman 1982). In other words, the growth of a global economy, the increase in capital mobility, the end of the Cold War, and the erosion of the social wage made Keynesianism inadequate in the postindustrial era.

Liberals or post-Keynesians have tried to devise industrial policies that enable established industrial nation states to compete more successfully in traditional "smokestack" industries and to stimulate new high technology industries, largely through increasing R&D and productivity (Porter 1990; Reich 1991; Tyson 1992). In this view the nation state plays a role in stimulating high technology innovation, in building human capital to exploit high technology in multinational corporations, and in creating a climate favorable to investment at home (Carnoy et al. 1993).

Although post-Keynesian political economists emphasize the stimulating and supportive role the state plays with regard to the economy, they simultaneously embrace free trade. For the most part, they eschew direct mechanisms for planning, relying instead on a bottom-up approach, in which industry, by taking advantage of government-subsidized opportunities for R&D stimulation—for example, the Advanced Technology Program in the United States—targets areas for state support in developing products for the global market (Etzkowitz 1994). A major problem for proponents of this type of post-Keynesian approach to the political economy is that the United States and United Kingdom had substantial increases in productivity in the late 1980s and early 1990s, but these did not translate into increases in wages and standards of living. According to the most recent Organization for Economic Cooperation and Development study (1990a), income distribution in Australia, the United Kingdom, and the United States showed a rise in inequality between the late 1970s and middle 1980s, particularly in the United Kingdom and the United States (Atkinson, Rainwater, and Smeeding 1995).

Post-Marxists continue to develop an important critique of global capitalism, even as they recognize that highly centralized state socialism is no longer a viable political economic alternative (Bowles 1992). Post-Marxists see the private sector working through the apparatuses of the several nation states and various international trade organizations and tribunals to level the playing field so that stateless multinational corporations can dominate the global economy, establishing a new international division of labor. In this new international division of labor multinational conglomerates move production facilities to those parts of the world which provide the most profitable combination of capital and labor, disproportionately to the lowest wage states that offer the greatest incentives to multinationals (Frobel, Heinrichs, and Kreye 1980; Chomsky 1994). Multinational CEOs are able to manage far-flung global production through the information superhighway and telecommunications. In this model, owners and managers of stateless multinationals, as well as owners and managers of the many ancillary businesses that serve them, are winners; and workers, whether high technology or low, and the unemployed, rooted or trapped in nation states, are losers.

The major problem for this explanation, as other post-Marxists as well as post-Keynesians have noted, is that there is little relationship between labor costs and international competitiveness. Much more important than labor costs in predicting an economy's productivity is the technological level of the industrial sector (Castells and Tyson 1988; Castells 1993). In other words, when multinationals relocate plants they choose industrializing countries with relatively high levels of technological development, avoiding the lowest cost, least developed countries, especially in Africa and in parts of South America, which political economic geographers now refer to as the *Fourth World* (Castells 1993).

Political economists who are neither post-Keynesians nor post-Marxists, but perhaps fall somewhere in between the two camps, argue for established industrial countries modeling themselves more closely on the Japanese and newly industrializing Asian countries and developing state planning capacities as well as mechanisms for capturing and redistributing more equitably the profits from multinational enterprises. They argue that national policies strongly influence competitiveness, especially national policies on labor availability and technological infrastructure, on R&D, on high technology and management training, and on protection from foreign competition and concessions from foreign multinationals (Harrison and Bluestone 1990; Carnoy 1993; Barnet and Cavanagh 1994). However, they do not speak to the political strategies and governmental mechanisms that would make such policies viable, particularly in countries such as the United States and the United Kingdom, which have traditionally tried to minimize the role of the government in economic planning.

Globalization and Higher Education

Globalization has at least four far-reaching implications for higher education. First is the constriction of moneys available for discretionary activities such as postsecondary education. Second is the growing centrality of technoscience and fields closely involved with markets, particularly international markets. Third is the tightening relationships between multinational corporations and state agencies concerned with product development and innovation. Fourth is the increased focus of multinationals and established industrial countries on global intellectual property strategies.

Despite the lack of a coherent conceptual understanding of why some countries are winners and others losers, three of the four established industrial nations that we studied, the exception being Canada, responded to increased global competition with conservative political economic policies. The policies are conservative in that they are aimed at regaining the nation's past positions, in the case of the United States and the United Kingdom, positions of global preeminence; in the case of Australia and Canada, positions that retain prosperity rooted in material abundance based on agricultural and extractive industries. In the 1980s and 1990s three of the four nations, the exception again being Canada, regardless of the political party in power, pursued supply-side economic policies, shifting public resources from social welfare programs to economic development efforts, primarily through tax cuts for the business sector but also through programs that stimulated technology innovation, whether through military or civilian R&D (Jessop 1993; Mowery 1994). (Although Canada was not able to institute such policies at the national level, a number of provincial governments did [Bell and Sadlak 1992; Michael and Holdaway 1992].) At the same time, all four countries attempted to reduce government expenditures to their national debt. As supply-side economic and debt-reduction policies were instituted, entitlement programs, particularly Social Security, Medicare, and primary and secondary education, expanded enormously, largely in response to demographic changes.

This combination of policies—supply-side economics, debt reduction, and increased entitlements—had powerful consequences for postsecondary education. Although postsecondary participation rates vary greatly among the four countries, none of the nations treats higher education as an entitlement program. Given the fiscal constraints imposed by conservative supply-side economic and debt-reduction policies, together with the growth of entitlement programs, less public money was available for postsecondary education, and what new money was available was concentrated in technoscience and market-related fields in what amounted to a higher education version of supply-side economics. In the words of a recent British white paper, postsecondary education in all four countries was directed toward national "wealth creation" and away from its traditional concern with the liberal education of undergraduates (White Paper 1993).

Whether scholars write about "high technology" (Reich 1991), the "information economy" (Castells 1993), or "technoscience" (Aronowitz and DiFazio 1994), they see as central to global competition national strength in computers, telecommunications, electronics, advanced materials, artificial intelligence, and biotechnology, whether as the basis for whole new industries or as a means for streamlining old industries. Technoscience makes impossible the separation of science and technology, basic and applied research, discovery and innovation (Touraine 1974; Lyotard 1984; Aronowitz and DiFazio 1994). Technoscience is at once science and product. It collapses the distinction between knowledge and commodity; knowledge becomes commodity. Telecommunications and biotechnology exemplify technoscience (Sassen 1991; Kevles and Hood 1992).

Although discussion of technoscience is usually confined to the physical and biological sciences that are related directly to manufacturing, the distinction between manufacturing and services is increasingly difficult to maintain (see Note 2), and the social sciences and professional schools are developing services with technoscience components which are marketed as products. Examples are legal tools and financial instruments as well as software packages that depend on sophisticated mathematical and statistical capabilities. In some ways technoscience is congealed intellectual labor, embodied in infrastructure, product, and software, authoritative, almost irrefutable, because its functions and formulas are inaccessible, distanced from ready manipulation and intuitive understanding (see Latour and Woolgar [1979] on the ability of technology to resist intellectual challenge). Universities, whether through R&D or education and training, are the font of technoscience for postindustrial economies.

As movement from bipolar to multipolar world trade heightens global competition, corporations and state agencies often work together to stimulate technoscience. Business leaders want increased civilian R&D to develop technoscience products competitive in global markets (Mowery 1994; Etzkowitz 1994; Slaughter and Rhoades 1996). Political leaders seek to stimulate technoscience as a way out of the impasse created by the failure of the Keynesian nation state. Leaders of nations, corporations, and universities hope that subsidy of technoscience innovation will recreate the prosperity of the post–World War II period (1945–70). Specifically, they see technoscience as generating numerous high paying jobs that will replace the well-paid blue collar manufacturing jobs characteristic of Fordism. In the four countries, leaders of state as well as business leaders have come together around programs to stimulate innovation, usually through building industry-government-academic partnerships led by industry, held together by government, and serviced by universities on the technoscience side (Business–Higher Education Forum 1983; Buchbinder and Newson 1990).

Because multinationals and nation states are pursuing technoscience as the way to increase shares of world markets, they are simultaneously pursuing intellectual property protection strategies. To reduce multipolar competition, especially from states with low labor costs and rising educational attainment, established industrial countries have worked assiduously to protect the intellectual property embodied in technoscience. The European Community (EC), General Agreement on Tariffs and Trade (GATT), and North American Free Trade Agreement (NAFTA) all recognize copyright and patents and attendant royalty and licensing agreements and have strong sanctions for violation.[6] Universities are a source that corporations and governments look to for discovery that will yield intellectual property. (To some degree, universities, at least in the United States, also compete with corporations, given that many universities have established technology licensing programs to increase institutional revenues [Slaughter and Rhoades 1993].) Leaders of corporations, government, and tertiary institutions increasingly see faculty work as possible intellectual property, more valuable in global markets as product or commodity than as unremunerated contribution to an international community of scholars.

Globalization theories underline the importance of higher education to technoscience, to industrial policy, and to intellectual property strategies. Universities are the central producers of technoscience, the primary product of postindustrial economies. At the R&D level, faculty and graduate students participate in innovation, increasingly working with industry on government-sponsored technoscience initiatives. Advances in R&D create new fields of knowledge—materials science, optical science, electronic communications, biotechnology—which reshape undergraduate education. Universities provide the high level of training, at the undergraduate and graduate levels, essential to technoscience. Increasingly the service component of universities is being rein-

6. Copyrights and patents are monopolies, protecting their holders from competition for various periods of time. Patents provide a seventeen-year period, with possible renewal at the end of that time. The Copyright Act of 1976 provides for copyright for the lifetime of the author plus an additional fifty years. During the period in which the patent or copyright is held, it is possible for the owner to gain control of markets and eliminate competition. The counterargument is that authors and inventors would not create intellectual property without the possibility of being rewarded through royalties and licenses derived from copyright and licensing, nor would businesses invest in new products unless they were able to reduce risk somewhat through purchase of copyrights and patents.

terpreted as contributing to national wealth creation (White Paper 1993). As Guy Neave puts it, "education is less part of social policy but is increasingly viewed as a subsector of economic policy" (1988, 274).[7]

National Higher Education Policies

To understand more concretely the impact that globalization has had on higher education policy, we review policy development in the four countries from 1980 forward. We look at both science and technology policy (research and graduate level education) and access, curricula, and financial aid policies (undergraduate education). We think that graduate and undergraduate policies cannot be understood separately, given the degree to which graduate education drives undergraduate, particularly at research universities. We also look closely at the way changes in higher education policy at the national level shape institutional and faculty autonomy. And, of course, we examine the degree to which national policies promote academic capitalism.

The United Kingdom

The United Kingdom demonstrates dramatically the pattern of change that has taken place in tertiary education in the four countries in response to global competition. With regard to access, in a twenty-year period the system moved from an elitist binary system, with the greatest numbers of students in the lower tier, to a unitary system that was expanded at the expense of the higher tier. In terms of career training and curricula, national policies privileged science and technology in terms of the numbers of student places and research. National research policies moved away from basic or curiosity-driven research to research tied more tightly to state initiatives aimed at increasing industrial competitiveness. Overall, the system lost autonomy because of major changes in governance structures, and professors lost many of their prerogatives with regard to control over their work.

Like many others, the British higher education system expanded greatly in the post–World War II period, nearly quadrupling in size between 1945 and

7. Neave writes about European countries generally rather than the four countries with which we are concerned. Overall, the European Community is developing policies on commercialization of science and technology congruent with those discussed here, strengthening the established industrial countries' attempts to maintain global shares through technoscience. There are, however, setbacks to the general direction of European Community policies, as in the case of the rejection of patents for living things, whether animal, plant, or person. The United States permits the patenting of life.

1970, doubling from 7 percent in 1964 to 13 percent in 1971 (Kogan and Kogan 1983; McFarland 1993). In 1963 the high point of expansion was probably reached with the Robbins Committee, which articulated the principle that all those who qualified for entry and wanted a place should be able to attend college or university. Universities were characterized by a powerful professional culture that explicitly rejected entrepreneurial initiatives and business goals (Robins and Webster 1985). Universities enjoyed a great deal of autonomy (Berdahl 1959). The University Grants Committee (UGC) acted as a buffer between the state and the institutions and had the authority to make decisions on institutional resource requests for research, drawing funds directly from the Treasury Department after making decisions about research funding on the basis of national needs for research in particular areas and on academic criteria for excellence in research (Shattock and Berdahl 1984).

Although tertiary education was not favored in terms of resources in the 1970s, higher education policy did not change dramatically in the United Kingdom until the 1980s. Thatcherism was the driving force behind the change (Gamble 1989). According to Michael Shattock (1989, 34),

> Within three days of Mrs. Thatcher's taking office in 1979, 100 million pounds were cut overnight from the universities' budgets, and, between 1980 and 1984, 17 percent was removed from the grants made by government to the UGC (University Grants Committee, which, at that point provided about 90 percent of the operating costs of British universities). . . . Four thousand academic posts were lost, mostly through government-funded early retirement. And, from 1985 onwards, the universities have lost a further 2 percent per annum from their budgets.

In the mid 1980s British business leaders worked with the Thatcher government to build an enterprise culture in tertiary education. In 1985 the push was articulated forcefully by the Jarrett Committee, chaired by a leading industrialist, which called for higher education to adopt more efficient managerial styles and structures. Business leaders organized the Council for Industry and Higher Education, an independent body supported by corporations. The council was composed of thirty-two heads of large companies and twelve heads of tertiary institutions. "Its aim was to encourage industry and higher education to work together, and its policy paper *Towards Partnership* (1987) argued for greater access to and more variety in higher education, as well as a shift toward science and technology provision" (Pratt 1992, 38). This group sought successfully to increase places in science and technology, particularly in the less costly polytechnic sector, and to increase civilian R&D, integrating it with economic development.

The work of politicians, industrialists, and higher education managers bore fruit in a 1987 white paper and the 1988 Education Act. The white paper called for "major changes . . . to improve the effectiveness and purposes of higher education." In particular, "higher education should serve the economy more effectively" and "have closer links with industry and commerce, and promote enterprise," and expand access "to take account of the country's need for highly qualified manpower," including studying the needs of the economy so as to achieve "the right number and balance of graduates." Research should be targeted "to prospects for commercial exploitation" (Secretary of State for Education and Science 1987).

The 1988 Education Act began to make these intentions law. It diminished differences between universities and polytechnics, abolishing the UGC along with the polytechnic board, and replacing them with smaller boards, dominated numerically by business leaders (Fulton 1991). This was a powerful attack on the autonomy of academics, symbolic of the end of an era of independent academic culture (Shattock 1994). Along with the demise of the UGC, the government directed that "state expenditures on higher education should be regarded as payments for services provided rather than as block grants to institutions" (Johnes 1992, 173). Universities and polytechnics were forced to develop competitive bidding schemes for students to increase institutional cost effectiveness.

In 1992 the binary system was abolished by the Department of Education and Science (DES). Teaching and research, once considered a single function in university funding, were differentiated and each allocated to institutions on a separate bidding system. Teaching moneys depended on numbers of undergraduate students and quality assessments, which looked at quantifiable outcomes and which were performed by agencies outside the institutions (Peters 1992). The research allocations previously incorporated in large institutional grants given automatically to universities were taken away, and competition for research was opened up to the system as a whole.

According to Martin Trow, Sir Peter Swinnerton-Dyer, head of the Universities Funding Council, which oversees the new unitary system, takes the following position,

(i) Enrollments in higher education in the U.K. are going to grow over the next decades. (ii) Public money for the system may grow also, but not at current cost levels and not as fast as enrollments. (iii) Therefore the unit of resource must and will continue to decline, although the Government is not prepared to say when the unit will hit bottom, nor is it prepared to discuss capital costs at this time. (iv) On the whole, capital growth will be a problem for the universities and not of the central government. (v) Public policy for higher education in this country has as its main goals to get more teaching and research for less public money, at less per unit of teaching and research. On the whole this is to be seen as an improvement in the efficiency of your institutions. (Trow 1992, 214)

In other words, abolishing the binary divide was a way of reducing the very high costs of universities by allowing less prestigious polytechnics and colleges to compete openly with them. By competing among themselves, institutions in the postsecondary sector would provide the finances for expansion of the system to meet rising enrollment demands by leveling down, not up, undercutting the rich resource base of the universities yet not providing the polytechnics with the same resources as universities.

The demise of the binary system and the institution of competition for research funds formalized the steady erosion of the research component of general university funds (GUF) throughout the 1980s. Between 1980 and 1987, GUF funding in the United Kingdom grew by 10 percent, while separately budgeted funding increased by 32 percent (Martin, Irvine, and Isard 1990). Rather than automatically receiving institutional funds for research, professors increasingly had to compete for funds targeted to strategic goals in technoscience areas. Following evolutionary theorists of science and technology, the government moved away from "the assumption of neoclassical economics that scientific and technological information moved freely between organizations" and instead viewed innovative technologies "as developing largely independently of science," or, when technology was related to science, as developing "in a more complex way than linear models suggest" (Gummett 1991; see also Gibbons et al. 1994). Government science and technology policy began to focus on "university-industry relations and upon the development of 'strategic' research to underpin new fields of technology, often across the boundaries of established disciplines," with special attention to "exploitable areas of science," and at the same time greatly increased assessment and evaluation of R&D programs (Gummett 1991, 35; see also Leydesdorff 1994). These policies led to a concentration of research resources in Interdisciplinary Research Centres won through competitive bidding and to the development of patent exploitation and technology licensing programs (Williams 1992; Gering and Schmied 1993). This direction was reaffirmed by a 1993 white paper that addressed the research function of postsecondary education and pressed universities and colleges to make a more direct contribution to wealth creation through research (White Paper 1993).

The United States

Although Mrs. Thatcher and Mr. Reagan had similar political philosophies and were heads of state at approximately the same time, their specific policies for higher education were quite different, at least in part because of dissimilar state structures, political economies, and academic cultures. In contrast to the United Kingdom, where change was systemic, initiated by the government through DES, and encompassed undergraduate education as well as graduate education and research, in the United States change at the federal level in the 1980s was piecemeal, emanating as much from the Congress as from the executive branch, and concentrated on the research function. Corporate leaders worked with political leaders and heads of universities to shift research away from basic and military research to civilian technoscience that met postindustrial needs (Etzkowitz 1994; Slaughter and Rhoades 1996).

With regard to student access, change started even earlier. In the early 1970s the Nixon administration, working with national policy groups such as the Committee for Economic Development, foundations such as the Carnegie Foundation for the Advancement of Teaching, and private and public higher education institutions, introduced the idea of market forces in higher education. Together they developed a high tuition–high aid policy through which government gave aid to students rather than institutions, thus making students consumers in the tertiary education marketplace. Institutions competed with each other to attract students and their Pell grants, which policy worked as long as grants matched costs and were equally available to students in all higher education sectors. (For an extended discussion of these policy changes and their consequences for research universities, see Chapter Three in this book.)

With regard to access, the numbers of students increased somewhat but varied greatly by sector. Community colleges absorbed the majority of *first generation* students and *students of color*—euphemisms for working and underclass college students (Grubb and Tuma 1991). In part these students concentrated in the lowest tier because costs were lower, especially in four-year institutions, although students in low-cost community colleges received the least aid of all postsecondary students because of eligibility rules that penalized part-time students and lack of financial aid services for students (Hearn and Longanecker 1993). High tuition–high aid policies did not cover the full costs of most students as the price of higher education rose, and the proportion of the costs borne by students increased concomitantly. As costs increased, federal legislation promoted loans as a way to bridge the growing gap between federal aid grants and college costs (Breneman 1993a).

Table 2.1   Selected U.S. Legislation Enabling a Competitiveness R&D Policy

1980	PL 96-480	Stevenson-Wydler Technology Innovation Act, as amended in 1986 and 1990
1980	PL 65-517	Bayh-Dole Act, and Reagan's 1983 Memo on Government Patent Policy
1982	PL 97-219	Small Business Innovation Development Act
1983	PL 97-414	Orphan Drug Act, as amended 1984, 1985, and 1990
1984	PL 98-462	National Cooperative Research Act
1986	PL 99-660	Drug Export Amendments Act of 1986
1987		Presidential Executive Order 12591
1988	PL 100-418	Omnibus Trade and Competitiveness Act
1993	PL 103-182	North American Free Trade Agreement
1993	PL 230-24	Defense Appropriations Act, Technology Reinvestment Program

In the 1980s and 1990s despite marked differences in the political institutions of the United Kingdom and the United States, leaders of large corporations, heads of universities, and political leaders in both countries used their unique institutions to develop competitiveness policies with regard to R&D. The vehicles for policy development were organizations such as the Business–Higher Education Forum (1983, 1986a, 1986b) and the Government-University-Industry Research Roundtable (1992), but these organizations were only two of many (see, e.g., Committee on Science, Engineering, and Public Policy 1992, 1993; President's Council of Advisors on Science and Technology 1992). Moreover, organizations that brought together leaders of industry, academia, and government developed in the several states in the 1980s and 1990s (Johnson 1984; U.S. Congress 1984; Lambright and Rahm 1991).

At the same time, a strong competitiveness coalition emerged in Congress and was ready to translate competitiveness policies into law (Slaughter and Rhoades 1996). (A selection of the many laws passed promoting technoscience research in universities and industry is presented in Table 2.1.) Generally, these laws allowed universities to participate in profit taking, permitted corporations exclusive access to government-funded research performed in universities and federal laboratories, and promoted joint ventures between universities and corporations, breaking down the relatively rigid organizational boundaries that had previously guarded universities' autonomy.

The Bayh-Dole Act of 1980 signaled the inclusion of universities in profit making. It permitted universities and small businesses to retain title to inventions developed with federal R&D moneys. In the words of the Congress, "It is the policy and objective of the Congress . . . to promote collaboration between commercial concerns and nonprofit organizations, *including universities"* ([emphasis ours] Bayh-Dole Act 1980). Before the Bayh-Dole Act, universities were able to secure patents on federally funded research only when the federal government, through a long and cumbersome application process, granted special approval. In a very real sense the Bayh-Dole Act encouraged academic capitalism.

The several technology transfer acts, beginning with the Stevenson-Wydler Act of 1980, pioneered the legal and administrative mechanisms for transfers between public and private entities. These acts were aimed primarily at federal laboratories but also touched on universities. For example, in the Federal Technology Transfer Act of 1986, federal laboratories were able to enter into cooperative R&D agreements with "other federal agencies, state or local governments, industrial organizations, public and private foundations, and nonprofit organizations, *including universities"* (emphasis ours).

The place of universities in the competitiveness agenda was underscored by the Small Business Innovation Development Act (1982). This act mandated that federal agencies with annual expenditures greater than $100 million devote 1.25 percent of their budgets to research performed by small businesses, which were deemed the engines of economic recovery. It passed despite the opposition of major research universities. The research universities wanted to retain the moneys for fundamental research, but the needs of business were paramount, outweighing claims for basic science (Slaughter 1990).

The Orphan Drug Act (1983) provided incentives for the development of drugs to treat rare diseases. Through tax advantages and market monopolies this act encouraged biotechnology firms—which drew heavily from academically based, federally funded R&D, whether through university spinoff companies or through licensing—to pursue niche markets for vaccines and diagnostics for diseases such as Huntington's chorea, which struck relatively small groups of victims. Such companies received a 50 percent tax credit for the cost of conducting clinical trials, often performed by universities, as well as a seven-year right to exclusivity in marketing the products (U.S. Congress 1991). University spinoff companies profited from the Orphan Drug Act, for example, Genentech, which was started by faculty at the University of California–San Francisco, where recombinant human growth hormone was first produced and then patented (Goggin and Blanpied 1986).

The 1984 National Cooperative Research Act afforded special antitrust status to R&D joint ventures and consortia. This act was crucial to university-industry collaborations. Previously, the courts had ruled that collaborations at the enterprise level were inappropriate, barring joint R&D efforts by firms in the same industries on grounds of restraint of trade. The National Cooperative Research Act made an exception for R&D, enabling broad government-industry-university funding of R&D, such as occurred with Microelectronics and Computer Technology Corporation.[8] Currently, there are more than one hundred such ventures (National Science Foundation 1989). The National Cooperative Research Act was also a counter in business leaders' strategy to overhaul national antitrust policy, promoting cooperation at home and competition abroad (Dickson 1984; Fligstein 1990).

A series of acts—the Drug Export Amendments Act of 1986, the Omnibus Trade and Competitiveness Act of 1988, NAFTA of 1993, GATT of 1994—embodied the global intellectual property strategy of the competitiveness coalition. By and large, these acts decreased regulation, specifically in the biotechnology area, and increased protection of intellectual property and enforcement of intellectual property rights. By emphasizing knowledge as a commodity, they reinforced the importance of academic capitalism in universities. (For a more detailed discussion of the provisions of these acts, see Slaughter and Rhoades 1996.)[9]

Neither President Reagan nor President Bush was enamored of a competitiveness policy if it in any way suggested that the United States was adopting an industrial policy. However, during the last two years of the Bush administration, his science and technology staff worked closely with the Council on Competitiveness in developing a bottom-up industrial policy that relied heavily on R&D (Slaughter and Rhoades 1996). In his campaign President Clinton borrowed heavily from these policy initiatives. He said, "We must go beyond sup-

---

8. Microelectronics and Computer Technology Corporation (MCTC) was a computer firm whose CEO, Admiral "Bobby" Inman, formerly of the Central Intelligence Agency, wanted to create a research consortia of U.S. electronics firms interested in developing technologies that would enable them to beat the Japanese in the race to develop a fifth generation. The consortia required modification of national antitrust rules. MCTC was ruled precompetitive and therefore allowable.

9. Legislation is only one aspect of the rule-making structures that shape competitiveness R&D policies in the United States. Other legal structures are administrative interpretations of new laws, rulings by administrative law judges, and litigation in civil courts. For example, the Internal Revenue Service does not tax the royalty income of universities, thus creating a strong incentive for universities to encourage patenting and copyrighting (Martino 1992). In 1980 in Charkabarty v. Diamond, the U.S. Supreme Court ruled that living organisms were patentable. In the same year the Patent and Trademarks Office issued the Cohen-Boyer patent on rDNA to Stanford. In 1988 the Patent and Trademarks Office issued Harvard a patent on the transgenic mouse (later globally marketed by DuPont as oncomouse, a laboratory animal for researchers). In 1990 the California Supreme Court ruled that a patient did not have a property right to his body tissues after they were used by researchers to develop a commercially important cell line (U.S. Congress 1991). Rule-making modalities other than legislation interact with new statutes to create a dense administrative-legal infrastructure for the new competitiveness policy.

port for basic research and a reliance on 'spinoffs' from defense R&D" (Clinton and Gore 1992, 2). As his position paper points out, "At present, 60 percent of the federal R&D budget is devoted to defense programs and 40 percent to non-defense programs. . . . At the very least, in the next three years the federal government should shift the balance between defense and nondefense programs back to a 50-50 balance, which would free up over $7 billion for nondefense R&D" (13–14).

In terms of university curricula and training there was little formal policy discussion at the national level in the 1980s and 1990s, in large part because higher education was the province of the several states, and curricula were set by faculty at the institutional level. However, federal grant and contract moneys for technoscience increased somewhat while moneys for the humanities and social sciences decreased dramatically (Rhoades and Slaughter 1996). Given that the number of places for graduate students was strongly—albeit indirectly—influenced by grant and contract moneys, the R&D function of universities concentrated increasingly on the sciences and engineering. In the period 1983–93 federal R&D in the science and engineering fields became more applied. Universities' share of basic research remained the same, but applied research increased by 6 percent and development by 4 percent (National Science Foundation 1993; see also Rhoades and Slaughter 1996).

Overall, in the 1980s and 1990s, U.S. policy at the federal level shifted so that colleges and universities were able to engage in academic capitalism. As in the United Kingdom, the U.S. federal science and technology policy promoted science and engineering that encouraged academic capitalism and rewarded universities that pursued these initiatives. Professors were discouraged from pursuing curiosity-driven research and were urged to engage in more commercial research (Etzkowitz 1994; Etzkowitz and Leydesdorff 1996). Given the power of the several states with regard to education, the U.S. government did not institute anything like quality assessments at the national level; however, a number of states began instituting the equivalent of quality assessments—rising junior exams, junior writing exams, value-added assessments, more standardized teaching evaluations, and performance-based budgeting—which regulated faculty's instructional work more closely (Guthrie and Pierce 1990). Although occurring in piecemeal fashion, policy changes in the United States were not dissimilar to those that took place in the United Kingdom.

Australia

During the 1980s and 1990s, Australia, like the United Kingdom and the United States, moved toward developing a closer relationship among industry, academe, and government in an effort to strengthen the national ability of private corporations to compete in a global economy. In many respects the Australian process was similar to that of the United Kingdom, although in some instances—for example, abolishing the binary divide—Australian policy developments preceded those in the United Kingdom (Williams 1992; Miller 1995). Like the United Kingdom, Australia, which also had a relatively low tertiary participation rate, saw breaking down its binary divide as a means of forcing institutions to compete with each other for students, thereby increasing the total skill output and expanding the overall number of places relatively cheaply, and to compete with each other for research moneys, ensuring more, if not cheaper, research. Unlike the United Kingdom, the Australian creation of a unified national system called for colleges of advanced education (CAEs), formerly in the lower tier of the binary system, to merge with universities, formerly in the higher tier. Before unification, Australia had eighty-five CAEs and thirteen universities. In 1987, after the organization of the unified national system, there were thirty-five universities. Because CAEs, historically concerned with vocational and technical education, were incorporated into the management and programming of universities, they tilted the system as a whole in the direction of technoscience.

Like the United Kingdom and the United States, Australia promoted science and technology at the graduate level, targeting specific areas and building university-industry-government centers and partnerships. Like the United Kingdom, the organization that buffered universities from the state was disbanded; and like the United Kingdom and United States, changes in organizational practice involved universities in academic capitalism. Unlike the United Kingdom and United States, these changes were instituted by a Labor government.

In 1988 the Hawke government instituted major organizational changes in higher education as part of an attempt to respond to the globalization of capital and labor (Pusey 1991). The Australian Labor government saw the rising productivity of nearby Asian countries as making Australian labor less competitive in southeast Asian markets. Australians were highly paid, with a minimum wage of A$11.85 (U.S.$10.00) per hour, and relatively poorly educated, with only about 10 percent of 18- to 21-year-old students going on to higher education. The Labor government saw reorganization of higher education as stimulating preparation of students in high technology fields and contributing to economic growth. "The society we want cannot be achieved without a strong economic base. In Australia this now requires a greatly increased export income, a far more favorable balance of trade and a considerable reduction in our external debt. Our industry is increasingly faced with rapidly changing international markets in which success depends on, among other things, the conceptual, creative and technical skills of the labour force and the ability to innovate and be entrepreneurial" (Dawkins 1988, 6).

To attain that end, the Labor government reorganized its education portfolio in 1987, replacing the Commonwealth Tertiary Education Commission (CTEC), an organization that, like the UGC in the United Kingdom, served to buffer higher education from other government bodies, with the National Board of Employment, Education, and Training, which included a Higher Education Council that provided advice but had no executive role. Generally, tertiary education was overseen by the Department of Employment, Education, and Training (DEET), foregrounding the economic component of education. The head of the new ministry, John Dawkins, made a number of organizational changes in higher education. Given that the federal government paid most of the bill for the tertiary sector, he had a relatively free hand. The three most significant changes for academic labor were: (1) amalgamating universities and CAEs; (2) developing policies that established targeted commercial research funding priorities; and (3) developing policies for establishing and monitoring institutional profiles (Dawkins 1988).

Creating a unified national system of higher education was probably the greatest of the three changes. Before the Dawkins organizational reforms, Australian higher education was organized into two sectors, universities and CAEs. The universities had a long history, often predating World War II, whereas the CAEs were relatively recent. The universities were geared toward research as well as teaching and focused particularly on preparation for entry into the established professions. The CAEs were focused on teaching and education for entry-level jobs in the more applied professions. The Dawkins reforms were an effort to eliminate these distinctions. Formerly, university professors were expected to do research one day in five, and they received a proportionately greater salary to cover this cost. The Dawkins reforms "clawed back" salaries from university professors and used the moneys retrieved for research for which professors throughout the unified system had to bid competitively. Similarly, professors in all universities had to compete for high status programs (Marginson 1995). The Labor government thought amalgamation would create more university places for students and stimulate more research. As in the United Kingdom, government resource flow did not match the increased number of university-level places, creating a situation in which the tertiary system was likely to be leveled downward rather than upward.

As amalgamation took place, Dawkins developed a policy of targeting research priorities, by and large concerned with political economic goals, such as technology to stimulate job growth, to protect the environment, and to build energy self-sufficiency. Intense competition for available moneys made professors more willing to consider new ways to fund research. By 1993, federal agencies funded only 20 percent of research grant applications (Wood, Meek, and Harman 1992). The most obvious pots of money were under the rainbows of the targeted areas, which usually focused on commercial endeavors that moved academe closer to the market. Securing these funds often involved university collaborations with industries and governments, usually through the formation of centers of excellence or centers in key technology areas (Turpin and Hill 1991; Hill 1993; Hill and Turpin 1993). At the same time, institutions, often working in concert with the several states, began to develop technology licensing programs and technology parks (Joseph 1989a, 1989b). Altogether, large amounts of research moneys spent previously on professors' curiosity-driven research were redirected toward government and industry goals that focused on building Australian competitiveness in global markets (Wood 1992).

As the unified system was directed toward more targeted research, DEET began to monitor institutions of higher education, whether universities or CAEs, more closely. Each year, universities and colleges were asked to develop institutional profiles in concert with the ministry as part of the federal funding process. As a condition of funding, institution and ministry had to reach common priorities. In 1993 DEET began conducting quality assurance exercises. These exercises reviewed internal university procedures for quality control, and institutions able to demonstrate efficacy with regard to quality procedures were eligible for a share of A$76 million that was set aside as a reward. Although these moneys were but a small part of university budgets, institutions that won them enhanced their student-drawing power immeasurably.

Before the 1990s, unlike those in the United Kingdom and the United States, the Australian private sector did not play much of a role in bringing tertiary education closer to economic development issues. In the early 1980s in countries other than Australia, business groups and organizations worked closely with the government and the tertiary education community to reform postsecondary education in ways that attended more closely to economic needs. In Australia peak business associations and other industry groups did not join with higher education leaders until 1990, when the Australian Business/Higher Education Round Table was organized (Marshall 1995). In other words, change in Australia was led by a Labor government concerned with industrial competitiveness rather than by industry or university groups.

As in the United Kingdom and the United States, the Australian government developed national policies that turned R&D away from basic or fundamental research and toward academic capitalism. Before the United Kingdom did so, Australia abolished its binary divide, expanding access by forcing institutions to compete with each other for student places and faculty to compete with each other for research dollars, overall giving rise to academic capitalism. At the same time, as in the United Kingdom at the national level and the United States at the level of the several states, the instructional and curricula work of faculty was monitored more closely through institutional profiling.

Canada

As in the United States and the United Kingdom, in Canada business leaders worked closely with university and government leaders to push for change in the tertiary system, and some changes were initiated at the federal level when the Conservative government took office in the mid 1980s (Miller 1995). As in the United States, change at the federal level was largely concerned with the research function because the Canadian division of powers between provincial and federal governments gave provinces the responsibility and budget for tertiary education.[10] As in the several states in the United States, a number of provinces in Canada pushed university-industry R&D programs that were aimed at stimulating regional economic development. Again, as in the United States, change was incremental. Despite the push by industry leaders and some university and federal government and provincial leaders, little change occurred in the higher education system, making Canada the outlier in that respect among the four nations.

In the early 1980s the Corporate–Higher Education Forum was organized; its membership consisted of corporate executives and university presidents. The goals of the Corporate–Higher Education Forum were similar to those of the Council for Industry and Higher Education in the United Kingdom and the Business–Higher Education Forum in the United States. "Corporate collaboration helps to optimize the use of Canada's limited human, financial, and physical resources in research and education while tuning the research effort and the university curriculum more closely to the needs of the marketplace" (Maxwell and Currie 1984, 2).

The agenda of the Corporate–Higher Education Forum was developed during a period of university underfunding by the federal and state governments

10. Unlike the United States, the Canadian provinces do not tax directly for all funds for higher education. Instead, the federal government reallocates tax moneys to the provinces for education, health, and social services. When these moneys are returned to the provinces, no strings are attached, and the provinces are able to decide how to allocate the moneys among functions. For a comprehensive account of Canadian funding of postsecondary education, see Elliott (1995).

(Elliott 1995). Because universities were searching for new streams of revenues the development of a partnership between higher education and business which led to academic capitalism had an almost inevitable logic (de la Mothe 1987; Buchbinder and Newson 1990; Newson 1994).

The government was a third party to the partnership between business and higher education. Like political leaders in the United States, the United Kingdom, and Australia, Canadian leaders viewed technoscience as a vehicle for creating high-paying jobs that preserved shares in the global market. A goal of the Mulroney government was to double the share of GNP spent on R&D by 1991. Mulroney established a National Council for Science and Technology, which he chaired, and a program to stimulate corporate giving for academic R&D. As a proportion of total R&D, Canada's privately funded R&D was the lowest of any major industrial country. The government tried to encourage contributions to R&D from the private sector by tying increases in university research support to corporate contributions to universities or the national research councils. As Julien (1989, 69) puts it, "The aims of this policy could not be clearer, the intention being, firstly, to encourage the private sector to fund university research and, by so doing, acknowledge its social and economic importance and, secondly, to strengthen the links between universities and the private sector and thereby promote and quicken the transfer of knowledge."

This policy was reflected in goals and priorities of the Science Council of Canada (1987, 17), an advisory body to government: "Teaching and basic research are major roles of the university and must remain so. But as knowledge replaces raw materials as the primer of the world economy, the universities' part in creating wealth—too often understated—becomes crucially important. The intellectual resources of the university are needed to help revitalise mature industries and generate the product ideas needed to create new ones. Canada's future prosperity increasingly depends on designing effective ways to integrate the university and the market place."

The federal government supported its commitment to harnessing research to economic innovation through a wide array of projects, often sharing costs with provincial and local governments. The InnovAction program, an agreement signed by the federal government and provincial and local governments, was an early example (Julien 1989; Buchbinder and Newson 1990). The federal government also worked in partnership with provincial governments to develop research parks and centers of excellence. In Canada research parks linked universities with high technology companies and promoted technology transfer from academy to corporation. In the early 1990s there were twelve such parks, with the majority started in the 1980s (Bell and Sadlak 1992).

"Centers of excellence," also called "university-industry research centers," were modeled on the U.S. National Science Foundation programs that had begun promoting university-industry interactions as early as the 1970s. Like the National Science Foundation centers, the Canadian centers were run by boards with university and industry representatives. The province of Ontario was especially active in creating centers of excellence in the 1980s, for example, the Ontario Laser and Lightwave Centre, the Waterloo Centre for Groundwater Research, the Manufacturing Research Corporation of Ontario, the Ontario Centre for Materials Research Centre, the Telecommunications Research Institute of Ontario, the Information Technology Research Centre, and the Institute for Space and Terrestrial Science. In the early 1990s the federal government began funding centers of excellence across the rest of the provinces (Bell and Sadlak 1992).

National commitment to science and technology innovation in commercial fields tipped Canadian R&D from fundamental to applied science. In a Natural Sciences and Engineering Research Council Survey in 1978–79, "33.6 percent [of scientists] stated they were doing applied work, and 66.4 percent characterized their work as toward the advancement of knowledge. By 1987–88 the figures had almost reversed themselves with 54.8 percent in the applied category and 45.2 percent in the advancement of knowledge category" (Buchbinder and Newson 1990, 375).

Throughout the 1980s, business and government leaders in Canada proposed initiatives to create industry–higher education–academic partnerships (Skolnik 1983a, 1983b, 1987). However, this policy direction was never adopted; instead, Canada gave the highest priority to increasing and widening access, overtaking the United States in terms of participation rates in 1988 (Jones and Skolnik 1992). Although Canadian scientists view themselves as doing more applied work, for the most part Canadian academics have resisted rapproachment with business, despite promptings from some federal agencies. In the words of Glen Jones (1991), there have been "modest modifications and structural stability." Canadian academics have perhaps been able to resist pressures by the business and the federal government because Canada has by far the most decentralized higher education system of the four countries (Skolnik 1990; Jones and Skolnik 1992).

Convergence of Higher Education Policies

In the 1980s and 1990s the higher education policies of three of the four countries, Canada being the exception, began to converge. The areas of convergence were science and technology policy, curriculum, access and finance, and degree of autonomy. For the most part, these policies are concerned with economic competitiveness: product and process innovation, channeling students and resources into curricula that meet the needs of a global marketplace, preparing more students for the postindustrial workplace at lower costs, and managing faculty and institutional work more effectively and efficiently. Each of the countries developed a number of policies outside these parameters which did *not* converge. Even in the areas of convergence, the four countries arrived at similar policies by very different paths. Australia and the United Kingdom used their ministries of education, the former led by a Labor government, the latter by a Conservative government. In Canada and the United States the provinces and the several states, as would be expected in relatively decentralized systems, often developed their own initiative to promote academic capitalism. In the United States, Congress was more aggressive than the executive branch in creating an infrastructure for academic capitalism. Despite the very real differences in their political cultures, the four countries developed similar policies at those points where higher education intersected with globalization of the postindustrial political economy. Tertiary education policies in all countries moved toward science and technology policies that emphasized academic capitalism at the expense of basic or fundamental research, toward curricula policy that concentrated moneys in science and technology and fields close to the market (business and intellectual property law, for example), toward increased access at lower government cost per student, and toward organizational policies that undercut the autonomy of academic institutions and of faculty.

R&D was probably the area in which the most dramatic policy changes occurred. In three countries national policy shifted from promoting basic or fundamental research to privileging science and technology policy aimed at national wealth creation. Even in the United States and the United Kingdom, where fundamental R&D in the postwar period was to some degree conflated with defense R&D, strong civilian science and technology policies emerged (Etzkowitz 1994; Slaughter and Rhoades 1996). The very words used to describe R&D changed. R&D was no longer focused on basic or fundamental research, which came to be referred to rather derisively as "professors' curiosity-driven research," but on precompetitive, strategic, or targeted research (Wood 1992; Etzkowitz 1994; Slaughter and Rhoades 1996).

Precompetitive research usually refers to research that benefits corporations at the enterprise level, before specific firms try to gain exclusive knowledge advantage. The Microelectronics and Computer Technology Corporation agreement in the United States (see Note 8) is a good example of precompetitive research. *Strategic research* refers to broadly targeted research, for example, some areas of biotechnology. *Targeted research* refers to narrower commercial programs, for example, the five areas identified by the Clinton administration as areas for R&D investment—areas addressed by the Advanced Technology Program. Similarly, we now speak of science and technology policy, not of science policy, stressing the product/manufacturing dimension of techno-science (Gummett 1991; Mowery 1994). So too, notions of the way science and technology move from academy to industry have become more complex, changing from *spinoff*, a concept that did not dwell on the causality of the leap from laboratory to commercial product, to *technology transfer*, which envisioned a relatively linear but highly managed transfer, to *evolutionary explanations*, which make the process more complex (Gummett 1991; Leydesdorff 1994). The three countries have adopted discourses on science and technology policy which go far beyond, sometimes even do away with, basic and fundamental research as central categories. All three countries see R&D as the font of technoscience, necessary for home-based multinationals to compete successfully in the global economy.

As part of the transformation of R&D, all four countries have seen the growth of technology parks, usually sited close to universities, sometimes partially funded by local or state/provincial governments, but often receiving some federal subsidy. So too all four countries have seen universities develop technology licensing schemes that join universities and corporations. Sometimes these are federally sanctioned, as was the case when the U.S. Congress turned patent ownership over to the institutions. More often, universities share royalties with the federal and state agencies that supported the research from which the invention was derived.

A number of these policy initiatives involve universities in profit making. The clearest cases are university technology licensing and university equity positions in faculty spinoff enterprises. In these instances universities profit to the degree that products sell. However, technology parks bring profits directly to universities, if only in the form of rent and sometimes through housing joint ventures. Centers of excellence, consortia with industry, and various university-industry partnerships most often provide multiyear government and corporate funding for commercially geared R&D but can utilize any of the profit-sharing schemes described above: share of royalty or licensing income, joint venture, or equity position. Changes in R&D policy in the several countries, then, have moved universities into academic capitalism.

Curriculum policies in all four countries have resulted in cutbacks in the arts and humanities (with the exception of Australia) and in the social sciences (Martin and Irvine 1992). In countries in which the power and budgets for tertiary education are not reserved for the states and provinces—namely, in Australia and the United Kingdom—the changes were made through allocation of student places (and, indirectly, faculty positions), with more students being funded in science and technology than in other areas. In the United Kingdom, for example, the fees allocated for social sciences and humanities students were cut by 30 percent, to £1,300, whereas fees for science and engineering laboratory courses rose to £2,772 per student (Halliday 1993). In the United States changes were made indirectly through cutbacks in research funding in non–science and technology areas, which resulted in fewer graduate student places.

In the United States, where salaries are partially determined by professors' viability in the market and through individual negotiation between professor and administration, marked increases in salaries in technoscience areas reallocated institutional resources to these fields, making them more attractive to students. Analysis of changes of U.S. faculty salaries by field from 1983 through 1993 shows that faculty with the highest salaries and percentage increase (70 percent and above) were in fields concerned with technology (engineering and computers), producer services (business and management, law) and health sciences, all fields focused on knowledge as commodity and on intellectual property strategies (see Table 2.2 and Slaughter and Rhoades 1996). The greatest gains were made by engineering, an applied science geared closely to R&D competitiveness policies, and by business, health sciences, computer and information science, and law, all also connected closely to R&D competitiveness policies; the physical sciences and mathematics, the doyens of "pure science," did not make nearly such dramatic gains. Even if salary level rather than percentage of increase is considered, the physical sciences and mathematics are substantially below the top tier, with $10,000 to $23,000 annual salary differences that range between them and salaries in the top tier. The lowest salaries and the lowest percentage increases are in the third tier, in fields furthest from the market, those closer to the social welfare functions of the state.[11] The difference in the percentage of salary increases between the lowest six fields in the third tier (philosophy and religion, foreign language, home economics, letters, education, and performing arts) and the five fields in the top tier ranges from 22 to 30 percent. As other countries move toward differential salaries, as the

11. With the exception of philosophy and religion, these fields have majority female student bodies. For an analysis of the gender implications of the restructuring precipitated in part by competitiveness R&D, see Slaughter (1993).

Table 2.2   Average Salaries of Full Professor by Field, 1983–1993

Field	Average salary	% Increase
	($75–90,000)[a]	
Law	$89,777	71.1
Engineering	$77,985	84.6
Health science	$77,913	78.7
Business and management	$77,535	79.0
Computers and information science	$75,964	74.8
	($60–74,000)	
Physical science	$65,914	63.2
Mathematics	$63,776	59.7
Psychology	$62,567	59.5
Public affairs	$62,435	57.6
Social science	$62,352	59.9
Library science	$61,827	59.5
Interdisciplinary	$61,808	59.0
	($50–60,000)	
Architecture	$59,322	57.0
Agribusiness	$59,178	63.8
Communications	$58,933	61.3
Philosophy and religion	$58,424	53.7
Foreign language	$57,344	52.4
Home economics	$57,157	54.3
Letters	$56,744	52.3
Education	$56,605	55.9
Performing arts	$52,495	61.4

Source: From the American Association of University Professors (1994) Annual report on the economic status of the profession, 1993–1994, *Academe* March/April: Table 5. Based on data from the National Association of State Universities and Land Grant Colleges.

[a] Average salary of full professor.

United Kingdom has, the resources concentrated in technoscience curricula, already rich in student places, will be concentrated further.

In all four countries, despite projections to the contrary, enrollments went up, tuition went up, government share of costs went down, and governments turned more to loans than grants to support students. Generally, working class and first generation college students were concentrated in the lower tiers of the system in all four countries. With the end of the binary divide in Australia and the United Kingdom, this may change somewhat, although it is likely that middle class students will move into the space created by competition among institutions, much as middle class students in the United States moved into state-funded four-year and comprehensive institutions, and less well-off students into the community colleges (National Center for Education Statistics 1995). As tuitions continue to increase and the rate of government spending continues to decrease, able students from families willing to purchase tertiary education are likely to occupy the most prestigious places.

The degree of autonomy possessed by institutions and professors has been reduced in the several areas discussed: R&D, curricula, and access. The loss of institutional autonomy was clearly seen with regard to R&D. In the United Kingdom the government agency responsible for buffering institutions from the state—the UGC—was abolished and replaced with agencies dominated by members of the business community. In Australia the CTEC, a body modeled on the British UGC, was abolished, and many of its functions were taken over by DEET, an agency the very title of which stressed the relationship between education and the economy (Marshall 1995). In the United States the agency concerned with pure science—the National Science Foundation—began to promote industry-led research (Slaughter and Rhoades 1996). To a substantial degree, the divisions between private and public organizations which had long protected institutional autonomy began to break down. The rule changes allowed public and nonprofit entities, whether universities, government agencies, or nonprofit research institutes, entry into the market, changing our commonsense understanding of what is public and what is private. Institutions still labeled public and nonprofit were able to patent and profit from discoveries made by their professional employees. Simultaneously, private, profit-making organizations were able to make alienable areas of public life previously held by the community as a whole: scientific knowledge, data bases, technology, strains and properties of plants, even living animals and fragments of human beings (Slaughter and Rhoades 1996). With the exception of Australia, this privatization was industry led, held together by government policies and government funding and serviced by tertiary institutions trying to augment funds.

Professors lost autonomy when research policies shifted from support for basic (professors' curiosity-driven) research to more applied research geared to economic development. Professorial autonomy with regard to curricula was also eroded. National competitiveness policies, supported by industrialists, government bureaucrats, university administrators, and some faculty, to a considerable degree determined the direction of curricula through resource flow. Decisions about the growth or decline of curricula were no longer made exclusively by faculty operating in collegium. Instead, decisions were made at a national level to strengthen technoscience in hopes of stimulating national wealth creation. As market considerations began to influence professorial salaries, the collegial model of governance was attenuated as faculty who professed certain curricula were, quite literally, valued more than faculty who professed in less well-funded fields.

Professors lost autonomy in other aspects of their work. The various quality assessment and accountability schemes developed in the four countries often called for evaluation from bodies outside tertiary institutions and frequently from bodies outside specific disciplines. As decisions about professors' performance of academic work were moved outside the purview of professional expertise, professors became more like all other informational workers and less like a community of scholars. Again, Canada was an exception; it has no external review at the federal level, and only one province has instituted an external evaluation system.

Since 1980, the higher education policies of three of the four countries have converged, although the countries remain divergent on a number of important dimensions: for example, degree of centralization, student participation rates, and student support. The United Kingdom and Australia dealt with higher education and academic science and technology policy through relatively centralized state agencies, the United States through less centralized state agencies. Although the United Kingdom and Australia disbanded the buffer organizations that protected higher education from the state, the same degree of centralization in these countries persisted throughout the 1980s and 1990s. The United States did not develop more centralized agencies, although its policies on the relation of education to the economy began to converge with those of Australia and the United Kingdom. Before the 1980s, Australia and the United Kingdom had relatively low higher education participation rates, with 10–12 percent of the 18- to 21-year-old cohort attending higher education institutions, whereas Canada and the United States had relatively high participation rates, with about 30 percent of the 18- to 21-year-old cohort attending. Canada overtook the United States in 1988 and now has the highest participation. Although all countries made plans to increase participation, given their very different starting points, enrollment patterns held throughout the 1980s and 1990s. With regard to student financial aid, the United States moved toward high tuition and toward loans rather than grants, and Australia and the United Kingdom explored similar policies while continuing to offer much more generous government support to students, as does Canada, than does the United States. In the United States, graduate students in technoscience fields are supported primarily from their professors' federal grants and contracts, whereas in the other countries graduate students are supported by policies of low or no tuition and often receive government stipends for living expenses (Lederman 1991).

Despite persistent divergence with regard to organization, access, and student support, a remarkable degree of convergence in higher education and R&D policy occurred in three of these four countries over the past twenty years. That convergence cannot be explained solely by the political party in power, given Australia's Labor government. We think that the convergence is best explained by globalization theory. The rise of multipolar global competition destablized Keynesian nation states, rendering problematic the implicit social contract between the citizenry and government with regard to entitlement programs and social safety nets. In the three countries, policy makers responded to increased competition for shares of global markets by reducing overall rates of increase in state expenditures and reallocating money among government functions. Generally, funds were taken away from discretionary programs, particularly from programs thought likely not to contribute in a direct way to technological innovation and economic competitiveness.

These macroeconomic policy changes had tangible consequences for tertiary education in the four countries. Academic R&D policies, the lifeblood of graduate education, became science and technology policies, more concerned with technoscience innovation and building links with the private sector than with basic or fundamental research that articulated more with learned and professional associations than with the economy. For the most part, technoscience fields gained funds while fields that were not close to the market, such as philosophy and religion, foreign languages, letters and performing arts, or fields that served the social welfare functions of the state, such as education and home economics, lost funds. Positions for faculty, places for students, and research money turned technoscience fields into growth areas in tertiary education.

Although technoscience areas generally received more money, and policy makers took the position that a postindustrial economy called for higher numbers of highly educated workers, policy makers in all four countries planned to expand student participation rates without comparably augmenting resources for tertiary education. The increase in student numbers together with the slowing in the rate of increase of state resources began to change the conditions of faculty labor in contradictory ways. On the one hand, faculty were encouraged to engage in academic capitalism. On the other hand, faculty became responsible for larger numbers of students and were watched more closely with regard to the instructional aspects of their work.

The exception was Canada. Although there was a decline in real operating funding per student and some targeted funding for high technology research and for collaborations with industry (see Chapter Three in this book), Canadian higher education did not undergo the same degree of change as the other countries. Even though the conservative Mulroney government tried to initiate a rapprochment among universities, industry, and government, for the most part there was little structural change in Canada. Canada's dissimilarity from the other countries is usually explained in terms of its extreme decentralization (Jones and Skolnik 1992). Canada, then, offers an alternative to the higher education policies developed by the other countries. The crucial question in the immediate future is whether this model can be maintained, given the size of Canada's national debt. Canada's national debt as a percent of GNP/GDP stood at 40.3 percent in 1990, almost ten percentage points higher than the other three countries (Oxley and Martin 1991, 148, Table 1).

The national policies of three of the four countries promoted academic capitalism—market and marketlike behaviors—on the part of faculty and institutions. In terms of access, institutions in Australia and the United Kingdom began to tender competitive bids for student places, contracting with the government to educate students for a fixed cost. In the United States, institutions increasingly compete to attract high tuition- and fee-paying students. In all three countries, curricula are supported differentially by the state. The United Kingdom has moved furthest in this direction, providing differential state support per student according to curricula. All four countries have instituted policies that treat R&D as a source of national wealth creation, although Canadian faculty and institutions are resisting this change. Faculty and institutions lost autonomy as higher education was integrated more closely with the market. Individual professors' freedom to pursue curiosity-driven research was curtailed by withdrawal of automatic funding to institutions to support this activity and by the increased targeting of R&D funds for commercial research. Faculty and institutions were pushed toward academic capitalism by policy directives and by shifts in the resource mix. And some faculty and institutions turned eagerly to academic capitalism, viewing it as an opportunity to exercise entrepreneurial skills, as a means to capture resources, or as a strategy for a prosperous future.

Although these countries promoted academic capitalism as a means of stimulating national growth, the success of these policies to date is mixed. Productivity and GDP increased somewhat in the 1990s, but income inequality increased in three of the four countries (Australia, the United Kingdom, and the United States, with the increases being greatest in the last two [Atkinson, Rainwater, and Smeeding 1995]). National wealth creation, as a policy, may be succeeding in terms of productivity and profitability, but recovery is not generating highly paid jobs. Indeed, relatively high levels of unemployment combined with the growth of poorly paid full-time jobs and an increasing number of part-time jobs have given rise to the concept of *jobless recovery* (Rifkin 1995). Even those with "some college and more" are no longer assured of a high return on their investment in higher education (Harrison and Bluestone 1990). (However, young workers entering the job market *without* some college or more are very likely to fare less well than their college-educated counterparts.) Paradoxically, national policies that promote technoscience and its attendant automation and corporate restructuring may play into the elimination of professional positions formerly filled by college-educated workers (Abbott 1988). The longevity of these trends and what they will mean in terms of popular support for higher education are not yet clear.

In sum, postindustrial economies are replacing industrial ones even as globalization of the political economy has destabilized traditional industrialized economies by replacing bipolar trading relationships with multipolar ones, causing the traditional industrialized nations to lose shares of global markets. In areas where higher education intersects with the global economy, three of the four countries have responded by developing policies that promote academic capitalism. Despite very different political cultures and institutions, the higher education policies of three of the four countries converged on science and technology policy, curriculum, access and finance, and degree of autonomy. These policies are, for the most part, geared toward increasing national economic competitiveness; they are concerned with product and process innovation, channeling students and resources into well-funded curricula that meet the needs of a global marketplace, preparing more students for the postindustrial workplace at lower costs, and managing faculty and institutional work more effectively and efficiently.

3

ORGANIZATIONAL TURBULENCE
AND RESOURCE DEPENDENCE

IN THIS CHAPTER WE explore the ways in which national policies in Australia, Canada, the United Kingdom, and the United States translate into higher education finance. We look at financial trends in postsecondary education over a twenty-year period, illustrating the way in which globalization of the economy resulted in a slowdown in the flow of public resources to postsecondary institutions, a slowdown most marked with regard to undesignated funds. Concomitantly, we examine the growth of alternative income streams. We make the case that national and state/provincial restriction of discretionary resources created increased resource dependence at the institutional level, causing institutions and professors to look to alternative revenue sources to maintain institutional income. These trends in postsecondary finance involved higher education more deeply in academic capitalism and pushed higher education closer to the market.

If global markets created national policies that channeled money away from social welfare and education functions of the state, specifically higher education, then how is this manifested at the national level? In other words, were the policy changes described in Chapter Two implemented in ways that could be measured empirically by higher education financial data? The theory that guides our interpretation of data in this chapter is that of resource dependence (Pfeffer and Salancik 1978; Pfeffer 1992). Our use of the notion of resource dependence (described later in this chapter) is tied tightly to political economic theories dealing with the emergence of a global economy, as discussed in Chapter Two. Whether responding to market pressures, movement of unrestricted capital, or political economic pressures from the business class, nation states developed policies in the 1980s which targeted public moneys for functions such as technology innovation, intellectual property management, and producer services development. These policy shifts served as a rationing device, shifting higher education moneys from block grants toward specific goals that were consistent with the new orthodoxy of making industry more competitive in the global market. Given that the federal governments, and, in the United States, the several states, paid the largest share of all higher education costs, government targeting of functions for research and program investment meant there were fewer unrestricted public resources available, thereby creating conditions of acute resource dependence in higher education systems.

Resource dependence theory suggests that as unrestricted moneys for higher education constrict, institutions within a national system will change their resource-seeking patterns to compete for new, more competitively based funds. To respond to new opportunities, institutions will have to shift away from basic research toward more applied science and technology. Further, they will likely increase tuition and become more active in expanding sales and services while lowering labor costs, primarily through replacing full-time faculty with part-time professors. To manage the shift from more unrestricted to more restricted moneys, institutions will likely spend more funds on administration as they attempt to oversee the transition as well as to manage new revenue-generating endeavors (such as institutional advancement—fund raising from private sources—and sales and services of their own educational activities) and academic capitalism (such as offices for patenting and licensing, technology transfer, arm's-length corporations, spinoff companies, and research parks). In other words, we believe that changes in the national financing patterns of higher education will promote academic capitalism.

If universities and faculty are shifting their efforts to maximizing external funding and lowering instructional labor costs, we should be able to see these trends in higher education financial data. Using Organization for Economic Cooperation and Development (OECD) data for the four countries, we consider changes in percent of gross national product (GNP) devoted to higher education, of general public funds allocated to postsecondary institutions, of tuition and fees charged by these organizations, and of other income generated. We then examine changes in indicator revenue categories: gifts, grants, and contracts; and sales and services. Finally, we look at expenditures: instruction, research, public service, administration, maintenance of plant, and student aid. Our method is not to compare countries across all of these dimensions, given that the quality of the data and the recording categories vary by country, but to look at change within each country to see if its postsecondary institutions are exhibiting resource-dependent behavior, winning an ever larger portion of support from sources other than block grant public funds and expending the resources in new ways.

Connections among Higher Education Revenues, Expenditures, and Academic Labor

Investigators, from journalists to prosecuting attorneys, learned long ago to follow money trails to track human behavior. In higher education, too, we know that income and spending patterns explain a great deal about organizational behavior. Sometimes we observe that financial patterns belie public statements as to official policy.

This principle, that financial behavior defines organizational behavior, is key to our thesis. Shifts in higher education institutional expenditures have occurred over time. *When connected to changes in revenues, changes in expenditures mean changes in the nature of academic labor.*

Expenditure shifts do suggest changes in the allocation of labor among functions or activities. For example, if in a given university, expenditures for research increase faster than the cost of research inputs then the *amount* of research being conducted will appear to have increased, regardless of how we choose to measure *amount*. Assuming for a moment that research *labor* costs have increased at the same rate as the cost of other research inputs, then increased research expenditures mean that the institution is committing more labor to research. Of course someone may be doing more teaching, too, or providing more service, but clearly there is more research going on: either more individuals are now doing research, the same individuals are doing more research, or fewer individuals are doing even more research.[1] If researchers are classified as academics, as they commonly are, then in absolute terms there is more research being done by academics. Still, on average, taken as a group, all academics may not be doing more research. If the *share* of expenditures going to research is increasing, however, all else equal, then the nature of what academics do is being altered in relative terms as well. Again, either more academics are doing research, the same number of academics are doing more research, or fewer academics are doing even more research; but now the nature of what academics do involves more research, on average. In simple terms the nature of what academics do, collectively, has been altered.

This illustration is no different from when spending is classified by object of expenditure (i.e., personnel, supplies, travel, etc.). When the cost of supplies is constant, if a given institution is spending more for supplies than it formerly was, then it has purchased more supplies. If the share of expenditures going for supplies is increasing, then the nature of institutional inputs is changing.

---

1. For definitions of the terms *faculty* and *academic*, see Chapter One, note 4.

The second connection between revenues and expenditures is similarly straightforward. To a greater or lesser degree, those who provide the resources to higher education expect certain efforts, if not results. In short, they expect that the university, more or less, will spend the money in the manner in which it was intended or required. The degree of latitude permitted in that spending, however, varies substantially. Sometimes the quid pro quo is explicit; sometimes it is only implicit; and it may even be quite vague. The amount of teaching expected of faculty by governments in return for general institutional aid is one example.

To meet whatever fiduciary responsibilities may be stipulated by resource providers, in the United States accountants have developed the terms *designated/nondesignated* and *restricted/unrestricted* to distinguish among the relative constraints invoked for various revenues. Those who provide contract money, for example, routinely specify the products or services expected in return. Normally, such moneys are considered restricted. Similarly, donors sometimes specify what their contributions are to be spent for, such as for scholarships to students possessing particular characteristics; at other times they give unrestricted grants that permit the institution broad or even total spending latitude. In the former case, assuming that the accountants are doing their jobs correctly, the donors' contribution will show up in the expenditure category *scholarships and fellowships*; in the latter case, the expenditures may be accounted for almost anywhere, but the spending will in fact be traceable to a particular defined function or functions.

Research grants tend to be similar to contracts in that grants increasingly have come to be awarded for specific research purposes, and notwithstanding the expenditure of research overhead, grant fund expenditures will almost certainly be found in the *research* spending category. Students have the expectation that their tuition money will be spent primarily for *instruction*, although many upperclasspersons, at least, will know that substantial portions of their tuition will go for other purposes. State governments tend to provide most of their support through *general institutional*—that is, unspecified—aid, although a modest share of state money usually is considered categorical— that is, designated—if not *restricted* (a term connoting less spending flexibility). In the former case, and as reflected in public opinion, the state expects that a good portion of expenditures will be used for *instruction* (a *functional* category, as are those that follow), with some amounts going to instructional support categories such as *academic support* and *student services*, but not to other functions such as *research* or *public service*, at least in any substantial amount. *Designated* funds from the state may be for these latter functions or purposes.

The terms employed by accountants may vary from nation to nation, but the concepts are applied universally. What is more likely to vary among nations is the degree of spending latitude which is afforded universities.

Resource Dependence Theory

Political economic theories that treat globalization (Chapter Two) enable us to understand changes occurring in national higher education policy. However, these theories do not speak to the ways in which higher education policies are translated into practice. Resource dependence theory helps us understand the changes occurring in the nature of academic labor in specific sets of institutions (Pfeffer and Salancik 1978).[2] In contrast with most organization theories, which deal with internal management strategies, resource dependence theory holds that the internal behaviors of organizational members are understood clearly only by reference to the actions of external agents. In the case of higher education, the external agents are the policy makers and policies described in Chapter Two. In particular, resource dependence holds that those who provide resources to organizations such as universities have the capability of exercising great power over those organizations. Stated in its simplest terms, "He who pays the piper calls the tune." As Pfeffer and Salancik put it, "The perspective developed denies the validity of the conceptualization of organizations as self-directed, autonomous actors pursuing their own ends and instead argues that organizations are other-directed, involved in a constant struggle for autonomy and discretion, confronted with constraint and external control" (1978, 257). There are two dimensions of resource exchange by which resource providers may impact organizations: the *relative magnitude* of the exchange and the *criticality* of the resource to the recipient (Pfeffer and Salancik 1978, 46).

Relative magnitude is measured in shares of resources provided. An organization receiving resources from only one source will be heavily dependent upon that supplier, which may exercise great power over that organization, should it desire to do so. Historically, public universities in most Western democracies have been heavily dependent financially upon their governments, which usually have allowed universities considerable operating autonomy. The principal mechanism that has enabled this autonomy has been the unstipulated or *block grant* mode of funding general institutional aid.

Criticality is the degree to which the organization may continue to function

2. Pfeffer and Salancik's work on resource dependence parallels the work of Herbert Simon who advises that organizations rarely gain major economies or directional shifts in the absence of intense external pressures.

in the absence of the resource. A steel plant cannot function without iron ore, coke, or electricity. The absence of any of these, no matter how small a share of overall resources represented, will place the plant in jeopardy. All are critical resources. For universities the critical resources include physical plant, faculty, students, utilities, and so forth, but in the end the issue is invariably money.

The ways in which resource providers exercise their control over internal organizational behaviors are both direct and indirect. Like all living organisms, organizations seek homeostasis or stability. They abhor disequilibrium or destabilization (Pfeffer and Salancik 1978). Unstable environments result in organizational turbulence. When resources are in a state of major flux, organizational stability is threatened. Organizational vulnerability occurs. Under such circumstances organizational efforts are directed at regaining stability, at removing the source of the threat to the organization. As put by Pfeffer and Salancik (1978, 2), "The key to organizational survival is the ability to acquire and maintain resources." The overriding long-term organizational goal is autonomy or independence: removing dependence upon resource providers to assure continuing stability and equilibrium (Pfeffer and Salancik 1978, 261).

In financial terms, organizational dependence is a function of (1) the importance of the resource to the organization (analogous to criticality); (2) the degree of discretion the organization has over the resource and its use; and (3) the existence of alternative revenues (Pfeffer and Salancik 1978, 45–46).

As Chapter Two suggests, it is our belief that changes in national higher education policies resulted in alterations in resource dependence which are driving changes within Western universities, rather than some self-induced change by the academy. Consider, for example and by way of contrast, that (alleged) faculty diversion of effort away from teaching toward research may be viewed either as reflecting faculty preferences (Massy and Zemsky 1990; Massy 1994) or, consistent with our view, as rational faculty response to resource changes (resource dependence).[3] Of course, each of these no doubt contributes to the full explanation, but we believe that the former is considerably less powerful and that vigorous pursuit of the remedies that logically follow (e.g., criticism, regulating teaching loads) would be largely unproductive. Indeed, the principal remedy, historically, hortatory solutions, has been employed for decades, without apparent impact.

As we shall see, financial conditions for public universities in most Western democracies in recent decades have become increasingly uncertain, if not tur-

3. This characterization is not entirely fair to Massy and Zemsky (Massy and Zemsky 1990; Massy 1994) who do acknowledge external forces even though they seem to favor faculty self-interest as the primary explanation for the shift from teaching to research.

bulent (OECD 1990a; Furstenbach 1993). Eicher and Chevaillier (1992) view conditions as in "crisis" and "much deeper than macrostatistics reveal." As we argued in Chapter Two, changes are *in kind* rather than degree. In the United States higher education is seen as entering a new era, and the financial problems are structural and will exist for the long term (Breneman 1993; Leslie 1995). In Europe at least, there is some sense of urgency. The 1994 Conference of European Rectors centered its discussions on how economic forces were "reshaping their institutions" (Bollag 1994).

The higher education policy changes described in Chapter Two were followed by changes in finance patterns. Financial support by governments declined, and alternative revenue sources were sought, with varying degrees of success. Perhaps more importantly, the *form* of financial support has changed, especially that from government, which has placed more conditions on the use of funds supplied. Further, increased reliance upon alternative revenue suppliers also has meant that increasingly a larger share of revenues has been stipulated, that is, categorical or conditional, as opposed to unstipulated or block grant.

The result is destabilization of universities, greater dependence upon revenue providers, and lost autonomy (Furstenbach 1993).[4] "We failed to recognize that our heavy dependence upon federal funding would encourage significant inroads by the government against the institution's autonomy" (Kennedy 1993, 148). Universities seek to regain their stability and their autonomy by reducing their financial vulnerability; however, the road to reestablished stability and independence is a difficult one. For U.S. higher education, Breneman (1993), for example, is "bearish" regarding increases from any revenue sources, even private ones, although he sees the possibility of substantial increases in tuition income for public universities.

As key organizational actors, academics are affected importantly by the changing environmental conditions. The nature of what is expected of them and what they take on for themselves is changing even more dramatically than the university revenue mix. "This challenge is a feature of academic life across the Western world," write Barnett and Middlehurst (1993). In a sense, faculty are victims of the changes, but they often are acquiescent. Clark Kerr (1994) perhaps said it best: "But the enticements are great. Knowledge is not only power, it is also money—and it is both power and money as never before; and the professorate above all other groups has knowledge."

With financing changes there has developed a multiplier effect by which

---

4. In addition to influences on autonomy Furstenbach lists changes in patterns of power within universities, in academic freedom, and quality implications as consequences of increased third-stream revenues.

what might appear to be relatively modest revenue changes have been translated into major alterations in how academics spend their time. Part of the reason is that by the mid 1990s universities in many OECD countries possessed little organizational slack. Most financial flexibility had been dissipated with the first few rounds of financial cutbacks. Additional revenue reductions had almost unprecedented consequences.

For public universities government block grants are the base of the revenue pyramid. Not only is the relative magnitude of such grants usually great, their criticality is high also because their (relatively) unconditional nature contributes to institutional independence. The decline of government support in Western democracies—and more so, the shift in remaining government support to conditional formats—greatly increases organizational turbulence because autonomy is threatened.

Universities seek to capture alternative revenues. But substitutes often carry stipulations; they require performance of certain acts. Collectively and individually, faculty perceive their greatest potential source of additional revenues to be in grants and contracts with government and with the private sector. *Taking government block grants (as well as student tuition revenues) as a given, they focus any marginal (additional) efforts on proposal writing, patenting, and developing and maintaining relations with potential funders.* Often these marginal efforts are directed at research that may result in scholarly publication, which serves the faculty reward structure well, further reinforcing the redirected faculty efforts. The end result is a measurable shift in faculty effort from activities financed by government block grants and tuition, specifically instruction and related activities, to activities designed to generate revenues in competitive, "marketlike"[5] areas and satisfy the conditions of those awards. In the words of Barnett and Middlehurst (1993, 110–11), "Both individually and collectively, academics are being challenged to take on new commitments and to reshape the balance of their professional activities. This challenge is a feature of academic life across the Western world. . . . Two obvious general challenges are that academics are having to be more *accountable* to external constituencies . . . and that the profession is having to be much more sensitive to the different markets." Evidence of the shift in both the sources and form of university funding is substantial.

5. Our usage of the term *market* is consistent with our audience here, comprised of academics in general. For economists, *market* is a technical term having specific meanings. For a discussion of these specific meanings in higher education, see Leslie and Johnson (1974). In describing types of higher education organizations, the OECD (1990a, 20) describes the systems of the OECD as mixed, in between the perfect market at the one end and the method of state planning at the other.

Separating Cause from Effect, and Data Problems

Before we proceed to a discussion of the degree to which sources of institutional revenues have been altered over recent decades, we need to examine whether those revenue shifts appear to be the *cause* of related actions or the *result*. We must also acknowledge the substantial data problems in reaching any conclusion at all.

Theory and empiricism are of considerable assistance in regard to the former. Most political economic theories (see Chapter Two) and empiricism support the conclusion that academics respond to changing revenue streams rather than cause the changes, although clearly the direction of the effect is, to some degree, two way. Almost certainly, the decline in revenues shares from state governments, the principal source of public higher education revenues in the United States, has been primarily the cause rather than the result of relative increases in other revenue categories. The same principle applies to national funding of higher education in Australia, Canada, and the United Kingdom.

In the United States, where the emerging financing trends common to most OECD countries probably began and, with some exceptions, may be further along than they are elsewhere (OECD 1990b), the roots of the recent patterns are traceable directly to changes brought about by national policy statements composed in the early 1970s by federal agencies and national policy groups, including the Committee for Economic Development and the Carnegie Foundation for the Advancement of Teaching. Perhaps the earliest of the pertinent federal policy papers, and the most telling, were the MEGA Documents, which were developed by the Nixon administration and whose thrust was to shift government support for higher education, most of which comes from the states, from institutions to students. Important gains were to be realized in the public higher education sector through the workings of the market. "The fundamental premise of this paper [MEGA Documents] is that a freer play of market forces will best achieve federal objectives in postsecondary education. . . . Accordingly, this paper describes what we should do to give individuals the general power of choice in the education marketplace and proposes levels and types of student support which will make most institutional aid programs unnecessary." The market direction fits nicely with the goals and aspirations of many institutions and faculty; many of the former aspire to research university status, and the latter benefit personally from grant and contract funding.

The common element of each of the proposed policy documents was the redirection of government support from institutions to students. Market forces would improve allocative efficiency in U.S. higher education in two important ways. By increasing tuition prices and diverting the savings in institutional aid (primarily at state level) to needy students, government subsidies would be better targeted to those less able to pay.[6] In short, government aid would not be "wasted" on upper and middle income individuals who could and would pay more. The second way, which involved private institutions, was only one step removed. At the time, the early 1970s, U.S. private institutions were in difficult and worsening financial condition (e.g., Jellema 1971, 1973). Fear was being expressed that many might even close. Shifting support from institutions to students would avoid constitutional and political constraints on government aid to private institutions, many of which were church related. This indirect subsidy of private institutions would enhance their long-term viability and prevent substantially increased public sector costs by keeping many students in the private sector. It was not incidental that many of the U.S. elites who led the policy change were graduates and benefactors of elite, private institutions.

The student aid initiative was critical, not so much for the consumer power gained by students, a gain that to date has been modest in public institutions, but rather for the broader market forces student aid set into motion. Indeed, student aid was no more, or less, than a market voucher. The first-level effect was relative decline in state block grant support. The second-level effect was diverting faculty and staff efforts into making up for the revenue losses.

In sum, this redirection of government aid from institutions to students, with its accompanying policy of higher tuition, would in one thrust greatly accelerate and perhaps most importantly legitimize the role of the market in U.S. higher education. (Canada may well be entering this same phase as we write this book.) The somewhat later government push in the science policy area fit beautifully with this new direction. Slaughter and Rhoades (1993, 287) characterize the transformation as follows: "Policies and statutes moved from an ideology that defined the public interest as best served by shielding public entities from involvement in the market, to one that saw the public interest as best served by public organizations' involvement in commercial activities." To many academics on campus, eventually, the chase for the dollar would no longer be questionable behavior. *These were the most important higher education policy changes of the postwar era.*

There was no discussion, and there were no claims, in these early delibera-

---

6. At the time the federal government was debating whether its aid would be primarily institution or student based. It chose the latter. Recognizing that most government aid was from the states, the federal government also saw federal need-based student aid as a way of leveraging the states to follow the federal lead.

tions, that the public colleges and universities either could "afford" reduced institutional aid or that shortfalls could be made up from other revenue sources. That the government action was to be the precipitator, the cause, of new financing directions was never in doubt. There was no observable evidence, nor was any such evidence ever cited, that university success in raising its own revenues was the cause of the plan to reduce government aid to institutions. In fact, all of American higher education was considered to be in financial crisis at the time (e.g., Cheit 1971). There was little if any expectation that institutions would increase their revenues from any other sources, save tuition.

From the institutional perspective, the new arrangement was solely between institutions and their students; losses in institutional aid were to be made up through increased student charges. Concerns that tuition increases might not keep up with institutional aid losses were dismissed out of hand, probably because the expected benefits were seen as far outweighing any likely negative effects.

Our thesis is that changes in national policy and declines in state share of support induce academic capitalism within institutions. Cause and effects are, nevertheless, almost certainly recursive, that is, circular. Generating additional tuition revenues is only one form. Higher tuition without obvious loss of student opportunity reduces political opposition and encourages future tuition increases, even if a net financial loss to institutions results. Any losses or reductions in rates of revenue increases create internal institutional pressures to increase revenues elsewhere. The only major resource the university has which would enable it to address new or expanded revenue sources is the human capital possessed by academics. The success of academics in raising alternative revenues not only reduces pressures on government to remedy past funding deficiencies but encourages additional state subsidy reductions.

If all elements in the public sector were equally capable of generating their own revenues, the pressures on higher education would be less intense. But most public expenditure is for transfer payments; the investment sector of government enterprise is quite limited. (Judging what is investment and what is a transfer payment [simply, money transfer; nothing is purchased] is sometimes debatable.) Burgeoning costs in entitlement areas such as health and welfare act to reduce resources for quasi-optional functions such as higher education. Academics and administrators read these signals clearly, and entrepreneurial efforts are doubled and redoubled. University successes in fund raising provide evidence that further government reductions are likely to cause little damage to the higher education enterprise. Marginal analysis easily supports the conclusion that increased subsidies to higher education are likely to yield greater damage in other public functions. A classic substitution effect occurs: institutions substitute self-generated revenues for losses in share of state institutional support; legislators substitute those increases for future government increases.

In our own work with legislative budget committees, we have regularly encountered evidence of legislative belief that universities can easily make up for reductions in the several states' share of subsidy through increases in alternative revenues. In response to budgetary pleadings, verbal and written references are made routinely, for example, to universities' external research support, research overhead revenues, and endowments. Revenues from athletic events often are cited, too, as are inflation-exceeding tuition increases, even though state governments themselves either set tuition prices directly or indirectly *effect* the increases through various kinds of budgetary pressures. Even though institutional claims of pending disaster are made by universities in each budget cycle, in fact the sky does not fall.

At the outset of this section, we mentioned data problems.[7] Fortunately, almost all of our analyses are within, rather than across, nations; thus, *international* data comparability is not important to our purposes. Further, we were able to obtain quite good data for Australia and the United States, where our field work was done. Nevertheless, interpretation of results may vary among readers of different countries.[8] It is common to experience data comparability problems even *within* a single country when data are examined over time, a problem that is important to this book.[9]

Our analysis rests primarily on changes *within* nations. The largest difficulties are likely to be in making interpretations. Nevertheless, regardless of how

---

7. Unfortunately, sources often do not report data for identical time periods. We have selected the most comparable time periods in the disparate data sources utilized.

8. To identify only a few of the difficulties, financial definitions can and do vary importantly, internationally, even among developed nations, such as the members of the OECD. What is considered to be revenue from "government" may vary widely, and when one attempts to discriminate among categories of government revenues, such as between general institutional aid and categorical institutional aid—a distinction that is germane to the theme of this book—the difficulties may be large. Expenditure classifications likely will be even more problematic because classification systems and definitions will vary widely. One nation may use functional expenditure categories, for example, *instruction, research,* and *service;* whereas another may use object-of-expenditure categories such as *salaries, travel, equipment,* or some combination of the two.

9. For example, the functional categories that are used almost universally today in the United States were defined differently in past years, although the problems are not serious until one goes more than twenty years back in time. Internal data comparability problems tend to be larger in many other countries simply because of the nature and consistency of data collection efforts.

the revenue and expenditure categories are defined within a country, provided that time series data largely are comparable or can be rendered comparable and that they exist, valid conclusions regarding the data can be reached.

Financing Higher Education

The United States

In this section we examine both the background data and the data showing the decline in government block grant funding of higher education in Australia, Canada, the United Kingdom, and the United States. Although our focus in this book is on public research universities, it is clear that other kinds of public institutions are experiencing similar revenue changes, and we hold that these changes support our general thesis. Further, some of the aggregated data do not permit separate examination of public universities. Finally, in some cases the aggregated figures include data for private institutions, a fact that calls for a careful examination but actually lends additional insight into resource dependence notions. (The fact that the patterns for the public universities persist even when the private universities and other public institutions are included testifies to the robustness of our observations.)

We should say a few additional words about the omission of private institutions from our focus. First, private colleges and universities are of very minor importance in three of our four nations. In the United States, where (all) private institutions serve approximately 20 percent of all students, the research enterprises of private universities are very substantial. Although limitations on our resources, alone, might have caused us to eliminate them from our study, there was an additional reason for our decision: private universities in the United States receive little in the way of government block grants; therefore, the major factor theorized to drive university destabilization does not pertain to them. Indeed, U.S. private universities have been operating in a highly competitive, relatively unprotected (by government) environment for many years, and as we shall see, they do exhibit some of the more important projected features. As a mater of fact, private universities in the United States might well be viewed as prototypes of where public universities are headed, and we reflect on this reality below.

In general, government support of institutions of higher education has declined within Australia, Canada, the United Kingdom, and the United States, although the magnitude and (importantly) *form* of the declines vary substantially. We began by examining information from the OECD, which probably devotes more attention than any other organization to collecting comparable data and to specifying international differences. Although the OECD data were quite informative, we decided to move the associated discussion to an appendix out of concern that we would overload the reader with information.

In the way of summary, although the OECD data are dated, by the mid 1980s it was already clear that there was a shift away from government funding (see Table A.1 in the Appendix). Generally, trends in the share of GNP devoted to higher education already supported our claim of reduced government support, and the balance of evidence showed a decline in *total expenditures per student* for higher education (for a more detailed treatment, see the Appendix). More importantly, revenues from governments had declined while overall expenditures actually had increased; clearly, private resources already were being substituted for government support, as per our claim. When inflation and enrollment increases were added in, these changes were dramatic.

For our more detailed analyses, we consider first the U.S. data for several reasons. First, the United States is probably the *frontier* nation in terms of market influences in higher education.[10] This is not necessarily to say that market forces are strongest in the United States but rather that those forces were evident earlier in the United States. Second, the U.S. government goes to unusual efforts to maintain compatible time series data. Thus, the U.S. data provide a good reference point. Third and particularly important, U.S. data are readily available to us, and we are familiar with whatever comparability problems exist.

The U.S. data support our thesis strongly. The most timely pertinent data available in the United States are state appropriations for public higher education,[11] the major revenue source (federal appropriations to institutions are almost inconsequential), and accompanying tuition and fee revenues. After a decline until the early 1980s, inflation-adjusted, per student, state appropriations increased for about three years, stabilized, and then turned down after 1988. The decline continues. *As a share of collected tax revenues* the decline has been quite steady and even more steep than the decline in absolute, inflation-adjusted, per student, dollars. However, similarly adjusted tuition revenues reveal a constant state of growth since the early 1980s. This is consistent with the revenue substitution hypothesis: actions are taken to make up for revenue short-

10. The term *frontier* is used in the research methods sense to connote an outlier or extreme case, studied to detect trends and to consider future implications of new developments.

11. This is because it is government revenues that are changing dramatically, especially general institutional aid, which is appropriated overwhelmingly to public institutions. U.S. private universities are probably even more market oriented than public universities because essentially all of the former's revenues are earned competitively, even those from government.

falls. The *net* effect of the appropriations and tuition changes has been to mod-ulate or temper the effects of the declines from the primary revenue source, government appropriations.

Other revenue, and all expenditure, data are available in a less timely man-ner. This time gap is important to our thesis because the largest declines in (theoretically) pivotal state appropriations have been in recent years, and we would *expect* some lag in the time required to increase self-generated funds from other sources.

Table 3.1 contains data for all revenue categories for *all* U.S. institutions of higher education. The data are only through academic year 1990–91, some four years prior to this writing. The table confirms the state appropriations and tuition and fees pattern described in the previous paragraphs. Further, the table shows companion declines in the share (from this source) of revenues from the federal government: from an institutional revenue share of 14.9 percent in 1980–81 to 12.2 percent in 1990–91. Theoretically, declines in state support should push higher education institutions to increase revenues from federal sources, but the amount of federal funds available is limited by congressional appropriations. In fact, exclusive of aid to students, the decline in the share of current fund revenues from federal sources, since 1969–70, has been the largest of all changes: from 19.2 to 12.2 percent (National Center for Education Sta-tistics 1993, Table 320). Although efforts to increase federal grants may be made by *institutions*, the fruits of such efforts will not be reflected in aggregate national data. (Note that federal student aid is categorized elsewhere; see Table 3.1, Footnote *b*.)

The revenue categories ultimately serving to test resource dependence the-ory best are private gifts, grants, and contracts; sales and services; and other sources.[12] Endowment income is not a good test because only endowment *earnings* are reflected in this category. Institutions are generally free to deter-mine how much of such earnings they will allocate to current fund budgets.[13]

12. Although institutional efforts to increase revenues from *discretionary* (nonappropriations) government sources no doubt are expanded, too, as appropriations decline, these efforts will not be reflected in aggregate U.S. data because public institutions can only succeed in attracting such revenues as are available. The amounts reflected in the government categories in Table 3.1 are those made available by government on an annual basis. To test resource theory one would need to ex-amine *institutional* accounts to determine whether changes in institutional revenues from discre-tionary categories are related to institutional revenue shortfalls in government appropriations.

13. Institutions have considerable flexibility in deciding how much of their endowment earn-ings will be retained in the endowment or will be allocated to competing fund groups, such as the plant (building) fund. Comparative annual additions to the endowment *principal* would be a good test of resource dependence theory, but the necessary data are not readily available.

Gifts, grants, and contracts from private sources show the hypothesized increase, from 4.8 to 5.6 percent of current fund revenues, over the time period. Sales and services exhibit increases also, from 20.9 to 22.8 percent, although this increase is due entirely to growth in revenues from hospitals, no doubt reflecting to a considerable degree rapidly escalating costs of medical care in the United States. Still, the revenue gains associated with hospitals, in part at least, may represent university efforts to increase revenues wherever they can.

Each percentage point change reflects more than $1 billion, so these are significant sums. The smaller increase—in other sources—is still large in absolute terms, reflecting hundreds of millions of dollars. This category is a largely discretionary catch-all that includes such revenue sources as interest earned and miscellaneous income.

The data for only public institutions are contained in Table 3.2; private institution data are in Table 3.3. The patterns for the public institutions are very similar to those in Table 3.1 because approximately 80 percent of U.S. students are enrolled in the public sector. What turns out to be very informative are the comparisons between the public and the private institutions. Because public institutions are far more dependent upon government appropriations (private institutions rely heavily on tuition and fees), we would expect resource dependence effects to be more extreme in the former, where state appropriation declines have been felt most severely. In fact, that is what occurs, and more.

Whereas state support of public institutions has declined, although small when expressed in percentage terms, such support has actually increased for the private sector, going from 1.9 to 2.3 percent of institutional revenues over the time period. In short, private institutions have not felt the impact of decreased revenues from the state. The growth in state revenues among private institutions is due primarily to increases in state-supported grants and loans to students, increases reflecting the new national policy direction of effecting market conditions by shifting state support from institutions to student consumers.

Other revenue comparisons are, for the most part, similarly instructive. Whereas revenue shares from private gifts, grants, and contracts grew by 1.3 percentage points in public institutions, such shares actually decreased by 0.7 percentage point in private institutions.[14] Whereas shares from sales and services increased by 3.1 percentage points in the public sector, they *decreased* by 0.4 percentage point in the private sector. Only in the other sources category

14. The data are in percentage points, not percentages. The difference is important. For example, suppose a revenue share from a given source is 30 percent and declines to 20 percent. This is a 10 percentage *point* (30 − 20 = 10) and a 33 *percent* decline (30 − 20 ÷ 30 = 0.33).

Table 3.1 Current Fund Revenue of U.S. Institutions of Higher Education, by Source: 1980–1981 through 1990–1991

Source	1980–1981	1983–1984	1984–1985	1985–1986	1986–1987	1987–1988	1988–1989	1989–1990	1990–1991[a]
					In thousands				
Total current fund revenue	$65,584,789	$84,417,287	$92,472,694	$100,437,616	$108,809,827	$117,340,109	$128,501,638	$139,635,477	$149,766,051
Tuition and fees	13,773,259	19,714,884	21,283,329	23,116,605	25,705,827	27,836,781	30,806,566	33,926,060	37,434,462
Federal government	9,747,586	10,406,166	11,509,125	12,704,750	13,904,049	14,771,954	15,893,978	17,254,874	18,236,082
Appropriations	1,346,835	1,426,539	1,570,590	1,617,510	1,656,245	1,664,054	1,677,430	1,890,046	1,840,694
Unrestricted grants and contracts	1,126,558	1,332,157	1,474,586	1,658,636	1,878,202	1,980,749	2,150,079	2,353,119	2,504,859
Restricted grants and contracts[b]	6,005,317	6,024,108	6,570,045	7,190,345	7,690,232	8,225,129	9,009,709	9,773,266	10,443,977
Independent operations (FFRDC)[c]	1,268,877	1,623,363	1,893,904	2,238,259	2,679,369	2,902,022	3,056,760	3,238,442	3,446,552
State governments	20,106,222	24,706,990	27,583,011	29,911,500	31,309,303	33,517,166	36,031,208	38,349,239	39,480,874
Appropriations	19,266,186	23,635,761	26,373,160	28,402,288	29,337,120	31,298,537	33,287,034	35,223,174	36,255,090
Unrestricted grants and contracts	84,848	120,546	135,139	154,109	213,461	217,208	357,221	411,757	366,206
Restricted grants and contracts	755,188	950,683	1,074,712	1,355,102	1,758,722	2,001,421	2,386,953	2,714,309	2,859,577
Local governments	1,790,740	2,192,275	2,387,212	2,544,506	2,799,321	3,006,263	3,363,676	3,636,902	3,931,239
Appropriations	1,482,536	1,826,590	1,973,284	2,153,160	2,294,133	2,470,439	2,758,086	2,919,447	3,177,696
Unrestricted grants and contracts	29,629	43,421	63,442	56,975	92,724	76,638	98,787	122,404	116,982
Restricted grants and contracts	278,575	322,264	350,485	344,371	412,465	459,186	506,803	598,051	636,561
Private gifts, grants, and contracts	3,176,670	4,415,275	4,896,325	5,410,905	5,952,682	6,359,282	7,060,730	7,781,422	8,361,265
Unrestricted	1,210,903	1,674,942	1,944,876	2,111,972	2,234,942	2,235,096	2,429,579	2,634,974	2,720,233
Restricted	1,965,766	2,740,333	2,951,448	3,298,933	3,717,741	4,124,186	4,631,151	5,146,448	5,641,032
Endowment income	1,364,443	1,873,945	2,096,298	2,275,898	2,377,958	2,586,441	2,914,396	3,143,696	3,268,629
Unrestricted	770,358	1,021,134	1,227,797	1,285,194	1,229,943	1,340,788	1,498,703	1,614,088	1,521,940
Restricted	594,085	852,811	868,501	990,704	1,148,015	1,245,654	1,415,694	1,529,608	1,746,690
Sales and services	13,677,366	18,467,779	19,701,912	21,274,265	23,283,927	25,492,435	28,162,465	30,787,233	34,107,502
Educational activities	1,409,730	1,970,747	2,126,927	2,373,494	2,641,906	2,918,090	3,315,620	3,632,100	4,054,703
Auxiliary enterprises	7,287,290	9,456,369	10,100,410	10,674,136	11,364,188	11,947,778	12,855,580	13,938,469	14,903,127
Hospitals	4,980,346	7,040,662	7,474,575	8,226,635	9,277,834	10,626,566	11,991,265	13,216,664	15,149,672
Other sources	1,948,503	2,639,973	3,015,483	3,199,186	3,476,760	3,769,787	4,268,618	4,753,051	4,945,998

Percentage distribution

Total current fund revenue	100.0	100.0	100.0	100.0	100.0	100.0	100.0	100.0	100.0
Tuition and fees	21.0	23.4	23.0	23.0	23.6	23.7	24.0	24.3	25.0
Federal government	14.9	12.3	12.4	12.5	12.8	12.6	12.4	12.4	12.2
Appropriations	2.1	1.7	1.7	1.6	1.5	1.4	1.3	1.4	1.2
Unrestricted grants and contracts	1.7	1.6	1.6	1.7	1.7	1.7	1.7	1.7	1.7
Restricted grants and contracts[b]	9.2	7.1	7.1	7.2	7.1	7.0	7.0	7.0	7.0
Independent operations (FFRDC)[c]	1.9	1.9	2.0	2.2	2.5	2.5	2.4	2.3	2.3
State governments	30.7	29.3	29.8	29.8	28.8	28.6	28.0	27.5	26.4
Appropriations	29.4	28.0	28.5	28.3	27.0	26.7	25.9	25.2	24.2
Unrestricted grants and contracts	0.1	0.1	0.1	0.2	0.2	0.2	0.3	0.3	0.2
Restricted grants and contracts	1.2	1.1	1.2	1.3	1.6	1.7	1.9	1.9	1.9
Local governments	2.7	2.6	2.6	2.5	2.6	2.6	2.6	2.6	2.6
Appropriations	2.3	2.2	2.1	2.1	2.1	2.1	2.1	2.1	2.1
Unrestricted grants and contracts	[d]	0.1	0.1	0.1	0.1	0.1	0.1	0.1	0.1
Restricted grants and contracts	0.4	0.4	0.4	0.3	0.4	0.4	0.4	0.4	0.4
Private gifts, grants, and contracts	4.8	5.2	5.3	5.4	5.5	5.4	5.5	5.6	5.6
Unrestricted	1.8	2.0	2.1	2.1	2.1	1.9	1.9	1.9	1.8
Restricted	3.0	3.2	3.2	3.3	3.4	3.5	3.6	3.7	3.8
Endowment income	2.1	2.2	2.3	2.3	2.2	2.2	2.3	2.3	2.2
Unrestricted	1.2	1.2	1.3	1.3	1.1	1.1	1.2	1.2	1.0
Restricted	0.9	1.0	0.9	1.0	1.1	1.1	1.1	1.1	1.2
Sales and services	20.9	21.9	21.3	21.2	21.4	21.7	21.9	22.0	22.8
Educational activities	2.1	2.3	2.3	2.4	2.4	2.5	2.6	2.6	2.7
Auxiliary enterprises	11.1	11.2	10.9	10.6	10.4	10.2	10.0	10.0	10.0
Hospitals	7.6	8.3	8.1	8.2	8.5	9.1	9.3	9.5	10.1
Other sources	3.0	3.1	3.3	3.2	3.2	3.2	3.3	3.4	3.3

Source: Digest of Education Statistics 1993, National Center for Education Statistics, U.S. Department of Education, October 1993.

Note: Because of rounding; details may not add to totals.

[a] Preliminary data.

[b] Excludes Pell grants; federally supported student aid that is received through students is included under tuition and auxiliary enterprises.

[c] Generally includes only those revenues associated with major federally funded research and development centers (FFRDC).

[d] Less than 0.05 percent.

Table 3.2 Current Fund Revenue of U.S. Public Institutions of Higher Education, by Source: 1980–1981 through 1990–1991

Source	1980–1981	1983–1984	1984–1985	1985–1986	1986–1987	1987–1988	1988–1989	1989–1990	1990–1991[a]
				In thousands					
Total current fund revenue	$43,195,617	$54,545,275	$59,794,159	$65,004,632	$69,613,289	$74,771,255	$81,927,371	$88,911,433	$94,904,506
Tuition and fees	5,570,404	8,123,318	8,647,637	9,439,177	10,198,633	11,184,657	12,435,763	13,820,240	15,258,024
Federal government	5,540,101	5,719,602	6,309,818	6,852,370	7,227,995	7,714,261	8,412,582	9,171,488	9,763,427
Appropriations	1,128,101	1,215,616	1,349,183	1,401,367	1,434,295	1,434,906	1,443,539	1,636,047	1,604,548
Unrestricted grants and contracts	529,424	642,117	723,509	816,364	907,299	989,781	1,083,575	1,214,836	1,319,035
Restricted grants and contracts[b]	3,812,197	3,774,093	4,120,266	4,481,723	4,662,798	5,095,910	5,656,468	6,106,112	6,629,484
Independent operations (FFRDC)[c]	70,379	87,777	116,860	152,916	223,602	193,664	228,999	214,493	210,360
State governments	19,675,968	24,157,316	26,965,417	29,220,586	30,439,878	32,437,504	34,835,716	37,052,307	38,239,973
Appropriations	19,006,716	23,340,360	26,065,494	28,071,070	28,974,665	30,917,534	32,929,719	34,858,904	35,898,653
Unrestricted grants and contracts	45,390	66,000	71,113	88,779	139,059	113,204	240,028	297,338	250,168
Restricted grants and contracts	623,863	750,956	828,810	1,060,737	1,326,154	1,406,946	1,665,969	1,896,065	2,091,157
Local governments	1,622,938	1,984,184	2,178,761	2,325,844	2,535,014	2,731,862	3,025,703	3,264,303	3,531,714
Appropriations	1,478,001	1,824,430	1,970,829	2,150,459	2,289,420	2,465,172	2,751,704	2,910,444	3,159,789
Unrestricted grants and contracts	9,915	18,856	35,398	27,352	56,781	41,940	64,455	82,405	73,281
Restricted grants and contracts	135,022	140,898	172,534	147,533	188,813	224,751	209,544	271,453	298,644
Private gifts, grants, and contracts	1,100,084	1,621,468	1,845,606	2,109,782	2,292,985	2,517,422	2,948,827	3,368,635	3,651,107
Unrestricted	110,462	204,441	236,385	279,381	297,163	305,457	362,011	436,028	529,496
Restricted	989,622	1,417,027	1,609,220	1,830,401	1,995,822	2,211,966	2,586,815	2,932,607	3,121,611
Endowment income	214,561	315,109	342,833	398,603	349,779	361,545	422,252	461,701	431,236
Unrestricted	102,388	137,945	147,237	181,624	125,165	127,361	149,650	164,242	147,363
Restricted	111,673	177,165	195,596	216,979	224,614	233,684	272,602	297,459	283,367
Sales and services	8,455,449	11,262,071	11,967,500	12,990,670	14,775,531	15,851,714	17,586,319	19,330,429	21,546,202
Educational activities	943,737	1,279,212	1,424,396	1,596,946	1,771,760	1,948,579	2,186,448	2,423,779	2,700,185
Auxiliary enterprises	4,614,561	5,947,717	6,296,312	6,684,794	7,092,985	7,306,302	7,309,234	8,473,282	9,058,745
Hospitals	2,397,151	4,035,142	4,246,293	4,703,330	5,910,785	6,596,733	7,591,087	8,433,369	9,787,271
Other sources	1,016,110	1,362,205	1,536,586	1,667,600	1,793,474	1,972,290	2,259,709	2,442,330	2,482,319

Percentage distribution

Total current fund revenue	100.0	100.0	100.0	100.0	100.0	100.0	100.0	100.0	100.0	100.0
Tuition and fees	12.9	14.9	14.5	14.5	14.7	15.0	14.7	15.2	15.5	15.1
Federal government	12.8	10.5	10.6	10.5	10.4	10.3	10.4	10.3	10.3	10.3
Appropriations	2.6	2.2	2.3	2.2	2.1	1.9	2.1	1.8	1.8	1.7
Unrestricted grants and contracts[b]	1.2	1.2	1.2	1.3	1.3	1.3	1.3	1.3	1.4	1.4
Restricted grants and contracts[b]	8.8	6.9	6.9	6.9	6.7	6.8	6.7	6.9	6.9	7.0
Independent operations (FFRDC)[c]	0.2	0.2	0.2	0.2	0.3	0.3	0.3	0.3	0.2	0.2
State governments	45.6	44.3	45.1	45.0	43.7	43.4	43.7	42.5	41.7	40.3
Appropriations	44.0	42.8	43.6	43.2	41.6	41.3	41.6	40.2	39.2	37.3
Unrestricted grants and contracts	0.1	0.1	0.1	0.1	0.2	0.2	0.2	0.3	0.3	0.3
Restricted grants and contracts	1.4	1.4	1.4	1.6	1.9	1.9	1.9	2.0	2.1	2.2
Local governments	3.8	3.6	3.6	3.5	3.6	3.7	3.6	3.7	3.7	3.7
Appropriations	3.4	3.3	3.3	3.3	3.3	3.3	3.3	3.4	3.3	3.3
Unrestricted grants and contracts	d	d	0.1	d	0.1	0.1	0.1	0.1	0.1	0.1
Restricted grants and contracts	0.3	0.3	0.3	0.2	0.3	0.3	0.3	0.3	0.3	0.3
Private gifts, grants, and contracts	2.5	3.0	3.1	3.2	3.3	3.4	3.3	3.6	3.8	3.8
Unrestricted	0.3	0.4	0.4	0.4	0.4	0.4	0.4	0.4	0.5	0.6
Restricted	2.3	2.6	2.7	2.3	2.9	3.0	2.9	3.2	3.3	3.3
Endowment income	0.5	0.6	0.6	0.6	0.5	0.5	0.5	0.5	0.5	0.5
Unrestricted	0.2	0.3	0.2	0.3	0.2	0.2	0.2	0.2	0.2	0.2
Restricted	0.3	0.3	0.3	0.3	0.3	0.3	0.3	0.3	0.3	0.3
Sales and services	19.6	20.6	20.0	20.0	21.2	21.2	21.2	21.5	21.7	22.7
Educational activities	2.2	2.3	2.4	2.5	2.5	2.6	2.5	2.7	2.7	2.8
Auxiliary enterprises	10.7	10.9	10.5	10.3	10.2	9.8	10.2	9.5	9.5	9.5
Hospitals	6.7	7.4	7.1	7.2	8.5	8.8	8.5	9.3	9.5	10.3
Other sources	2.4	2.5	2.6	2.5	2.6	2.6	2.6	2.8	2.7	2.6

Source: Digest of Education Statistics 1993, National Center for Education Statistics, U.S. Department of Education, October 1993.

Note: Because of rounding, details may not add to totals.

[a] Preliminary data.

[b] Excludes Pell grants; federally supported student aid that is received through students is included under tuition and auxiliary enterprises.

[c] Generally includes only those revenues associated with major federally funded research and development centers (FFRDC).

[d] Less than 0.05 percent.

Table 3.3   Current Fund Revenue of U.S. Private Institutions of Higher Education, by Source: 1980–1981 through 1990–1991

Source	1980–1981	1983–1984	1984–1985	1985–1986	1986–1987	1987–1988	1988–1989	1989–1990	1990–1991[a]
					In thousands				
Total current fund revenue	$22,389,172	$29,872,012	$32,678,536	$35,432,985	$39,196,539	$42,568,854	$46,574,267	$50,724,044	$54,861,545
Tuition and fees	8,202,855	11,591,566	12,635,691	13,677,429	15,507,194	16,652,124	18,370,803	20,105,820	22,176,439
Federal government	4,207,485	4,686,564	5,199,307	5,852,380	6,676,054	7,057,693	7,481,396	8,083,386	8,472,654
Appropriations	218,733	210,923	221,407	216,143	221,950	229,148	233,891	254,000	236,146
Unrestricted grants and contracts	597,134	690,040	751,076	842,272	970,903	990,968	1,066,504	1,138,283	1,185,824
Restricted grants and contracts[b]	2,193,119	2,250,015	2,449,780	2,708,622	3,027,434	3,129,219	3,353,241	3,667,154	3,814,493
Independent operations (FFRDC)[c]	1,198,498	1,535,586	1,777,044	2,085,343	2,455,767	2,708,358	2,827,761	3,023,949	3,236,192
State governments	430,253	549,673	617,593	690,914	869,424	1,079,562	1,195,492	1,296,932	1,240,896
Appropriations	259,470	295,401	307,666	331,219	362,454	381,183	357,315	364,270	356,437
Unrestricted grants and contracts	39,458	54,546	64,026	65,330	74,402	104,004	117,193	114,419	116,038
Restricted grants and contracts	131,326	199,727	245,902	294,365	432,568	594,475	720,984	818,244	768,421
Local governments	167,801	208,091	208,451	218,662	264,307	274,400	337,973	375,599	399,525
Appropriations	4,535	2,160	2,455	2,701	4,713	5,267	6,383	9,003	17,907
Unrestricted grants and contracts	19,714	24,565	28,045	29,123	35,943	34,698	34,332	39,999	43,701
Restricted grants and contracts	143,552	181,366	177,951	186,838	233,651	234,435	297,258	326,598	337,917
Private gifts, grants, and contracts	2,076,585	2,793,807	3,050,719	3,301,124	3,659,697	3,841,360	4,111,904	4,412,787	4,710,158
Unrestricted	1,100,441	1,470,501	1,708,491	1,832,592	1,937,778	1,929,639	2,067,568	2,198,946	2,190,736
Restricted	976,144	1,323,306	1,342,228	1,468,532	1,721,919	1,912,220	2,044,336	2,213,841	2,519,421
Endowment income	1,149,883	1,558,836	1,753,465	1,877,295	2,028,179	2,224,896	2,492,144	2,681,995	2,837,394
Unrestricted	667,471	883,190	1,080,560	1,103,570	1,104,778	1,212,926	1,349,053	1,449,846	1,374,572
Restricted	482,412	675,646	672,905	773,725	923,400	1,011,970	1,143,091	1,232,149	1,462,322
Sales and services	5,221,917	7,205,708	7,734,412	8,283,595	8,508,396	9,640,720	10,575,646	11,456,804	12,561,301
Educational activities	465,993	691,535	702,032	776,548	870,145	969,411	1,129,717	1,208,322	1,354,518
Auxiliary enterprises	2,672,729	3,508,652	3,804,098	3,989,342	4,271,203	4,641,476	5,046,296	5,465,187	5,844,382
Hospitals	2,083,195	3,005,520	3,228,282	3,517,705	3,367,048	4,029,333	4,400,178	4,783,295	5,362,401
Other sources	932,392	1,277,768	1,478,897	1,531,586	1,638,287	1,797,498	2,008,909	2,310,720	2,463,178

Percentage distribution

Total current fund revenue	100.0	100.0	100.0	100.0	100.0	100.0	100.0	100.0	100.0
Tuition and fees	36.6	38.8	38.7	38.6	39.6	39.1	39.4	39.6	40.4
Federal government	18.8	15.7	15.9	16.5	17.0	16.6	16.1	15.9	15.4
Appropriations	1.0	0.7	0.7	0.6	0.6	0.5	0.5	0.5	0.4
Unrestricted grants and contracts	2.7	2.3	2.3	2.4	2.5	2.3	2.3	2.2	2.2
Restricted grants and contracts[b]	9.8	7.5	7.5	7.6	7.7	7.4	7.2	7.2	7.0
Independent operations (FFRDC)[c]	5.4	5.1	5.4	5.9	6.3	6.4	6.1	6.0	5.9
State governments	1.9	1.8	1.9	1.9	2.2	2.5	2.6	2.6	2.3
Appropriations	1.2	1.0	0.9	0.9	0.9	0.9	0.8	0.7	0.6
Unrestricted grants and contracts	0.2	0.2	0.2	0.2	0.2	0.2	0.3	0.2	0.2
Restricted grants and contracts	0.6	0.7	0.8	0.8	1.1	1.4	1.5	1.6	1.4
Local governments	0.7	0.7	0.6	0.6	0.7	0.6	0.7	0.7	0.7
Appropriations	[d]	[d]	[d]	[d]	[d]	[d]	[d]	[d]	[d]
Unrestricted grants and contracts	0.1	0.1	0.1	0.1	0.1	0.1	0.1	0.1	0.1
Restricted grants and contracts	0.6	0.6	0.5	0.5	0.6	0.6	0.6	0.6	0.6
Private gifts, grants, and contracts	9.3	9.4	9.3	9.3	9.3	9.0	8.8	8.7	8.6
Unrestricted	4.9	4.9	5.2	5.2	4.9	4.5	4.4	4.3	4.0
Restricted	4.4	4.4	4.1	4.1	4.4	4.5	4.4	4.4	4.6
Endowment income	5.1	5.2	5.4	5.3	5.2	5.2	5.4	5.3	5.2
Unrestricted	3.0	3.0	3.3	3.1	2.8	2.8	2.9	2.9	2.5
Restricted	2.2	2.3	2.1	2.2	2.4	2.4	2.5	2.4	2.7
Sales and services	23.3	24.1	23.7	23.4	21.7	22.6	22.7	22.6	22.9
Educational activities	2.1	2.3	2.1	2.2	2.2	2.3	2.4	2.4	2.5
Auxiliary enterprises	11.9	11.7	11.6	11.3	10.9	10.9	10.8	10.8	10.7
Hospitals	9.3	10.1	9.9	9.9	8.6	9.5	9.4	9.4	9.8
Other sources	4.2	4.3	4.5	4.3	4.3	4.2	4.3	4.6	4.5

Source: Digest of Education Statistics 1993, National Center for Education Statistics, U.S. Department of Education, October 1993.

Note: Because of rounding, details may not add to totals.

[a] Preliminary data.

[b] Excludes Pell grants; federally supported student aid that is received through students is included under tuition and auxiliary enterprises.

[c] Generally includes only those revenues associated with major federally funded research and development centers (FFRDC).

[d] Less than 0.05 percent.

were the patterns essentially the same. Clearly, the national data support the thesis that the decline in state support, the primary source of revenues for U.S. public institutions of higher education, has been associated with compensating increases in other public institution revenue categories. Of course part of this growth in revenue shares is an artifact of the decline in state support rather than an actual increase in revenues from other categories.[15]

As postulated, expenditure changes follow revenue changes. Expenditure changes are substantial and, based upon recent dramatic changes in government support, are expected to grow larger, at least in the public sector.

Considering all institutions, public and private, expenditures for instruction decline moderately, from 32.4 percent of current fund expenditures in 1980 to 31.1 percent in 1990–91 (Table 3.4). The share devoted to instruction had been 36.4 percent in 1969–70 and 43.7 percent in 1929–30 (National Center for Education Statistics 1993, Table 320). Given that the recent decades were periods of major enrollment growth in the United States, these are profound declines. Correspondingly, *increases* for research, public service, academic and institutional support (administration), and student services also are moderate, whereas decreases for operation and maintenance of the plant and increases for student aid are large (Table 3.4).

What is most enlightening in this regard are the comparative changes for the public and private sectors (Tables 3.5 and 3.6). For all public institutions, the expenditure share for instruction over the time period reflected in the tables declined from 35.1 to 33.7 percent; the decline for private institutions was only 0.4 percentage point. Comparative changes in most other categories also demonstrate the greater stress experienced in the public sector.

Within the public sector, between 1982–83 and 1990–91, the rate of change for instruction was 79.66 percent, the smallest of all increases except maintenance and operation of the physical plant, and which in the short term offered the most discretion in spending. Increases for research and public service were 40 and 30 percent *greater* than for instruction, respectively. Another interesting category is that of scholarships and fellowships, which showed the largest increase of all. This increase is consistent with the policy change of the early 1970s by which governments would substitute student aid for institutional aid in order to capture the benefits of market functioning.

Expenditure data according to institutional *type* within the public sector permit further exploration and allow us, finally, to focus on the public univer-

15. If revenues from source A are merely constant while revenues from source B decline, the *share* of revenues from A will increase. What the data in these tables show usually is *relatively* less growth in state categories; absolute declines in state support occurred in only a single year.

sity sector. We would expect those institutions experiencing the greatest financial stress *and* the greatest potential for readjustment to demonstrate the greatest alterations in expenditure patterns. Over the period reflected in the tables, public universities probably experienced no more stress than did four-year or two-year institutions; however, the university capability for raising external funds presumably was somewhat greater. Its potential sources of additional revenues certainly were more varied. In public universities current fund expenditure shares going to instruction declined by 2.2 percentage points between 1980–81 and 1990–91 (Table 3.7) compared with only 0.5 percentage point in public four-year colleges (Table 3.8) and 0.7 percentage point in public two-year colleges (Table 3.9). In short, all three institutional types reallocated money out of the primary expenditure category supported directly by state governments, but the possibilities for making up the lost revenue were somewhat different for the three institutional types, as the data reflect.

Expenditure shares for research increased by 2 percentage points in public universities and a slightly smaller 1.6 percentage points in four-year colleges (Tables 3.7 and 3.8); differences in the absolute dollar increases are much larger because relatively little research occurs in four-year colleges (research is almost nonexistent in two-year institutions). The larger change differences are in other categories. Whereas public service declined by 0.1 percentage point in public universities, the *increase* for public four-year colleges is 0.9 point. Although the two-year college public service change is only +0.2 percentage point, the more recent and pertinent (to our thesis) increase is a much larger 0.9 point (since 1982–83). In other words, in public research universities, where negative effects of research dependence on public service should be the greatest, this is precisely what occurs; in fact, in the other public institutions, public service expenditure shares actually increase. Increases for administration are substantially larger in public two- and four-year colleges than in universities. It is not clear why this should be so. Meanwhile, the most discretionary spending, for libraries and operation and maintenance of the plant, decreases in all three types of institutions,[16] whereas spending for scholarships and fellowships increases in all three types, again a reflection of the national policy change toward higher tuition and more need-based student aid. Clearly, the changes support our theme: state appropriations decline relatively in all three types of public institutions; institutions seek alternative revenues, exploiting their major potential sources; and evolved expenditure patterns reflect the changes.

16. Former Stanford president Donald Kennedy (1993) writes about the related "chronic, deterioration of institutional infrastructures," which he sees as an outgrowth of the university financing changes that serve as the base for the ideas expressed in this book.

Table 3.4 Current Fund Expenditures of U.S. Institutions of Higher Education, by Purpose: 1980–1981 through 1990–1991

In thousands

Purpose	1980–1981	1983–1984	1984–1985	1985–1986	1986–1987	1987–1988	1988–1989	1989–1990	1990–1991
Total current fund expenditures	**$64,052,938**	**$81,993,360**	**$89,951,263**	**$97,535,742**	**$105,763,557**	**$113,786,476**	**$123,867,184**	**$134,655,571**	**$146,087,836**
Educational and general expenditures	50,073,805	63,741,276	70,061,324	76,127,965	82,955,555	89,157,430	96,803,377	105,585,076	114,139,901
Instruction	20,733,166	26,436,308	28,777,183	31,032,099	33,711,146	35,833,563	38,812,690	42,145,987	45,496,117
Research	5,657,719	6,723,534	7,551,892	8,437,367	9,352,309	10,350,931	11,432,170	12,505,961	13,444,040
Public service	2,057,770	2,499,203	2,861,095	3,119,533	3,448,453	3,786,362	4,227,323	4,689,758	5,076,177
Academic support	4,273,286	5,531,152	6,074,253	6,667,392	7,575,451	8,141,581	8,904,279	9,437,644	10,050,773
Libraries	1,759,784	2,231,149	2,361,793	2,551,331	2,441,184	2,836,498	3,009,870	3,254,239	3,343,892
Student services	2,908,998	3,797,935	4,178,236	4,562,938	4,975,913	5,396,520	5,780,837	6,388,148	7,025,482
Institutional support	5,772,515	7,763,325	8,587,216	9,350,786	10,084,663	10,774,495	11,529,119	12,674,031	13,726,484
Operation and maintenance of plant	5,350,310	6,729,825	7,345,482	7,605,226	7,819,032	8,230,986	8,739,895	9,458,262	10,062,581
Scholarships and fellowships	2,504,525	3,301,673	3,670,355	4,160,174	4,776,100	5,325,358	5,918,666	6,655,544	7,551,184
From unrestricted funds	1,080,614	1,738,188	1,961,597	2,285,116	2,644,615	2,941,143	3,282,698	3,853,904	4,445,106
From restricted funds[b]	1,423,911	1,563,485	1,708,758	1,875,059	2,131,486	2,384,215	2,635,969	2,801,640	3,106,078
Mandatory transfers	815,516	958,321	1,015,613	1,192,449	1,212,488	1,317,633	1,458,397	1,629,742	1,707,063
Auxiliary enterprises	7,288,089	9,250,196	10,012,248	10,528,303	11,037,333	11,399,953	12,280,063	13,203,984	14,272,247
Mandatory transfers	508,377	576,066	597,344	617,171	633,461	629,369	744,752	836,852	936,376
Hospitals	5,433,111	7,379,654	8,010,141	8,692,113	9,173,014	10,406,461	11,824,782	12,679,286	14,325,365
Mandatory transfers	57,963	88,447	130,892	123,333	151,071	178,472	240,278	222,192	274,452
Independent operations (FFRDC)[c]	1,257,934	1,622,233	1,867,550	2,187,361	2,597,655	2,822,532	2,958,962	3,187,224	3,349,824
Mandatory transfers	643	2,110	1,899	3,432	2,292	4,306	6,987	5,812	5,645

Percentage distribution

Total current fund expenditures	100.0	100.0	100.0	100.0	100.0	100.0	100.0	100.0	100.0
Educational and general expenditures	78.2	77.7	77.9	78.1	78.4	78.4	78.2	78.4	78.1
Instruction	32.4	32.2	32.0	31.3	31.9	31.5	31.3	31.3	31.1
Research	8.8	8.2	8.4	8.7	8.8	9.1	9.2	9.3	9.2
Public service	3.2	3.0	3.2	3.2	3.3	3.3	3.4	3.5	3.5
Academic support	6.7	6.7	6.8	6.8	7.2	7.2	7.2	7.0	6.9
Libraries	2.7	2.7	2.6	2.6	2.3	2.5	2.4	2.4	2.3
Student services	4.5	4.6	4.6	4.7	4.7	4.7	4.7	4.7	4.8
Institutional support	9.0	9.5	9.5	9.6	9.5	9.5	9.3	9.4	9.4
Operation and maintenance of plant	8.4	8.2	8.2	7.3	7.4	7.2	7.1	7.0	6.9
Scholarships and fellowships	3.9	4.0	4.1	4.3	4.5	4.7	4.8	4.9	5.2
From unrestricted funds	1.7	2.1	2.2	2.3	2.5	2.6	2.7	2.9	3.0
From restricted funds[b]	2.2	1.9	1.9	1.9	2.0	2.1	2.1	2.1	2.1
Mandatory transfers	1.3	1.2	1.1	1.2	1.1	1.2	1.2	1.2	1.2
Auxiliary enterprises	11.4	11.3	11.1	10.8	10.4	10.0	9.9	9.8	9.8
Mandatory transfers	0.8	0.7	0.7	0.6	0.6	0.6	0.6	0.6	0.6
Hospitals	8.5	9.0	8.9	8.9	8.7	9.1	9.5	9.4	9.8
Mandatory transfers	0.1	0.1	0.1	0.1	0.1	0.2	0.2	0.2	0.2
Independent operations (FFRDC)[c]	2.0	2.0	2.1	2.2	2.5	2.5	2.4	2.4	2.3
Mandatory transfers	d	d	d	d	d	d	d	d	d

Source: Digest of Education Statistics 1993, National Center for Education Statistics, U.S. Department of Education, October 1993.

Note: Because of rounding, details may not add to totals.

[a] Preliminary data.

[b] Excludes Pell grants.

[c] Generally includes only those expenditures associated with major federally funded research and development centers (FFRDC).

[d] Less than 0.05 percent.

Table 3.5   Current Fund Expenditures of U.S. Public Institutions of Higher Education, by Purpose: 1980–1981 through 1990–1991

Purpose	1980–1981	1983–1984	1984–1985	1985–1986	1986–1987	1987–1988	1988–1989	1989–1990	1990–1991 [a]
					In thousands				
Total current fund expenditures	$42,279,806	$53,086,644	$58,314,550	$63,193,853	$67,653,838	$72,641,301	$78,945,618	$85,770,530	$92,961,093
Educational and general expenditures	34,173,013	42,593,562	46,873,546	50,872,962	54,359,434	58,639,468	63,444,908	69,163,958	74,395,428
Instruction	14,849,822	18,592,391	20,287,410	21,880,782	23,359,057	24,954,204	26,893,691	29,257,209	31,371,394
Research	3,813,350	4,559,531	5,119,191	5,705,144	6,258,625	6,976,925	7,796,952	8,542,235	9,364,213
Public service	1,718,924	2,049,032	2,316,270	2,515,734	2,727,593	2,986,164	3,351,950	3,688,664	3,990,232
Academic support	3,029,284	3,809,572	4,267,698	4,693,543	5,048,232	5,436,155	5,941,906	6,535,076	6,933,847
Libraries	1,187,116	1,463,500	1,557,489	1,685,052	1,619,353	1,853,410	1,956,497	2,102,672	2,167,161
Student services	1,950,566	2,460,204	2,684,343	2,921,758	3,158,991	3,482,112	3,678,419	4,021,328	4,398,365
Institutional support	3,563,194	4,679,824	5,191,693	5,667,144	6,042,593	6,470,162	6,876,360	7,490,137	8,030,642
Operation and maintenance of plant	3,681,921	4,577,702	5,040,869	5,177,254	5,308,631	5,601,732	5,913,267	6,333,582	6,655,605
Scholarships and fellowships	1,064,864	1,276,644	1,374,803	1,575,909	1,751,671	1,941,389	2,150,350	2,386,493	2,688,532
From unrestricted funds	367,476	518,626	569,058	696,973	750,931	830,195	944,001	1,099,425	1,270,158
From restricted funds [b]	697,388	758,018	805,745	873,935	1,000,740	1,111,194	1,206,349	1,287,068	1,418,374
Mandatory transfers	501,087	588,662	591,269	735,695	704,040	790,624	842,012	909,234	962,598
Auxiliary enterprises	4,658,140	5,901,869	6,431,577	6,830,235	7,135,393	7,237,366	7,744,725	8,282,332	9,049,935
Mandatory transfers	344,043	367,956	387,585	410,777	409,726	412,006	512,413	551,331	623,146
Hospitals	3,377,972	4,503,492	4,914,560	5,353,699	5,904,212	6,532,905	7,533,912	8,113,989	9,315,902
Mandatory transfers	26,613	37,003	69,072	75,569	102,623	106,131	159,507	156,029	195,961
Independent operations (FFRDC) [c]	70,681	87,720	94,867	131,956	254,799	231,063	222,072	210,252	199,827
Mandatory transfers	322	656	451	846	194	2,063	1,787	2,276	1,201

Percentage distribution

Total current fund expenditures	100.0	100.0	100.0	100.0	100.0	100.0	100.0	100.0	100.0
Educational and general expenditures	80.8	80.2	80.4	80.5	80.3	80.7	80.4	80.6	80.0
Instruction	35.1	35.0	34.8	34.6	34.5	34.4	34.1	34.1	33.7
Research	9.0	8.6	8.8	9.0	9.3	9.6	9.9	10.0	10.1
Public service	4.1	3.9	4.0	4.0	4.0	4.1	4.2	4.3	4.3
Academic support	7.2	7.2	7.3	7.4	7.5	7.5	7.5	7.6	7.5
Libraries	2.8	2.8	2.7	2.7	2.4	2.6	2.5	2.5	2.3
Student services	4.6	4.6	4.6	4.6	4.7	4.8	4.7	4.7	4.7
Institutional support	8.4	8.8	8.9	9.0	8.9	8.9	8.7	8.7	8.6
Operation and maintenance of plant	8.7	8.6	8.6	8.2	7.8	7.7	7.5	7.4	7.2
Scholarships and fellowships	2.5	2.4	2.4	2.5	2.6	2.7	2.7	2.8	2.9
From unrestricted funds	0.9	1.0	1.0	1.1	1.1	1.1	1.2	1.3	1.4
From restricted funds[b]	1.6	1.4	1.4	1.4	1.5	1.5	1.5	1.5	1.5
Mandatory transfers	1.2	1.1	1.0	1.2	1.0	1.1	1.1	1.1	1.0
Auxiliary enterprises	11.0	11.1	11.0	10.8	10.5	10.0	9.8	9.7	9.7
Mandatory transfers	0.8	0.7	0.7	0.7	0.6	0.6	0.6	0.6	0.7
Hospitals	8.0	8.5	8.4	8.5	8.7	9.0	9.5	9.5	10.0
Mandatory transfers	0.1	0.1	0.1	0.1	0.2	0.1	0.2	0.2	0.2
Independent operations (FFRDC)[c]	0.2	0.2	0.2	0.2	0.4	0.3	0.3	0.2	0.2
Mandatory transfers	d	d	d	d	d	d	d	d	d

Source: Digest of Education Statistics 1993, National Center for Education Statistics, U.S. Department of Education, October 1993.

Note: Because of rounding, details may not add to totals.

[a] Preliminary data.
[b] Excludes Pell grants.
[c] Generally includes only those expenditures associated with major federally funded research and development centers (FFRDC).
[d] Less than 0.05 percent.

Table 3.6   Current Fund Expenditures of U.S. Private Institutions of Higher Education, by Purpose: 1980–1981 through 1990–1991

Purpose	1980–1981	1983–1984	1984–1985	1985–1986	1986–1987	1987–1988	1988–1989	1989–1990	1990–1991[a]
					In thousands				
Total current fund expenditures	$21,773,132	$28,906,716	$31,636,713	$34,341,889	$38,109,719	$41,145,174	$44,921,566	$48,885,041	$53,126,743
Educational and general expenditures	15,900,792	21,147,714	23,187,778	25,255,003	28,596,121	30,517,962	33,358,469	36,421,118	39,744,472
Instruction	5,883,343	7,843,917	8,489,773	9,151,318	10,352,089	10,879,358	11,918,999	12,888,779	14,124,723
Research	1,844,369	2,164,003	2,432,701	2,732,222	3,093,684	3,374,006	3,635,218	3,963,726	4,079,827
Public service	338,845	450,171	544,825	603,799	720,860	800,198	875,373	1,001,094	1,085,945
Academic support	1,244,002	1,721,580	1,806,555	1,973,849	2,527,219	2,705,426	2,962,374	2,902,568	3,116,927
Libraries	572,667	767,649	804,304	866,279	821,831	983,087	1,053,372	1,151,567	1,176,731
Student services	958,432	1,337,731	1,493,893	1,641,180	1,816,922	1,914,409	2,102,418	2,366,819	2,627,117
Institutional support	2,209,321	3,083,501	3,395,523	3,683,642	4,042,069	4,304,333	4,652,759	5,183,893	5,695,842
Operation and maintenance of plant	1,668,389	2,152,123	2,304,612	2,427,972	2,510,400	2,629,254	2,826,628	3,124,680	3,406,945
Scholarships and fellowships	1,439,661	2,025,028	2,295,551	2,584,266	3,024,430	3,383,968	3,768,316	4,269,051	4,862,651
From unrestricted funds	713,138	1,219,562	1,392,539	1,588,143	1,893,684	2,110,948	2,338,697	2,754,479	3,174,947
From restricted funds[b]	726,523	805,466	903,012	996,123	1,130,746	1,273,021	1,429,619	1,514,572	1,687,704
Mandatory transfers	314,429	369,659	424,344	456,754	508,448	527,009	616,385	720,508	744,465
Auxiliary enterprises	2,629,948	3,348,327	3,580,671	3,698,067	3,901,940	4,162,087	4,535,337	4,921,653	5,222,312
Mandatory transfers	164,335	208,110	209,760	206,394	223,736	217,364	262,339	285,521	313,730
Hospitals	2,055,139	2,876,161	3,095,581	3,333,414	3,268,802	3,873,556	4,290,869	4,565,297	5,009,963
Mandatory transfers	31,349	51,444	61,819	53,264	48,449	72,291	80,771	66,164	78,491
Independent operations (FFRDC)[c]	1,187,253	1,534,513	1,772,683	2,055,405	2,342,856	2,591,569	2,736,890	2,976,973	3,149,996
Mandatory transfers	321	1,454	1,449	2,586	2,098	2,244	5,200	3,535	4,444

Percentage distribution

Total current fund expenditures	100.0	100.0	100.0	100.0	100.0	100.0	100.0	100.0	100.0
Educational and general expenditures	73.0	73.2	73.3	73.5	75.0	74.2	74.3	74.5	74.3
Instruction	27.0	27.1	26.8	26.6	27.2	26.4	26.5	26.4	26.6
Research	8.5	7.5	7.7	8.0	8.1	8.2	8.1	8.1	7.7
Public service	1.6	1.6	1.7	1.8	1.9	1.9	1.9	2.0	2.0
Academic support	5.7	6.0	5.7	5.7	6.6	6.6	6.6	5.9	5.9
Libraries	2.6	2.7	2.5	2.5	2.2	2.4	2.3	2.4	2.2
Student services	4.4	4.6	4.7	4.8	4.8	4.7	4.7	4.8	4.9
Institutional support	10.1	10.7	10.7	10.7	10.6	10.5	10.4	10.6	10.7
Operation and maintenance of plant	7.7	7.4	7.3	7.1	6.6	6.4	6.3	6.4	6.4
Scholarships and fellowships	6.6	7.0	7.3	7.5	7.9	8.2	8.4	8.7	9.2
From unrestricted funds[b]	3.3	4.2	4.4	4.5	5.0	5.1	5.2	5.6	6.0
From restricted funds[b]	3.3	2.8	2.9	2.9	3.0	3.1	3.2	3.1	3.2
Mandatory transfers	1.4	1.3	1.3	1.3	1.3	1.3	1.4	1.5	1.4
Auxiliary enterprises	12.1	11.6	11.3	10.3	10.2	10.1	10.1	10.1	9.8
Mandatory transfers	0.8	0.7	0.7	0.6	0.6	0.5	0.6	0.6	0.6
Hospitals	9.4	9.9	9.8	9.7	8.6	9.4	9.6	9.3	9.4
Mandatory transfers	0.1	0.2	0.2	0.2	0.1	0.2	0.2	0.1	0.1
Independent operations (FFRDC)[c]	5.5	5.3	5.6	6.0	6.1	6.3	6.1	6.1	5.9
Mandatory transfers	[d]	[d]	[d]	[d]	[d]	[d]	[d]	[d]	[d]

Source: Digest of Education Statistics 1993, National Center for Education Statistics, U.S. Department of Education, October 1993.

Note: Because of rounding, details may not add to totals.

[a] Preliminary data.

[b] Excludes Pell grants.

[c] Generally includes only those expenditures associated with major federally funded research and development centers (FFRDC).

[d] Less than 0.05 percent.

Table 3.7　Educational and General Expenditures of Public Universities, by Purpose: 1976–1977 through 1991–1992

Year	Total	Instruction	Administration[a]	Student services	Research	Libraries	Public service	Operation and maintenance of plant	Scholarships and fellowships	Mandatory transfers
					Educational and general expenditures					
					Expenditures, in thousands of current dollars					
1976–77	$9,413,626	$3,570,554	$1,222,410	$346,906	$1,727,807	$331,614	$763,809	$857,577	$377,749	$115,099
1977–78	10,220,191	4,009,870	1,344,538	388,262	1,896,578	343,198	803,309	938,952	389,682	105,803
1978–79	11,284,191	4,408,025	1,478,568	419,231	2,136,135	363,875	920,726	1,046,740	396,356	114,533
1979–80	12,540,072	4,860,411	1,572,523	473,460	2,444,471	463,642	1,012,376	1,148,942	439,461	124,786
1980–81	13,951,029	5,374,271	1,795,504	525,891	2,743,145	451,978	1,158,512	1,270,339	492,225	139,164
1981–82	15,077,263	5,852,958	1,974,219	566,366	2,903,178	488,939	1,223,417	1,412,557	525,498	130,131
1982–83	16,089,168	6,247,358	2,107,933	604,657	3,086,846	528,470	1,300,353	1,512,947	562,903	137,702
1983–84	17,234,711	6,646,501	2,263,565	643,614	3,295,053	577,136	1,385,191	1,627,702	624,642	171,306
1984–85	18,960,810	7,257,618	2,598,784	701,451	3,682,755	609,365	1,519,324	1,745,825	677,533	168,155
1985–86	20,716,657	7,807,522	2,882,006	762,324	4,076,258	669,253	1,664,917	1,831,618	780,080	242,679
1986–87	22,023,387	8,368,187	3,088,348	819,829	4,399,405	677,531	1,725,613	1,829,880	847,328	267,266
1987–88	23,848,427	8,902,624	3,311,806	889,528	4,911,929	762,858	1,857,008	1,934,489	949,438	328,746
1988–89	26,138,665	9,623,797	3,638,424	975,801	5,476,936	813,888	2,096,267	2,069,744	1,096,447	347,362
1989–90	28,077,757	10,269,007	3,867,818	1,028,463	5,997,942	860,981	2,263,623	2,200,111	1,199,643	390,170
1990–91	30,367,325	11,012,373	4,157,677	1,103,058	6,599,209	906,506	2,479,956	2,305,115	1,367,754	435,676
1991–92[b]	31,565,791	11,373,749	4,198,990	1,161,633	6,937,360	946,098	2,609,520	2,323,220	1,556,868	458,354
					Percentage distribution					
1976–77	100.0	39.0	13.0	3.7	18.4	3.5	8.1	9.1	4.0	1.2
1977–78	100.0	39.2	13.2	3.8	18.6	3.4	7.9	9.2	3.8	1.0
1978–79	100.0	39.1	13.1	3.7	18.9	3.2	8.2	9.3	3.5	1.0
1979–80	100.0	38.8	12.5	3.8	19.5	3.7	8.1	9.2	3.5	1.0
1980–81	100.0	38.5	12.9	3.8	19.7	3.2	8.3	9.1	3.5	1.0
1981–82	100.0	38.8	13.1	3.8	19.3	3.2	8.1	9.4	3.5	0.9
1982–83	100.0	38.8	13.1	3.8	19.2	3.3	8.1	9.4	3.5	0.9
1983–84	100.0	38.6	13.1	3.7	19.1	3.3	8.0	9.4	3.6	1.0

Year										
1984–85	100.0	38.3	13.7	3.7	19.4	3.2	8.0	9.2	3.6	0.9
1985–86	100.0	37.7	13.9	3.7	19.7	3.2	8.0	8.8	3.8	1.2
1986–87	100.0	38.0	14.0	3.7	20.0	3.1	7.8	8.3	3.8	1.2
1987–88	100.0	37.3	13.9	3.7	20.6	3.2	7.8	8.1	4.0	1.4
1988–89	100.0	36.8	13.9	3.7	21.0	3.1	8.0	7.9	4.2	1.3
1989–90	100.0	36.6	13.8	3.7	21.4	3.1	8.1	7.8	4.3	1.4
1990–91	100.0	36.3	13.7	3.6	21.7	3.0	8.2	7.6	4.5	1.4
1991–92[b]	100.0	36.0	13.3	3.7	22.0	3.0	8.3	7.4	4.9	1.5

Expenditure per full-time equivalent student in constant 1991–92 dollars

Year										
1976–77	$13,308	$5,189	$1,728	$490	$2,443	$469	$1,080	$1,212	$534	$163
1977–78	13,449	5,277	1,769	511	2,496	452	1,057	1,236	513	139
1978–79	13,939	5,445	1,826	518	2,639	449	1,137	1,293	490	141
1979–80	13,811	5,353	1,732	521	2,692	511	1,115	1,265	484	137
1980–81	13,581	5,232	1,748	512	2,670	440	1,128	1,237	479	135
1981–82	13,390	5,198	1,753	503	2,578	434	1,086	1,254	467	116
1982–83	13,374	5,193	1,752	503	2,566	439	1,081	1,258	468	114
1983–84	13,711	5,288	1,801	512	2,621	459	1,102	1,295	497	136
1984–85	14,382	5,505	1,971	532	2,793	462	1,152	1,324	514	128
1985–86	14,992	5,650	2,086	552	2,950	484	1,205	1,325	565	176
1986–87	15,225	5,785	2,135	567	3,041	468	1,193	1,255	586	185
1987–88	15,611	5,828	2,168	582	3,215	499	1,216	1,266	621	215
1988–89	15,832	5,829	2,204	591	3,317	493	1,270	1,254	664	210
1989–90	15,827	5,788	2,180	580	3,381	485	1,276	1,240	676	220
1990–91	16,101	5,839	2,204	585	3,499	481	1,315	1,222	725	231
1991–92[b]	16,061	5,787	2,137	591	3,530	481	1,328	1,182	792	233

Source: Digest of Education Statistics 1994, National Center for Education Statistics, U.S. Department of Education, October 1994.

Note: Data in this table may differ slightly from data appearing in other tables. Data for 1976–77 through 1985–86 include any institutions that provided both enrollment and finance data. The Higher Education Price Index was used to convert the per student figures to constant dollars. Because of rounding, details may not add to totals.

[a] Includes institutional and academic support less libraries.

[b] Preliminary data.

Table 3.8 Educational and General Expenditures of Public Four-Year Colleges, by Purpose: 1976–1977 through 1991–1992

Year	Total[a]	Instruction	Administration[b]	Student services	Research	Libraries	Public service	Operation and maintenance of plant	Scholarships and fellowships	Mandatory transfers
					Educational and general expenditures					
					Expenditures, in thousands of current dollars					
1976–77	$8,682,538	$4,027,051	$1,445,651	$500,832	$607,235	$340,002	$250,152	$1,001,848	$338,432	$171,335
1977–78	9,568,977	4,423,487	1,598,092	572,193	677,414	369,408	274,314	1,118,393	332,899	202,777
1978–79	10,455,134	4,770,598	1,789,534	651,541	786,072	395,299	301,387	1,214,996	337,588	208,119
1979–80	11,750,398	5,271,621	2,029,327	733,557	937,874	448,190	359,467	1,375,308	383,036	212,019
1980–81	13,139,618	5,890,759	2,258,987	807,249	1,043,614	511,817	407,816	1,563,514	412,972	242,890
1981–82	14,321,586	6,537,888	2,518,182	834,225	1,086,146	536,080	440,736	1,738,210	403,069	227,050
1982–83	15,286,145	6,980,269	2,660,360	904,745	1,150,011	559,353	469,841	1,857,151	450,067	254,349
1983–84	16,538,128	7,464,035	3,013,666	1,041,488	1,246,289	622,879	513,732	1,873,528	473,503	288,908
1984–85	18,333,578	8,211,171	3,370,676	1,140,312	1,420,844	669,518	603,018	2,137,225	489,188	291,626
1985–86	19,860,947	8,945,373	3,658,627	1,235,418	1,618,737	712,112	648,178	2,118,522	569,841	354,139
1986–87	21,490,078	9,608,239	4,019,850	1,318,666	1,846,712	695,692	766,865	2,226,599	660,940	346,515
1987–88	23,124,455	10,310,532	4,261,440	1,434,726	2,053,638	774,274	864,347	2,340,495	711,704	373,299
1988–89	24,639,653	10,991,086	4,496,286	1,504,869	2,305,152	813,801	941,434	2,429,103	754,412	403,508
1989–90	27,210,634	12,079,093	5,076,792	1,648,526	2,525,080	888,526	1,088,113	2,607,385	871,944	425,175
1990–91	28,903,790	12,818,677	5,374,417	1,800,723	2,745,613	888,162	1,145,892	2,728,949	963,436	437,921
1991–92[c]	30,720,827	13,270,992	5,305,724	1,868,329	2,986,474	945,097	1,310,700	2,782,200	1,248,220	503,091
					Percentage distribution					
1976–77	100.0	46.4	16.7	5.8	7.0	3.9	2.9	11.5	3.9	2.0
1977–78	100.0	46.2	16.7	6.0	7.1	3.9	2.9	11.7	3.5	2.1
1978–79	100.0	45.6	17.1	6.2	7.5	3.8	2.9	11.6	3.2	2.0
1979–80	100.0	44.9	17.3	6.2	8.0	3.8	3.1	11.7	3.3	1.8
1980–81	100.0	44.8	17.2	6.1	7.9	3.9	3.1	11.9	3.1	1.8
1981–82	100.0	45.7	17.6	5.8	7.5	3.7	3.1	12.1	2.8	1.6
1982–83	100.0	45.7	17.4	5.9	7.5	3.7	3.1	12.1	2.9	1.7
1983–84	100.0	45.1	18.2	6.3	7.5	3.8	3.1			

1984–85	1.6	2.7	11.7	3.3	3.7	7.7	6.2	18.4	44.8	100.0
1985–86	1.8	2.9	10.7	3.3	3.6	8.2	6.2	18.4	45.0	100.0
1986–87	1.6	3.1	10.4	3.6	3.2	8.6	6.1	18.7	44.7	100.0
1987–88	1.6	3.1	10.1	3.7	3.3	8.9	6.2	18.4	44.6	100.0
1988–89	1.6	3.1	9.9	3.8	3.3	9.4	6.1	18.2	44.6	100.0
1989–90	1.6	3.2	9.6	4.0	3.3	9.3	6.1	18.7	44.4	100.0
1990–91	1.5	3.3	9.4	4.0	3.1	9.5	6.2	18.6	44.3	100.0
1991–92c	1.6	4.1	9.1	4.3	3.1	9.7	6.1	18.9	43.2	100.0

Expenditure per full-time equivalent student in constant 1991–1992 dollars

1976–77	$191	$378	$1,120	$280	$380	$679	$560	$1,516	$4,501	$9,704
1977–78	208	341	1,146	281	378	694	586	1,637	4,532	9,804
1978–79	201	327	1,176	292	383	761	631	1,732	4,617	10,119
1979–80	185	334	1,199	313	391	818	640	1,770	4,597	10,246
1980–81	187	318	1,206	314	395	805	622	1,742	4,542	10,132
1981–82	160	284	1,224	310	377	765	587	1,773	4,603	10,082
1982–83	164	290	1,197	303	360	741	583	1,714	4,497	9,849
1983–84	174	285	1,129	309	375	751	627	1,815	4,496	9,961
1984–85	168	281	1,228	346	385	816	655	1,937	4,718	10,534
1985–86	195	313	1,164	356	391	890	679	2,011	4,917	10,917
1986–87	175	335	1,129	389	353	936	668	2,037	4,870	10,892
1987–88	179	341	1,123	415	371	985	688	2,044	4,946	11,094
1988–89	178	333	1,072	415	359	1,017	664	1,984	4,850	10,373
1989–90	172	352	1,054	440	359	1,020	666	2,052	4,881	10,996
1990–91	162	356	1,009	424	328	1,015	666	1,987	4,738	10,684
1991–92c	178	441	983	463	334	1,055	660	2,051	4,689	10,854

Source: Digest of Education Statistics 1994, National Center for Education Statistics, U.S. Department of Education, October 1994.

Note: Data in this table may differ slightly from data appearing in other tables. Data for 1976–77 through 1985–86 include only institutions that provided both enrollment and finance data. The Higher Education Price Index was used to convert the per student figures to constant dollars. Because of rounding, details may not add to totals.

a Excludes universities. See Table 3.7.
b Includes institutional and academic support less libraries.
c Preliminary data.

Table 3.9 Educational and General Expenditures of Public Two-Year Colleges, by Purpose: 1976–1977 through 1991–1992

Year	Total	Instruction	Administration[a]	Student services	Research	Libraries	Public service	Operation and maintenance of plant	Scholarships and fellowships	Mandatory transfers
						Educational and general expenditures				
				Expenditures, in thousands of current dollars						
1976–77	$4,875,998	$2,490,274	$882,813	$409,217	$15,698	$171,409	$97,635	$547,515	$142,827	$118,618
1977–78	5,336,153	2,700,489	1,035,206	437,060	9,333	188,201	112,944	605,464	117,996	129,458
1978–79	5,734,611	2,877,651	1,119,840	482,323	21,289	193,703	110,918	650,447	127,633	150,807
1979–80	6,334,777	3,185,815	1,204,082	547,457	26,288	202,583	141,000	743,014	147,865	136,673
1980–81	7,063,474	3,575,743	1,347,020	615,869	26,591	222,391	152,597	844,781	159,474	119,008
1981–82	7,757,435	3,947,065	1,473,733	684,650	15,632	262,597	147,385	952,591	160,109	113,473
1982–83	8,292,446	4,218,388	1,620,644	741,179	18,090	248,682	123,722	1,016,267	175,069	130,403
1983–84	8,820,575	4,481,854	1,748,535	775,084	18,189	263,485	150,109	1,076,371	178,500	128,448
1984–85	9,560,507	4,806,050	1,929,968	841,101	15,591	278,363	193,903	1,156,074	207,975	131,482
1985–86	10,252,955	5,116,884	2,122,060	920,299	10,136	295,691	202,440	1,220,646	225,979	138,820
1986–87	10,845,969	5,382,531	2,363,275	1,020,496	12,508	246,131	235,115	1,252,152	243,402	90,258
1987–88	11,666,586	5,741,049	2,479,661	1,157,858	11,358	316,278	254,809	1,325,748	280,247	88,578
1988–89	12,666,590	6,278,809	2,727,058	1,197,748	14,864	328,809	314,250	1,414,420	299,491	91,142
1989–90	13,875,566	6,909,109	2,977,932	1,344,339	19,213	353,165	336,927	1,526,086	314,906	93,889
1990–91	15,124,313	7,540,344	3,265,233	1,494,583	19,390	372,492	364,384	1,621,542	357,343	89,001
1991–92[b]	16,242,146	8,167,389	3,403,593	1,659,746	24,747	392,728	365,281	1,582,319	450,040	96,303
				Percentage distribution						
1976–77	100.0	51.1	18.1	8.4	0.3	3.5	2.0	11.2	2.9	2.4
1977–78	100.0	50.6	19.4	8.2	0.2	3.5	2.1	11.3	2.2	2.4
1978–79	100.0	50.2	19.5	8.4	0.4	3.4	1.9	11.3	2.2	2.6
1979–80	100.0	50.3	19.0	8.6	0.4	3.2	2.2	11.7	2.3	2.2
1980–81	100.0	50.6	19.1	8.7	0.4	3.1	2.2	12.0	2.3	1.7
1981–82	100.0	50.9	19.0	8.8	0.2	3.4	1.9	12.3	2.1	1.5
1982–83	100.0	50.9	19.5	8.9	0.2	3.0	1.5	12.3	2.1	1.6
1983–84	100.0	50.8	19.8	8.8	0.2	3.0	1.7	12.2	2.0	1.3

Year									
1984–85	100.0	50.3	20.2	8.8	0.2	2.9	2.0	12.1	2.2	2.2	1.4
1985–86	100.0	49.9	20.7	9.0	0.1	2.9	2.0	11.9	2.2	2.2	1.4
1986–87	100.0	49.6	21.8	9.4	0.1	2.3	2.2	11.5	2.2	2.2	0.8
1987–88	100.0	49.2	21.3	9.9	0.1	2.7	2.3	11.4	2.4	2.4	0.6
1988–89	100.0	49.6	21.5	9.5	0.1	2.5	2.5	11.2	2.4	2.4	0.7
1989–90	100.0	49.8	21.5	9.7	0.1	2.5	2.4	11.0	2.3	2.3	0.7
1990–91	100.0	49.9	21.6	9.9	0.1	2.5	2.4	10.7	2.4	2.4	0.8
1991–92[b]	100.0	50.3	21.0	10.2	0.2	2.4	2.2	10.4	2.8	2.8	0.6

Expenditure per full-time equivalent student in constant 1991–92 dollars

Year									
1976–77	$5,230	$2,671	$947	$439	$17	$184	$105	$587	$153	$127
1977–78	5,267	2,665	1,022	431	9	186	111	598	116	128
1978–79	5,447	2,733	1,064	458	20	184	105	618	121	143
1979–80	5,363	2,697	1,019	464	22	172	119	629	125	116
1980–81	5,134	2,599	979	448	19	162	111	614	116	86
1981–82	5,129	2,610	974	453	10	174	97	630	106	75
1982–83	4,858	2,471	949	434	11	146	72	595	103	76
1983–84	4,931	2,506	978	433	10	147	84	602	100	72
1984–85	5,414	2,721	1,093	476	9	158	110	655	118	74
1985–86	5,592	2,791	1,157	502	6	161	110	666	123	76
1986–87	5,672	2,915	1,236	534	7	129	123	655	127	47
1987–88	5,587	2,749	1,187	554	5	151	127	635	134	42
1988–89	5,623	2,787	1,211	532	7	146	140	628	133	40
1989–90	5,483	2,730	1,177	531	8	140	133	603	124	37
1990–91	5,541	2,762	1,196	548	7	136	133	594	131	33
1991–92[b]	5,296	2,663	1,110	541	8	129	119	548	147	31

Source: Digest of Education Statistics 1994, National Center for Education Statistics, U.S. Department of Education, October 1994.

Note: Data in this table may differ slightly from data appearing in other tables. Data for 1976–77 through 1985–86 include only institutions that provided both enrollment and finance data. The Higher Education Price Index was used to convert the per student figures to constant dollars. Because of rounding, details may not add to totals.

[a]Includes institutional and academic support less libraries.

[b]Preliminary data.

It will be useful here to make some explicit connections to resource dependence theory. What resource dependence theory suggests is that the shift in revenue sources, specifically the decline in revenue shares from general purpose state appropriations, has destablized public universities. These universities have responded as best they can, by raising tuition (directly or indirectly) and, most significantly, by increasing shares from sources that require specific products and services under the terms of related agreements. Both the shifting revenue shares among resource providers and the different nature of the expectations of those providers are significant. Losses from state governments are destabilizing in and of themselves, causing considerable expenditure of university human and financial resources in attempts to make up for those losses; but worse, the terms of the agreements associated with the substitute revenues mandate specific actions on the part of university staff, thereby accelerating internal changes in the work that must be performed. The end result of these changes has been reduced university effort in the area of primary state (and student) interest: instruction and increased effort particularly in the area stipulated in contractual agreements, research. The shift away from instruction may have negative direct consequences not only for students, but it also contributes to increased university alienation from the general public, thereby reinforcing secular tendencies to reduce state general support even more, which in turn further destabilizes the universities and ultimately renders them more dependent upon and answerable to contracting and granting organizations.

Public two-year colleges in the United States are a particularly interesting case in the context of our thesis. Although these institutions conduct little research, they are considered almost unique in their ability and willingness to adapt. For example, over roughly the past two decades, in response to growth in student demand which has vastly surpassed government willingness to increase funding, public two-year colleges have come to rely heavily on poorly paid, part-time faculty. The increased reliance largely explains the two-year colleges' relative decrease in spending for instruction.

These changes in community college personnel policies may reflect another facet of resource dependence theory: the tendency for organizations to take on the characteristics of their resource providers. Community colleges have greatly expanded their instructional services to business; thus, one might expect these institutions to take on the staffing characteristics of the business sector. This has indeed happened as both types of organization have substituted part-time for full-time employees.

Increasing reliance on part-time faculty also may be viewed more simply as an outgrowth of resource dependence theory, as an alternative to raising more revenues. A complementary perspective, which has been applied to higher education (Leslie and Miller 1974; Miller 1976), was developed in 1934 by Joseph Schumpeter to describe how private sector firms respond to fiscal stress: they seek new markets, develop new products, reorganize and restructure, improve productivity, and seek new sources of supply of factors of production. Only the last type of adjustment is a direct reflection of resource dependence theory, although all of these adjustments may be viewed as logical outgrowths of that theory.

The United Kingdom, Australia, and Canada

Initially we were not at all sure how the four nations would array themselves with regard to likely changes in academic labor as reflected in revenue and expenditure data. We had reason to suspect that U.S. academics were the most heavily engaged in academic capitalism; after all, the United States usually is viewed as the prototypic free market system, and much recent U.S. higher education literature has dealt with topics such as technology transfer, industrial parks, and faculty entrepreneurship within universities. However, the national policy changes in the four countries discussed in Chapter Two suggested that major higher education financing changes were likely in the United Kingdom and to some degree in Australia, and perhaps in Canada.

Discussions with British academics and subsequent research in Australia, however, left us wondering. From academic perspectives in the United Kingdom, reductions in government support of universities were being viewed as draconian, and our early impressions in Australia were that academic conditions were not all that different from those in the United States. Indeed, we observed that the Australian universities might be well ahead of U.S. universities in implementing market mechanisms. Only in Canada did the data suggest and colleagues assure us that the financial changes impacting the United States were largely yet to be felt, although alarm was already being expressed about higher education cuts in government funding.

In the end we relied on our theory. If it is really resources that drive academic behaviors, then relative decline in government support of institutions, generally, and in the form of government support, specifically, should dictate the degree of change in what academics do. If this reasoning is correct, then subjectively we probably would expect the array of national higher education systems to show the greatest changes in the United States, followed fairly closely by the United Kingdom, with Australia some distance behind, and Canada clearly being the most stable system.

We remain less than confident in the positioning of the national systems on this continuum, however, because the appropriate relative weights of the factors involved are unclear. Further, there is the problem of the insider/outsider perspective: one's views usually reflect one's closer familiarity with changes in one's own system than with changes in other systems. Our interviews and conversations with our international informants suggested that they tended to view changes in their own country as quite large even though the same changes might have been seen as quite small in other countries. Such perspectives are due not only to one's vested interest in the financing system of one's own nation but also in the configuration of one's national financing system. For example, reductions in government support and increases in alternative sources of support which might have been seen as quite minor by a U.S. observer were seen as major by Canadian and Australian observers in part because of the historic almost total reliance upon block grant funding from the central government in the latter countries.

Then there is the folklore of national systems. Although we came away from our interviews, site visits, and data analyses almost shocked by the degree of academic capitalism which had emerged in the higher education systems in the United Kingdom and Australia (more insider/outsider disparities, no doubt), it was clear that almost all of our informants in these countries assumed that the U.S. system was much more market oriented than their own. We were not so sure. Although market forces have been in existence in U.S. higher education for some time and although the trend is relatively new in the other countries, the rate of implementation of market mechanisms in the United Kingdom and Australia has been very high.

In any case, we turn next to the United Kingdom as probably the next most market-oriented higher education system. In terms of *recent* changes and perhaps in absolute terms, the United Kingdom is probably the most heavily impacted of the four nations. (For an extended treatment of the policy changes in the United Kingdom, see Chapter Two.) Fortuitously, Gareth Williams (1992) collected and tabulated most of the British data and information pertinent to our thesis. Williams's book, *Changing Patterns of Finance in Higher Education*, describes the major financing changes that transpired in the United Kingdom in the 1980s, and his theme that changes in funding mechanisms have led to important internal changes in British institutions of higher education essentially is identical to our own. Again, changes in financing the entire higher education system are important as background, even though our focus is on universities.

After reminding us of definitional problems in international treatises on higher education (see page 2), Williams describes the 1980s as "a period of great turbulence, uncertainty and change" as well as growth in British higher education (3). He notes that the 1980s began with a planned higher education expenditure reduction of 20 percent, entailing abandoning subsidies for overseas students and cuts in support of institutions. These were the largest reductions in real *actual* expenditures ever encountered in Britain (the effective cut was 8 percent) and were accompanied by major increases in enrollments. The reductions heralded a "watershed in higher education policy," in Williams's words (3), with routine increases in government support no longer to be taken for granted and new expectations of institutions by government to become the norm, "to help reduce public expenditures; and to increase efficiency by encouraging institutions to 'earn' a larger proportion of their income from both government and nongovernmental sources, and to be explicitly accountable for it" (3–4). Williams observes, "It is misleading to consider the 1980s simply as a period of cuts in higher education resources. It was rather . . . one of changing patterns of finance" (12).

The altered government policy in regard to overseas students is a poignant illustration of the nascent market role in higher education funding in the United Kingdom, as well as in Australia, but one that has not yet been pursued aggressively by public institutions in the United States.[17] In the United Kingdom and Australia, higher education is seen as an export commodity, a generator of foreign exchange. British and Australian higher education is viewed as a valuable national asset to be exploited along with raw materials and manufactured goods. In the United States, comparatively, enrollment of oversees students is still seen more as a foreign policy device than as a service for export, with many such students, especially graduate students, being largely supported directly or indirectly by U.S. federal and state government and institutional funds.[18] From a market perspective, an essential difference among the three countries is that in the United Kingdom and Australia, but not in the United States, the full-cost fees collected from overseas students are shared with the academic units enrolling the students. That the United Kingdom and Australian policies can be effective is evidenced by large increases in enrollments of overseas students in both countries, after initial declines when full fees were introduced.

The data Williams has compiled reveal that planned public expenditures on core higher education activities in Britain (comparable to the annual operating budgets for educational and general expenditures in the United States) de-

17. A thorough discussion of this development is contained in Rhoades and Smart (1996).

18. According to Williams (1992, 15), the British government still pays approximately 12 percent of fees of overseas students.

clined in real, per student terms in the 1980s in large part because of enrollment increases (Williams 1992, 4–7, Tables 1.1–1.4 and Figure 1.1). Demonstrating the marketlike responses of institutions, the decline in revenues per student was much greater in polytechnics and colleges than in universities because the University Grants Committee, the primary source of university funds before its abolition in 1988, threatened financial sanctions if universities exceeded specified enrollments, whereas the former institutions found it necessary to increase enrollments to maintain their shares of government subsidies, which were awarded competitively, based on enrollment shares (Williams 1992, 4–6). In other words, it was the changes in the denominator, not the numerator, of the expenditure per student calculation which differentiated the relative decline in financial health of the polytechnics and colleges from the universities.

It was less decline in government support per se, however, than shifts in the forms of government subsidy which appear to have had the greatest effects on U.K. institutions, and that best illustrate the resource dependence thesis among universities. During the 1980s university block grants from the government declined in constant dollars from about 75 to 55 percent of institutional revenues, whereas government research council and other government categorical (i.e., specified purpose) awards increased substantially (Williams 1992, Table 1.3). Further, university block grants, which previously had been essentially unstipulated as to use, now were designated separately for research or teaching (9). Williams characterized the changes as being "the forerunners of what came to be a more systematic policy of government to steer resources according to its own strategic priorities" (9). Concomitantly, revenues from other sources showed increases that ranged from large to huge. While other income increased by about 20 percent, contributions from overseas students more than doubled, as did income from industry (Table 1.3). The only revenue category that explicitly reflects *expenditures*, as the term is used in the United States, is research, which witnessed an increase from 13 percent of university revenues in 1980–81 to 20 percent in 1988–89.

In the polytechnics and colleges similar patterns were observed (although data problems clouded the issues somewhat). Enrollment levels became far more important in determining government funding, and financial supplements were added to accomplish particular ends. Bidding for marginal funding of student places was implemented, with program cost being a partial determinant of success (7). What had been viewed, in both sectors, as "hard" money, now was viewed as "soft," being dependent upon, as Williams says, "provision of specific services for which there is an economic demand" (14).

Williams writes that by the end of the 1980s, British institutions of higher education essentially were contracting with government for the education of specified numbers of students in specified academic programs (9). This same arrangement was only beginning to be advocated in the United States as a means of setting government financing expectations of higher education institutions so that the institutions would be free to develop other revenue sources without fear that government would substitute those revenues for their own (Leslie 1995).

The trends continue in the United Kingdom. In 1992 the government committed to transferring substantial shares of its subsidies from institutions to students and to the research councils. Considering student fees as earned income, Williams estimates that as much as 70 percent of university income soon will fit this description, along with 40 percent of the income of the nonuniversities (39).

Change is well under way in Australia.[19] Actions by the ruling Labor Party have set a new direction for Australian higher education. In national policy statements higher education is to be a major vehicle for national economic growth. Government subsidies to universities for research, seen almost as entitlements historically by many Australian academics, are offered increasingly in competitive forms. The federal (commonwealth) government has set a policy of substantially increasing higher education enrollments while limiting federal appropriations increases. Not only are universities to become more efficient, they are to compensate through such means as charging students, engaging the private sector in joint money-making activities, and otherwise raising revenues in whatever ways they can. (For an extended treatment of recent higher education policy changes in Australia, see Chapter Two.)

Among the key developments foreseen by the government in the 1990s are:

> greater emphasis on continuing education and skills upgrading; a more competitive and focussed research effort; increased emphasis on improved management procedures; . . . a more outward orientation, reflected in the development of closer links with industry, TAFE [technical and further education], and other organisations; and an expansion of international contacts in teaching and research. (Department of Employment, Education, and Training [DEET] 1993, xxvii)

The first six factors listed in the description of the associated, new model for allocating commonwealth funds to institutions are:

19. An excellent summary of the more recent developments in Australia is contained David Mahony's 1994 paper in the *Journal of Higher Education*.

State views on priority regions for growth; demographic trends, unmet demand, trends in retention rates and participation rates in the institution's catchment areas; the ability of the institution to sustain growth within national priority areas; past performance in achieving growth in the priority areas; demand for external places; and institutional bids and justification. (DEET 1993, 90)

Unquestionably, this is a market-oriented list of considerations for institutional funding.

By most measures government financial support of higher education in Australia has been relatively generous in recent years. As a share of all federal outlays, higher education had done reasonably well, increasing in every year but one between 1987–88 and 1992–93 (DEET 1993, Table 4.9). (Comparatively, shares of government outlays have declined markedly in the United States.) Commonwealth subsidies for operating budgets increased between about 2 and 3 percent per year during the last half of the 1980s, on a constant dollar basis (DEET 1993, Table 4.3), and this too compares very favorably to the United States (most recent data available from government publications). Only in funding per student is the seemingly favorable picture in Australia altered; this anomaly is a function of unusual enrollment growth, which is a reflection of changed federal policy.

Commonwealth-provided total operating resources per equivalent full-time student declined steadily on a constant dollar basis between 1980 and 1991, although such funding was projected to increase from 1993 through 1995 (DEET 1993, Table 4.10). Between 1983 and 1991, dollars per equivalent full-time student decreased 11.2 percent (Mahony 1994). Total resources from the commonwealth essentially were stable in the early years of the data series, grew in the late 1980s and early 1990s, and are projected to continue to grow through 1995.

Although most university income continues to the present to come from government and although the major financing change over recent decades is the role that is served by the federal versus state governments, revenue shares from other sources have increased rapidly in accordance with the new policies. Although government funding of higher education has increased in most recent years, as in the United States, government rate of growth has slowed, and on a per person basis in Australia the government funding levels of 1975 were not attained again until 1989 (DEET 1993, Table 4.4). Recent changes have paralleled and surpassed those in the United States. As a share of total university income, government contributions declined from 90.1 to 78.5 percent between 1981 and 1990. Correspondingly, between 1981 and 1990 shares increased from 0.0 to 5.9 percent for student contributions (comparable to tuition and fees); from 4.4 to 7.6 percent for investments, endowments, and donations;

and from 5.5 to 8.1 percent for other income (DEET 1993, Table 4.6). By government policy there is to be increasing "diversification of funding sources" (DEET 1993, xxvii). The forces that could set in motion changes in academic labor in Australia without question are present, even though declines in government support are not as large as in the United States.

Second-level analyses comparable to those for the United States are not possible from available Australian financial data. Australia has a very small *private* higher education sector, and its former colleges of advanced education, which were similar to U.S. four-year colleges, were merged with the universities in the 1980s. Although its TAFEs are somewhat analogous to U.S. two-year colleges, the former are considered as part of the Australian postsecondary (rather than higher) education system, and data for this postsecondary sector are lacking.

Although national *expenditure* data are not published, some evidence of a few expenditure trends does exist (DEET 1993, Table 4.10). For example, consistent with the most recent federal policy direction, according to DEET, funding for research has grown and was to continue to grow until at least 1995, when a decrease was planned.[20] (Australia uses a triennial funding system.) This growth is particularly relevant to our theme that the nature of academic labor is changing because the role of government in Australia is very large relative to the United States (as is the government role in the United Kingdom and Canada). Proportionately, more research money comes from the commonwealth government, the amount of commonwealth research funding is growing, and amounts available are being dispensed on increasingly competitive grounds.

In sum, the ingredients for important changes in the nature of academic labor are present in Australia, although conclusions specific to the university sector are hazardous because of our inability to disaggregate data. Whether the ingredients are stronger than those in the United States and the other countries is difficult to say. On the one hand, fiscal stress is obviously present in Australia, although recent financial trends appear to be more favorable than those in the United States and the United Kingdom.[21] On the other hand, reliance on gov-

20. Australians knowledgeable about these data point out that a substantial portion of the growth merely reflects a change in accounting procedures. It would appear that $79 million of the apparent growth represented a transfer of funds from the operating grants of the universities to the competitive grants offered by the Australian Research Council (DEET 1993, 89).

21. Australian academics with many years of experience in financial matters advise caution in interpreting government statistics. The academics cite a "pliable" commonwealth bureaucracy that is encouraged strongly by the pertinent minister to present data in a light favorable to the government. These academics believe that the financial plight of Australian universities is substantially greater than indicated.

ernment is substantially greater in Australia, and the government message to universities is clear: "Enter the marketplace and raise more of your own money." Shifting revenue streams confirm that the government message is being heard. Certainly, our preconception that the United States was at the forefront of higher education commercialization was severely shaken by our experiences in and new-found knowledge about Australia.

Authorities on Canadian higher education finance are aware of the aforementioned changes in the United States and United Kingdom, but most do not think such developments are yet very far along in their country. They do not disagree that the changes are on the horizon for Canada, however; in fact, they point to related Canadian developments that are so recent that they do not yet appear in the published data. For example, they cite a flattening and then decline in the government (higher education) subsidies curve over the first three years of the 1990s and a major fee hike that was to be implemented in the fall of 1994. They see the recession that hit the Western democracies in the early 1990s and which arrived somewhat earlier and was more severe in Canada as a partial explanation for the recent financial developments in Canadian higher education. Statistics for more recent years, they say, would show increases in the share of institutional revenues from student fees, even if the substantial fee increases had not been imposed, because of the decline in government support. (This is the statistical artifact mentioned earlier.)

The Canadian higher education system is relatively decentralized. The federal government gives the provinces block grants for health, postsecondary education, and social welfare, and the provinces then decide how much to allocate to postsecondary education. The federal government also provides research money through a competitive grants process. Until recently, levels of higher education were such that academics did not generate many alternative revenues. However, during the eighteen months in which this book was in progress, evidence of change in Canada had begun to appear in the literature. (For recent changes in Canadian higher education policies, see Chapter Two.)

In our first draft of this chapter we observed that "there was no emergent government policy for universities to self-finance, as there was in Australia and the United States."[22] This view may now be obsolete. A paper appeared in 1993

22. This was not to say that there were no government efforts along these lines, although the relationships of such efforts to government were sometimes indirect. For example, in 1986 the Ontario government established *centres of excellence*, which were to conduct research "in areas of strategic importance to the province." The centres, however, were to be kept at arm's length from the government.

which discussed the (current) transition of the Canadian university out of a tradition of welfare liberalism into the *service university*, a term that resulted from the Science Council of Canada's work to link universities and industry (Buchbinder and Rajagopal 1993, 273). The authors saw the increased linkage of universities toward the market and several implications of the development of entrepreneurial professors for the nature of academic labor (273).

Clearly, there is growing Canadian attention to the role of universities in economic growth. A large source of Canadian research funding, The National Research Council, has shifted its orientation from basic research to applied research and technology, in a fashion similar to that of the U.S. National Science Foundation under the Clinton administration and the Australian Research Council under the Labor government.

Further, the Canadian government now has proposed a new student loan system that is to be coupled with a decline in federal (in favor of provincial) support of higher education which is to reach zero by 2006. It has been suggested that the loan proposal is a harbinger of higher student tuition charges, which in turn could signal structural changes to come, for it was changes in student funding which greatly accelerated the move in the market direction in the United States (Lewington 1994).

Although available Canadian financial statistics are more dated than those of the United States and Australia, some useful information is available. Expenditures on postsecondary education were 2.0 percent of Canadian GDP (gross domestic product) in 1980–81 and were still at that level in 1989–90 (Statistics Canada 1992). Share of total expenditures[23] provided by the federal, provincial, and municipal governments increased slightly, growing from 83.3 to 84.0 percent between 1980–81 and 1988–89. This increase was at odds with share declines in Australia and the United States. Despite this small share change, current dollar increases averaged 8.4 percent in the 1980s and increased in the last three years of the data from a trough in the mid 80s.

The small government revenue *share* increase was, of course, accompanied by small *share* decreases in other (combined) categories. While government subsidies to institutions were increasing by 90 percent (in absolute, not share, terms), income from fees and other sources were growing by 115 and 47 percent, respectively. Although small in absolute dollars, the forerunners of the sorts of large increases in student charges now manifest in the United States and Australia may already have been evident in the Canadian data. The

23. Whereas the data reported for the United States and Australia were shares of annual operating budgets, the Canadian data included capital expenditures. This should not pose an important problem for intranational comparisons but would if international comparisons were desired.

government *share* increase of 0.7 percentage point was complemented by a share increase of 1.1 percentage points in fees and a *decrease* of 1.9 points for other income. In contrast to the United States and Australia, Canadian higher education came to rely slightly *more* upon government rather than less, although the Canadian data are more dated. This difference in periods covered is important because the Canadian data do not cover any of the recession of the early 1990s.

For Canada there are some data by institutional type. Although Canada, too, lacks a substantial private sector, Canadian data for the nonuniversity sector do permit comparisons between institutional sectors. Canadian universities, by far the largest component of Canadian higher education, of course closely follow the total higher education pattern. The share of total revenues coming from government is two percentage points smaller for universities than for the total system, but is very stable. Fees increase from 9.0 to 10.6 percent of revenues, and other revenues decline from 9.8 to 7.9 percent, consistent with the patterns noted previously. The nonuniversity sector shows a bit more change. Nonuniversities get more of their revenues from government, and the share is increasing moderately. The share from fees *declines* noticeably, as does the share from other sources. Here some correspondence with Australian government policy appears evident: the technical and applied nonuniversity sector is relatively favored by government, and correspondingly, the fees charged students decline proportionately. (Again, these are 1980–81 through 1988–89 data.)

Another inconsistency in the general pattern and one that supports the suggestion of changing government priorities is the disproportionate increase in sponsored research within universities, some 145 percent between 1980–81 and 1988–89. This increase is substantially larger than the increase in any other revenue category. The money for sponsored research in Canada comes largely from government, and coupled with declines in other revenue shares, this supports the notion that government levels of funding were such that faculty were not impelled to find alternative sources of revenues.

The roots of possible change also may be seen in the expenditure data for universities. Between 1980–81 and 1989–90, expenditures for instruction, which serves as our reference point, grew by 99 percent. Larger increases were observed for sponsored research expenditures, 167 percent; student services, 133 percent; administration, 112 percent; and other, 190 percent. Clearly, resources had been shifted from instruction in a pattern similar to that in the United States. The functional areas slighted even more than instruction were those least relevant to generating alternative revenues: libraries, maintenance, and capital (84, 74, and 66 percent increases, respectively).

Overall, the (unfortunately rather dated) statistics support the perspectives of Canadian financial observers. With regard to revenues, before 1990 at least, stability had been the case for Canada; there was, as of that year, little evidence of changing funding patterns. However, as noted in Chapter Two, Canada's net government debt as a percent of GNP/GDP increased from 26.1 percent in 1984 to 40.3 percent in 1990, by far the highest of the four countries. We would expect debt reduction efforts to precipitate changes in federal and provincial funding for higher education. Expenditure patterns provided evidence of the beginnings of change. Internal resource allocations within universities suggested that growing attention was being paid to diversifying university revenue bases, probably through entry into competitive arenas. The changes in revenues which reputedly have now occurred but are not yet reflected in revenue data may greatly hasten any change. Assuming that the expenditure changes signal changes that now are reflected in evolving revenue patterns, Canada by now may have joined the United States, the United Kingdom, and Australia in altering historical traditions for funding higher education. If so, important impacts upon the nature of academic labor are likely to follow.

Conclusions

Although our ability to reach conclusions about changes in revenue patterns among public research universities is sometimes hampered by the form and recency of data available, essentially all information points in the direction predicted: reductions in shares of resources from government, in particular in critical, block grants, and resulting alterations in the nature of work performed within universities, as evidenced by changes in expenditure patterns. We believe these changes in revenue patterns promote academic capitalism because they push faculty and institutions into market and marketlike behaviors to compensate for loss of share from block grants.

The magnitude and nature of changes in the financing of public higher education in Australia, the United Kingdom, and the United States appear to meet Pfeffer and Salancik's (1978) conditions for organizational turbulence easily. Such changes may have begun in Canada but are not yet clearly visible in available data. Resource dependence theory suggests that this organizational turbulence is having major impacts on the internal operation of higher education institutions, especially universities, in at least the first three of these countries.

Among these impacts are major changes in the nature of academic labor: changes in what academics do, how they allocate their time, changes that may be much greater than most academics realize as they undertake their work on a day-to-day basis. These changes are reflected clearly in the financial data for several countries. In the following chapters we will draw out the implications of the changes in some detail.

4

ADVANTAGES AND DISADVANTAGES OF ACADEMIC CAPITALISM

In Chapter Three we looked at changes in revenue patterns among research universities in four countries over a twenty-year period. In all four countries we found similar higher education finance patterns: reductions in shares of resources from government, in particular in block grants. Because block grants were reduced, faculty began to compete for targeted government funds and funds from sources external to colleges and universities to maintain institutional equilibrium. In other words, faculty increased their participation in academic capitalism. In this chapter we look at how resource dependence plays out in two universities in one country, Australia. We interviewed faculty at both institutions in academic units (departments and centers) involved in academic capitalism to find out how they viewed the increase of market and marketlike activity prompted by changes in the institutional resource mix. Specifically, we asked them to identify the advantages and disadvantages of academic capitalism.

Resource dependence theory guides this chapter. Resource dependence theory suggests that organizations deprived of critical revenues will seek new resources. In the late 1980s Australian national higher education policies abolished the binary system and created a unified national system. (For a detailed account of these changes, see Chapter Two.) In the unified national system the practice of automatically giving universities research money for each faculty member was eliminated. Instead, university faculty had to compete for research funds with many professors from former colleges of advanced education who were now part of the greatly expanded system. These government research funds were targeted increasingly on national priorities that were often concerned with Australian economic development. At the same time, professors and institutions were encouraged by government to bring in funds from outside the government. Faculty and institutions began to generate funds from external sources by recruiting overseas students who would pay full fees, by developing partnerships with industry for research and training, and by developing products and processes suitable for the market.

In other words, universities and faculty had to compete—engage in market and marketlike behavior—for critical resources. Research money is a critical resource for universities because universities are prestige maximizers. Since most faculty teach, and many faculty perform public service, but fewer win competitive research funds from government or industry, research is the activity that differentiates among universities. Resource dependence theory suggests that faculty will turn to academic capitalism to maintain research resources and maximize prestige. Put another way, if faculty were offered more resources to teach more students, it is not clear that they would compete for these moneys with the same zeal with which they compete for external research dollars targeted for government priorities or commercial endeavors.

In this chapter we report on perspectives of faculty and professional officers (academic staff who are not tenure track) who are in units generating revenues from many entrepreneurial sources. It is important to note that these were "mainstream," not highly entrepreneurial, universities. We examined the financial records of two Australian universities, identified units that self-generated more than a few thousand dollars annually, and then interviewed representative project managers and staff who participated in entrepreneurial agreements as well as unit members who were *not* a party to these agreements or the related work. The two universities, Oceania University and Snowy Mountain University, were, respectively, an urban and a rural university. Oceania University was ranked near the middle and Snowy Mountain University near the bottom among Australian universities in terms of revenues received for basic research.

We began our inquiry by asking central administrators about the effects of faculty entrepreneurism within the university, which departments were most active, and how we might obtain pertinent financial records. We then used unit budgets to select the sample for intensive examination; roughly, 1 percent of budget, or at least $20,000, had to be derived from entrepreneurial activity for the unit to be included. The budgets and related documents yielded information as to the source of revenues and objects of expenditure for the entrepreneurial funds. Next, we interviewed the unit head and the unit financial officer (usually a department staff member) to help identify the departmental activities that met our operational definition of *entrepreneurism*: activities undertaken with a view to capitalizing on university research or academic expertise through contracts or grants with business or with government agencies seeking solutions to specific public or commercial concerns. Activities such as consulting were included as long as the associated revenues entered university accounts, university expertise was directly involved, and the activities were applied or developmental in nature. In this chapter we exclude basic research[1] as well as efforts to generate university revenues through recruitment of students who would pay full or high fees.

We began faculty interviews with the persons identified as project directors. In these and subsequent interviews we identified other faculty entrepreneurs and nonentrepreneurs and then sought out and interviewed unit personnel critical of the entrepreneurial activities. Because we limited the sample to units engaged significantly in entrepreneurism, however, there were few such critics, although there were many faculty who had some reservations. The first part of each interview was a subjective discussion of the impacts of entrepreneurism on the unit and the university. The second part employed a technique used in economics research to impute quantitative values for qualitative variables (e.g., Dunn 1997; McMahon 1982; Haverman and Wolfe 1984). Subjects were asked to rate, on a scale of −10 to +10, the extent to which the revenues associated with entrepreneurial activity contributed to the university's mission. Using this as a reference point, subjects then rated the relative benefits and costs of the qualitative criteria. This permitted a very rough means for assigning dollar values to the qualitative criteria and for calculating a cost-benefit ratio.

We performed our study of Oceania University and Snowy Mountain University in 1991, when Australian faculty first responded to changes in national policy which favored more entrepreneurial activity. In 1994 a study by Philpott[2] asked most of the same questions within a university that had been highly entrepreneurial for some time. Indeed, this university, unlike other Australian

---

1. Distinguishing between applied and basic research is always troublesome. We employ the National Science Foundation (United States) definition: "original investigation for the advancement of scientific knowledge . . . which do(es) not have immediate commercial objectives." We explore the limits of this definition more fully in subsequent chapters.

2. Rodger Philpott was a student of Larry Leslie's and used essentially the same method as did Leslie, creating a faculty cost-benefit taxonomy based on interviews. His findings were more similar to those presented in Chapters Five and Six than in this chapter. Unlike this chapter, which deals with all units on the two campuses which generated more than 1 percent of their budget from academic capitalism, Chapters Five and Six deal with units on campuses which were involved primarily in market rather than marketlike activities. In other words, the units in these chapters were developing products and processes for commercial markets. Faculty in these units experienced a great deal of stress, and some were quite critical of academic capitalism, as were the faculty in Philpott's study at the university that had taken its direction from the market. Intense involvement in market activities may create more problems than routine activities such as consulting or government grant and contract work.

universities, claims to take its direction from the market. Philpott's respondents had considerably more experience with academic capitalism than ours; his university had become more dependent on securing such funds. The two studies, Philpott's and ours, offer an informative contrast between internal university conditions early and somewhat later in faculty responses to a competitive funding environment.

Entrepreneurial Academic Units

Our study may be the first broad attempt to examine the economic consequences of academic capitalism within universities. An extensive search of the literature revealed several university case studies of a particular form of academic capitalism—development of intellectual property (Blumenthal, Epstein, and Maxwell 1986; Weiner 1987; Matkin 1990; Slaughter and Rhoades 1990; Rhoades and Slaughter 1991a, 1991b)—but no studies having either broad or in-depth analysis of a financial nature. This situation stands in contrast to that in commercial endeavors in the private sector, where several studies have examined the social returns to research and development across large numbers of companies and across industries (e.g., Minasian 1962, 1969; Terleckyj 1974; Griliches 1980; Mansfield 1980, 1989).

From the university perspective, what are the costs and benefits of academic capitalism activities? As nonprofit organizations, universities are presumed to be revenue maximizers in order to serve their clients: students, government, other patrons, and the larger public interest. Universities are known also to be prestige maximizers (Weiner 1986; Fairweather 1988; Winston 1994), to possess an overriding preference for those engaging in activities that contribute to high status among universities. Given that most faculty in postsecondary institutions teach and usually engage in public service, research is the activity that differentiates among institutions, conferring high status and prestige. From a public policy perspective, however, university costs and benefits must be evaluated on the basis of the extent to which they satisfy all components of institutional missions: teaching, research, and service. In our interviews we asked respondents to assume this perspective and speak to the effects of academic capitalism on those components.

Academic capitalism contributed importantly to university income. Even though the two universities constituting the case studies were described by informed observers as "not major players" in self-generating revenues from external sources, the amounts involved were substantial. At Oceania University the sums were $16.3 million in 1989, and at Snowy Mountain University the sums were $12.3 million in 1990.[3] These figures represented a respective 10 and 12 percent of total university operating revenues and were 18 and 19 percent as large as the recurrent funding provided by the commonwealth.[4] Clearly these were important activities from a revenue perspective.

By no means were the $16.3 and $12.3 million distributed evenly across the departments of the universities (Table 4.1). Less than half of the university departments self-generated significant revenues, and activity was highly concentrated in a few departments. (Only departments raising substantial revenues are represented in Table 4.1.) The humanities and social sciences were unlikely to have more than a few thousand dollars in such funding. The same was true of most professional fields related to the social sciences, although a few notable exceptions existed. More surprising, the more basic natural science disciplines such as chemistry, physics, botany, and zoology tended to generate fairly modest sums, too (even for basic research, which was excluded from our analysis). It was in the applied fields—applied natural sciences, agricultural sciences, and engineering—where revenues from contracts and grants with businesses and governments were substantial. Fairweather (1988) observed a similar pattern in the United States, which Levin et al. (1987) confirmed from their survey of businesses regarding the relevance of various scientific fields to technical advances.

Overall, departments identified as having self-generated substantial amounts averaged 22 percent of their revenues from these sources, with shares running nearly 50 percent and more in several departments in the applied sciences and agriculture.[5] Centers and institutes organized specifically to generate revenues often derived 100 percent of their income through academic capitalism.[6] The concentration of academic capitalism in the centers and institutes is hardly surprising, given that their creation and maintenance often are for the sole pur-

3. Data were for different years because at Oceania University the 1990 data were not yet available, and 1989 was an anomalous year for Snowy Mountain University because of institutional amalgamation with colleges of advanced education. The inconsistency posed no major problems because the primary purposes of the study were not of a comparative nature and because most research questions concerned revenue shares rather than absolute numbers.

4. This term is comparable to *current funds* in the United States.

5. At Oceania University, all centers and institutes were amalgamated with departments, whereas at Snowy Mountain University most centers and institutes were free standing. Had university policies been consistent, shares of department expenditures related to commercial activities would have been much higher at Snowy Mountain.

6. The difference in the separateness of centers and institutes at Oceania University versus Snowy Mountain greatly affects the interpretation of the data in Table 4.1. At Snowy Mountain University the utility of the center- or institute-based revenues to *departments* ranges from only moderate to almost nil. From the *university* perspective, the centers and institutes may contribute to research and service in much the same way as do department-based efforts.

Table 4.1   Commercialization of Science Revenues and Expenditures: Totals and by Department in Two Australian Universities

	University A		University B		All	
	Revenue dollars[a]	*Percent of total*[b]	*Revenue dollars*	*Percent of total*	*Revenue dollars*	*Percent of total*
Agriculture science departments						
1	623	37	874	55		
2	1,148	49	1,387	55		
3	441	38	680	47		
Applied natural science departments						
1	366	11	1,308	52		
2	1,104	41	55	3		
3	75	5	616	45		
Basic natural science departments						
1	28	1	379	29		
2	30	1	30	3		
3	102	6	75	9		
4	47	3	392	30		
5	241	6				
6	113	6				
Engineering departments						
1	1,478	30	100	16		
2	1,156	34				
3	624	18				
Social science departments/professional units						
Departments						
1	34	1	117	30		
2	153	7	40	7		
3			134	11		
Professional units						
1	260	9	81	7		
2	981	29	93	6		
3	440	100				
Independent center units						
1	6,822	100	2,407	100		
2			1,018	100		
3			591	87		
4			204	100		
5			638	100		
6			323	100		
7			707	98		
Total	16,266	25	12,249	45	28,515	36
Total, departments only	9,444	22	6,361	23	15,805	22

Note: Data are for 1989 in University A and 1990 in University B.
[a] In thousands.
[b] Percent of departmental total expenditures.

pose of responding to external funding opportunities (Hill 1993; Hill and Turpin 1993; Stahler and Tash 1994).

Although less likely, it is by no means impossible to gain significant revenues outside the applied sciences. Two of the most impressive successes in the case studies were in a physical education department and a special criminology unit. The physical education department had generated millions of dollars over the past ten years, primarily through swimming lessons and exercise and recreation videotapes. The special criminology unit had obtained from the government a single multimillion dollar grant to gather and maintain crime statistics, and this small unit was essentially living off the interest of the block grant which had been paid "up front." (This was in an era of very high interest rates.) In these units organizational dynamics were unusual. In the former, some hostility had developed toward the entrepreneurial head, whom some faculty thought had subverted traditional academic values. In the criminology unit it is not an overstatement to say that most typical academic functioning was absent. There were, for example, no regular faculty other than the unit head.

Costs and Benefits

The utility of academic capitalism activities to the university may be seen as direct or indirect. In the pilot phase of the study, when we asked faculty and administrators about the value of the revenues generated, both often prefaced their response by emphasizing that benefits extended far beyond the money itself. These were what Feller referred to as the important "second order consequences" of advanced technology programs (Feller 1988a, 248). Put more directly, the quality of academic life was seen to be affected in indirect ways by academic capitalism; indeed, the indirect effects were viewed as the essence of how academic capitalism impacted academic labor. Thus, it was clear that an adequate estimate of benefits and costs, and in turn the implications for academics, must include the indirect effects, which could be seen as relating strongly to the overall market positions of the departments and the universities.

To capture some sense of the relative importance of the indirect benefits and costs involved in academic capitalism, we asked interviewees to relate direct benefits and costs of the associated revenues to a list of indirect benefits and costs. (We compiled the list from the literature and from the pilot interviews.) Always, the criterion was the extent to which, from the interviewee's perspective, the projects impacted the university's mission.[7] The process was first to

---

7. We instructed interviewees to focus explicitly on the *university* mission; however, it was clear from responses that many interviewees reacted partially from a unit or even personal perspective.

gain the interviewee's scaled estimate of the direct benefit of the revenues themselves and then, using this estimate as a reference point, to gain a similarly scaled estimate of the indirect benefit associated with each item on the indirect benefits list.

Respondents attached a high value to the *direct* benefits of the $28.6 million generated through university commercial ventures. These were the direct benefits associated with the contracts and grants: individuals employed, departmental operating expenses contributed, travel paid for, and so forth. (Salaries and wages accounted for about 50 percent and equipment about 4 percent of expenditures at Oceania University; expenditure breakdowns were not available for Snowy Mountain.) On a scale of 0 to 10, the mean value assigned to the extent to which the ventures contributed to university mission accomplishment was 7.0. The mean value for Oceania University, the more "standard" university in that curricula were more broadly balanced and most research was basic, was 7.1; for Snowy Mountain, which was very modestly involved in engineering and was heavily involved in agriculture, the mean was a slightly lower (and statistically insignificant) 6.9.

Analogously, the indirect benefits associated with the revenues were put by the faculty and departmental administrators at 1.83 times as important, or $52.3 million, for a total benefit of $80.9 million.[8] For Oceania University the indirect to direct benefits ratio was 1.66:1; for Snowy Mountain University it was 1.98:1, probably reflecting the latter's relatively larger revenues from academic capitalism; that is, the larger the revenues, the greater the likely utility. Again, these figures can only be taken as crude estimates, but they are instructive.[9] The general view is that indirect benefits of academic capitalism clearly outweigh the direct, monetary benefits. Of sixty individuals responding to both questions, forty-seven considered the indirect or spillover benefits to be equal or more important. The pattern of responses was consistent across basic

---

This does not necessarily lead to interpretation problems because universities may be seen as collections of academic and support units—and ultimately of individuals—but it is an issue about which the reader should be aware and take interpretive caution.

8. We eliminated one very large outlier each from the benefit and cost data. If the very large values are included, the indirect to direct benefit ratio rises to almost 2.0:1, and the (indirect) cost-benefit ratio declines from 2:5 to 1:3.

9. Although the interviewees appeared to assign values to the total indirect benefits thoughtfully and thus the monetary values were generally valid, they seemed to be more liberal in assigning values to individual *indirect* benefits. As an illustration, it seemed somewhat questionable that, having placed a direct benefit value of 7 on $100,000 in commercially obtained revenue, they would then assign a 7 to recruitment of students—that is, that they truly valued the enhanced student recruitment equally with the $100,000 in revenue.

and applied researchers regardless of the degree of personal involvement in commercial projects.[10]

When costs were taken into account, again analogously, net benefits declined to $64.2 million; the cost to benefit ratio was approximately 1:3.[11] For Oceania University the cost-to-benefit ratio was 1:3.7, and at Snowy Mountain University it was 1:2.9, reflecting primarily larger perceived costs at the latter. The difference in cost perceptions may have reflected increased sensitivities at Snowy Mountain University, where the commercial activities were relatively dominant; in other words, as a university becomes more heavily involved in academic capitalism, some of the pitfalls may become more apparent. This generalization is supported strongly by Philpott's (1994) findings at a university considered a *frontier* institution, in academic capitalism terms.

For the two universities, total indirect costs were put at $16.7 million. Only three of fifty-nine respondents held the costs of academic capitalism activities to be in excess of benefits. None of these three was personally involved in commercial activities, and all three were in departments where such activities were considerable but in which the financial fruits were not shared widely. Two of the three seemed to be disgruntled regarding related departmental policies, whereas the third simply thought that applied research shifted the university focus away from "the more important" basic science objective. Philpott's study (1994) showed that this kind of dissatisfaction increases as staff are expected to generate more and more revenues.

Cost-Benefit Taxonomy

The cost-benefit taxonomy reflects respondents' assessments of the costs and benefits of academic capitalism, as identified in the literature and added to by the interviewees in the pilot study.[12] Items are arranged in descending order of importance, as viewed by the respondents, and statistically significant differences between universities are noted. The references that follow the mean values relate to literature sources that suggested the particular cost or benefit.

10. A recent survey of approximately one hundred universities in the United States demonstrated that faculty, *regardless of field or involvement with academic capitalism,* thought that the benefits from university cooperation with industry were substantial. For details, see Campbell (1995).

11. Only indirect benefits to costs are reflected. Since all revenues generated (direct benefits) are expended (direct costs) in the nonprofit universities, only the indirect benefit to cost ratio has a clear policy implication.

12. Specifically, we conducted an exhaustive search of the literature for possible costs and benefits, the respondents identified a few additional costs and benefits, and the respondents assigned weights to each of these.

Relations with External Bodies (Mean, 7.0) (Blumenthal, Epstein, and
Maxwell 1986; Feller and Seshadri 1989)

Faculty and administrators believed strongly that university commercial activities enhanced university relations with external groups such as business firms, the public, and government agencies. The mean value for this item was essentially equal to that assigned to the direct benefits of the revenues themselves. Interviewees cited the enhanced stature of the university in the eyes of client groups, government ministries, and the community. They believed that commercial contracts and grants strengthened the university's political base by enhancing its credibility as a "relevant" social actor. Only rarely did interviewees speak of negative client interactions that might be detrimental to university external relations. Of course, by implication, the respondents were saying that their personal stature was being enhanced, both externally and within the university, through this work. It was clear that it was largely individuals, not the university, who maintained the relationship with clients. A literal translation of the value assigned to this indirect benefit would be $28.6 million.[13]

Prestige (Mean, 7.0) (Weiner 1986; Fairweather 1988)

That universities are prestige maximizers was supported very strongly by the interviewees, whether vice-chancellor, department head, or faculty member. Clearly, this is a major driving force behind academic capitalism. As one vice-chancellor put it, "It's not the money; it's to make your mark as a university." Or as put in reverse and critically by an accountant who had recently joined a university research center, "That's the problem. The faculty aren't trying to make money as they should be. They're simply striving for excellence. That's the test. They constantly do more than is required under the contract."

The one or two respondents who held that academic capitalism actually reduced the unit's prestige across the campus were individuals at odds with the entrepreneurial direction of the unit. They believed that the units were reduced in status by their involvement in academic capitalism. However, even most of the individual critics of academic capitalism conceded that it enhanced

13. We report this value for illustrative purposes only; we do not provide values for other specific items because of transformational problems. The problem occurred primarily at the low end of the scale, particularly for costs, which were rated relatively low. A common respondent answer to a low rated cost item was "Oh, very minor [cost] if any—1 or 2 [rating]." In other words, the respondent viewed the cost as insignificant or nearly so; but because of the scaling, even values of 1 or 2 represented millions of dollars in costs—clearly much more than the respondent intended. At the low end of the scale, imputed amounts could represent costs greater than the university's total expenditure on the activity, for example, administration.

Oceania University and unit prestige, at least under present conditions. The mean value assigned to prestige was significantly higher at Snowy Mountain University than Oceania University. This was as would be expected, since Snowy Mountain University was relatively more heavily engaged in academic capitalism.

What does this mean for the individual academic? There was never a question, in the interviews, that *personal* prestige was enhanced by successful revenue generation. The assumption was implicit and often explicit: "Clyde is a doer. He is into everything. In a sense he is a role model for our younger staff. He is well known in Canberra, and he can call his own shots in the university. His opinions are never ignored." Individuals who were successful in academic capitalism had very considerable prestige both within Oceania University and externally. Logically, we may conclude that as the importance of self-generated revenues increases, the prestige of entrepreneurs increases commensurately. It follows also that those who do not so succeed will enjoy less prestige, all else equal. It was observed at the two universities that disparate success led to status bifurcation within academic units.

Spillovers to Research (Mean, 6.5) (Blumenthal, Epstein, and Maxwell 1986; Blumenthal et al. 1986a; Geiger 1989; Crean 1990)

Under our operational definition, most academic capitalism involved (applied) research, and as such the spillovers to basic research were usually substantial. In many units respondents reported that the commercial research projects added greatly to the research atmosphere of the unit. Among staff of applied science units, a common response was that unit purpose *was* applied research and that this was the only research funding available to them. Distinctions made between basic and applied research had little meaning in these units. The mean value assigned to spillovers to research was significantly higher at Oceania University than at Snowy Mountain, perhaps reflecting the considerably greater emphasis on basic research in the former. The one unavoidable conclusion from the responses was that academic capitalism increased the share of academics' time and university resources devoted to the associated functions.

Spillovers to Teaching (Mean, 5.9) (Blumenthal, Epstein, and Maxwell 1986; Fairweather 1989; Crean 1990)

"What I learn from my projects is what I teach my students" was a comment made by a professor of an applied science department. In contrast, a senior lecturer in a basic science department responded, "The applied research involved is far too esoteric for the undergraduates I teach, the only [teaching] spillover being an occasional reference to my work." These disparate comments reflected a fundamental dichotomy in the benefit to teaching of the commercial activities: some activities were seen as highly relevant to teaching; others were not. The mean value assigned to this variable was significantly higher at Oceania University than at Snowy Mountain. This difference may have had to do with the greater integration of academic capitalism in academic units at Oceania versus the organizational separateness of many entrepreneurial activities at Snowy Mountain.

Future Consulting Opportunities (Mean, 5.6) (Omenn 1982; Fairweather 1988; Slaughter and Rhoades 1990)

Successful academic capitalists quickly become aware that success breeds success. Commercial contracts and grants build one's reputation and often lead to consulting opportunities.[14] Academics' personal incomes are enhanced through consulting as well as through research contracts and grants, and improved personal financial status translates into reduced control of academics by universities.

Employment of Graduates (Mean, 5.0) (Gilley 1986; Feller 1988a; Geiger 1989)

Interviewees usually were quite clear that the projects enhanced the employability of department graduates, either through the imparting of marketable skills and knowledge or through contacts established with contracting and granting agencies or businesses. This is consistent with a major aim of employers: to "promote [at universities] state-of-the-art research and to upgrade the training of graduate students" (Feller 1988a, 243). As one very successful faculty academic capitalist said, "These students are by definition working at the cutting edge of knowledge in our field. Without these experiences they have only textbook, often out-of-date, knowledge. It is very common for our graduates to go to work in precisely the same knowledge areas as [those] they are involved in [in] our projects."

Yet, it was also clear that such "value added" to graduates was not universal. The many low values assigned to this item suggest that many commercial projects do not operate in areas that promise jobs for graduates.

14. We asked respondents to ignore the benefits to the university of consulting fees paid directly to faculty consultants. Our reasoning was that respondents would not be knowledgeable as to the amounts of such fees and that the benefit to the university would be very difficult to estimate.

One of the personal implications of graduate placement for academics is in the possibility of future contractual work. The placement of a former student may enhance one's likelihood of future grant and contract success with the employing organization (through personal influence), thus increasing further both the time the academic commits to such activities and the resources and associated financial independence gained.

Student Recruitment (Mean, 4.8) (Blumenthal et al. 1986b; Stauffer 1986; Fairweather 1989)

It was strongly held by respondents that departmental commercial activities were important to the recruitment of postgraduate, but not undergraduate, students. This difference largely explained the middle range mean value assigned to this item. Often the individuals employed to work on projects were postgraduate students. Further, a significant number of commercial relationships resulted in the sponsorship of postgraduate fellowships by business or government. But most important was the view that the projects gave the departments the visibility and the perceived quality that were instrumental to the attraction of postgraduate students. Again, item overlap was noted. The mean for student recruitment was significantly higher for Snowy Mountain University than Oceania, a result that was consistent with the greater commercial activity at Snowy Mountain.

Successful academic capitalists are aware of the importance of their personal success to attracting top graduate and postdoctoral students. Not only do such students contribute significantly to research and other work performed, their success also benefits their faculty mentors. Over a career span, academics come to be known in part by the quality of their former students and often by subsequent work conducted with those graduates. Those personal relationships pay dividends in various ways. In the end it is in increased personal status, income, and independence that the dividends of academic capitalism are captured.

Services Contributed by Project Personnel (Mean, 4.5) (Fairweather 1989)

In larger projects and in units where commercial activity was substantial, it was fairly common for the added personnel to work with one or two postgraduate or honors students in their research. Less frequently, project personnel did some teaching for the department. In one department contributed services were so great that all faculty experienced substantially reduced teaching loads. This, however, was the exception. Generally, even though the numbers of project personnel were quite large, usually only one or two of these persons were involved importantly in academic affairs, and quite frequently no personnel were so involved; therefore, respondents assessed this benefit as minor.[15] The mean value assigned at Oceania University was significantly higher than that assigned at Snowy Mountain. It was clear from the interviews that Oceania University capitalized more on project personnel than did Snowy Mountain.

Academic capitalism leads to the employment of staff who relieve academics of some of their responsibilities. Perhaps most commonly, graduate assistants employed for projects assist academics in their research, whether in the laboratory or the library, but also sometimes they are used as assistants more broadly, for example, in preparing for and teaching courses. Project staff aid faculty in a wide variety of nonteaching tasks, from gathering data to building apparatus for research to running workshops for unit clients. Project staff relieve faculty of these duties so faculty can continue to teach while they are involved in entrepreneurial activity. Project staff may serve as guest lecturers, especially while faculty are on travel, and academics may "buy out" all or some of their teaching responsibilities by using grant and contract funds to hire replacements. Undoubtedly, this is part of the explanation for why research university faculty teach fewer class hours than in an earlier time. Further, the overhead from grants and contracts is often used by departments to employ teaching and research assistants, thereby reducing the requirements placed upon academics. In this general area are seen major impacts of academic capitalism on the nature of what academics do.

Equipment Gains (Mean, 4.4) (Stauffer 1986; Fairweather 1989)

Considered here was equipment available to the universities after project completion plus equipment donated or offered to the universities at reduced prices. Responses to this question were distributed bimodally, with one group indicating very little equipment purchase with these funds, and the other group saying that such funds were the only means of gaining significant equipment in the present funding environment. (Some grantors prohibited equipment purchases under the terms of their awards.) Of course, response patterns also depended upon the capital intensiveness of the discipline. A few respondents reported that the university had provided extra money for expensive equipment only so that commercial ventures could be maintained or pursued. The mean value assigned at Oceania University was significantly higher than at Snowy Mountain.

15. This is in contrast with the American university system, where successful grantees/contractees often buy out some of their teaching time, and project personnel commonly teach entire courses. In general, Australian use of project personnel is much less than in the United States. Differences in the mix of regulations and traditions explain the contrasts.

The effects on individual academics are noteworthy. In many areas special equipment is essential to one's research and thus to success in one's academic career. Even in nontechnical fields, the equipment benefits from academic capitalism may be substantial. Successful academic entrepreneurs in the social sciences and humanities, for example, often are able to purchase state-of-the-art personal computers and software only through their own efforts. Although it may be argued that such entrepreneurial success merely allows the state to substitute self-generated revenues for its own support, these are the realities faced by many academics: either pay for equipment through your own efforts, continue to use obsolete tools, or do without.

Employment of Students (Mean, 4.2) (Blumenthal et al. 1986b; Fairweather 1988)

Usually commercial activities made it possible for units to employ departmental students, thus serving an important role in student matriculation and persistence. This was particularly true at the postgraduate level, but undergraduates also gained project employment, particularly in the summer. The benefit to the university was perceived as moderate. The benefits to individual academics of attracting students were discussed earlier.

Recruitment of Faculty or Staff from Clients (Mean, 0.9) (Fairweather 1988, 1989)

Harvard University is said to have reversed its decision to refrain from commercializing its biotechnology research out of fear that doing so would result in the loss of some of its best medical and associated faculty to biotechnology firms (Fairweather 1988; Feller 1988b). Such losses would represent a cost to academic capitalism. When this item was suggested as a possible cost in the first research center visited, the response was that the center had recruited from, not lost its staff to, its clients. Although this item subsequently was added to the list of benefits, very few individuals responded that their units had recruited personnel from client groups. The small number who did so reported that their recruiting success reflected personnel preferences for the university over the business or government environment.

Other Benefits

Occasionally, respondents suggested additional benefits that were derived from the commercial projects. Cited frequently was the general infusion of enthusiasm and a research ethos into the department, into the university, and even into individual staff members. As one center director put it, "Great excitement has been added to the university." Many reported that the activities had created a dynamic atmosphere with greatly improved morale yielding a generally more favorable work environment. Other significant comments were that the revenues added importantly to university autonomy, that the funds were responsible for building a research infrastructure that would not have existed otherwise, that the projects resulted in additional faculty positions, and that unit status had been greatly enhanced on campus. Patent development and international service also were cited, as was the projects' provision of badly needed field experiences for students (e.g., geology) and the manufacture of equipment for campus use (a computer-assisted design and manufacture unit). Other comments were more negative; these are included below, under "Costs."

In assessing costs of academic capitalism we asked interviewees to assume that direct project costs were paid by project funds, leaving only indirect costs to be estimated by the interviewees. Often, the response was that all or most indirect costs were accounted for under the contracts, and in such cases individual indirect costs were estimated to be quite small or nonexistent. Overall, costs were seen as small in relation to benefits. There was one exception.

Academic Resources Consumed (Mean, −3.1)

Most interviewees agreed that commercial projects consumed substantial university and department resources not covered by the contracts. Most often the item was valued at 1 or 2 on the scale, with about one in four respondents viewing the cost as significant—almost always in response to a specific problem or inconvenience encountered. Secretarial time, telephone costs, copying, and, most of all, physical space were cited. "Space! Space!" exclaimed one department head, as he observed that the projects consumed large amounts of space and that the university lacked the funds to build more.

Generally, Philpott's cost results (1994) are substantially larger than ours. Philpott's research was done several years after ours at a university heavily involved in academic capitalism. The apparent explanation for why he found greater costs is that as the scale of academic capitalism increases, the costs become more apparent. Now consumption of unit resources becomes a substantial problem. Annoyances multiply. Although it would seem to be a fairly simple matter to reimburse units fully for project costs, incidental expenses are often overlooked or underestimated in project proposals, occasionally funders refuse to pay for such costs, or competition is for *particular* unit resources (e.g., a specific piece of equipment, a specific secretary). At times the result is that the successful entrepreneur purchases his or her own incidentals out of external funds, leaving others to compete for those of the unit, further contributing to an internal dichotomy between "haves" and "have-nots." The have-nots may benefit from reduced competition for unit resources, but they nevertheless may resent the relative resource abundance enjoyed by the haves.

Loss of Time for Basic Research (Mean, −2.8) (Blumenthal, Epstein, and Maxwell 1986; Blumenthal et al. 1986b; Anderson and Sugarman 1989; Geiger 1989; Fairweather 1989; Matkin 1990)

This is the major concern about academic capitalism which is expressed in the literature. Stated dramatically, the argument is that "a greater emphasis on applied science will deflect resources from more basic, fundamental research and thus destroy the 'seed corn' of technological progress" (Matkin 1990, 10–11).

A few faculty and administrators held that the cost of applied commercial activities to basic research was high; a larger number put the cost in the mid range; and most put the cost quite low, holding that commercial activities actually stimulated basic research activity. Little cost was seen by individuals working in applied fields. The difficulties were seen as somewhat greater at Snowy Mountain University, which was more applied in orientation but had a larger commercial bent than Oceania. (The relationship between basic and applied research is examined more fully in Chapter Six.)

Time of Academic Support Personnel (Central Administrators) (Mean, −2.2) (Feller 1988b; Rosenthal and Fung 1990)

The pattern of responses to this item was similar. A very few respondents put the costs at the high end of the range, usually observing that a great deal of department head and central administration time was consumed. A few more saw the costs in the mid range, but most perceived these costs as minimal or nonexistent. Most opinions were either along the lines expressed by a senior lecturer that "central administrators have little enough productive work to do as it is," or that the value of such time was small and was often covered by imposed management fees.

Philpott's findings (1994) are again more extreme than ours. Philpott found that antagonisms toward administrators were substantial and increasing. Overhead costs charged by the university administration were resented more and more as academic units were expected to raise more of their own funds. (For a fuller discussion of tensions between faculty and administrators, see Chapter Five.)

Revenue Substitution (Mean −2.1) (Blumenthal et al. 1986b; Fairweather 1988; Feller and Seshadri 1989)

There was mixed and tentative concern about this item, which was presented as a hypothesis that university success in generating revenues through academic capitalism might result in reduced subsidies from the commonwealth government. Evidence to date in the United States indicates either no (Feller and Seshadri 1989) or some (Jaschik 1987) increase in state expenditures for higher education, overall, in relation to university research contract and grant income.

To some respondents revenue substitution was accepted as an eventuality; they believed that the commonwealth simply could not meet all of the claims upon it and that universities would have to do more for themselves. A variation of this response was to agree with the eventuality but to take a much more pessimistic view of the implications for universities. Only a few respondents were concerned seriously about the likelihood of a revenue substitution effect, but it was clear that most simply had not thought about the issue. In rejecting the hypothesis several individuals in vice-chancellories cited commonwealth funding regulations that in fact financially rewarded success in raising external revenues through commercial ventures. These individuals, however, seemed focused on their university's relative *share* of the commonwealth revenue pie rather than how large the pie was.

At the worst, most respondents believed that the forces balanced out; that is, there was some substitution of self-generated for government revenues, but some additional government funds resulted from university success in revenue self-generation. Those more concerned sometimes cited statistics showing declines in commonwealth support per student, along with other financing trends, such as the newly instituted HECS (higher education contribution scheme) charges to students and rapid growth in full-fee courses, which suggested to them a clear government intent to promote substitution of self-generated revenues for commonwealth appropriations. Others pointed to specific cases; an example was the alleged relatively lower than normal capital appropriations to a university that possessed a substantial endowment. It was noteworthy that most expressed concerns were by individuals at Snowy Mountain, which raised considerably more money through academic capitalism and where budget cuts had been announced recently.

Substitution of self-generated revenues for block grant funds is, of course, the essence of what is transpiring in most of the Organization for Economic Cooperation and Development countries, including Australia, the United Kingdom, and the United States. It was noteworthy that at neither of these two universities did a large number of staff connect revenue self-generation to relative decline in commonwealth support, at least in an important way; nor did staff see revenue substitution as a particular problem; few if any seemed aware of the consequences of resource dependence changes.

Equipment (Mean, –2.0)

Included here were marginal costs for university equipment, such as wear and tear and increased demand. Only infrequently were these costs seen as significant. Just as often it was observed that some equipment would otherwise have remained underutilized.

Loss of Teaching and Teaching Preparation Time (Mean, –1.9) (Blumenthal, Epstein, and Maxwell 1986; Blumenthal et al. 1986a; Anderson and Sugarman 1989)

Fairweather (1989), in particular, is concerned that activities associated with revenue self-generation will lead to reduced faculty attention to teaching; however, respondents generally did not share his concern, nor is his concern generally supported in the empirical literature (e.g., Blumenthal et al. 1986a). The most common interview response to this item was a momentary stare at the interviewer, followed by a comment to the effect that any research or service work is in addition to one's teaching responsibilities. Representatively, an associate professor of engineering observed, "One simply cannot short one's teaching." Such responses were usually followed by an assignment of 0 (no cost) to this item. Others were less sure of the effects, although in most cases the usually small negative values assigned seemed to be in relation to the extent to which other faculty, not themselves, probably spend less time in teaching preparation as a result of academic capitalism.[16]

Again, Philpott (1994) is less sanguine. His findings suggest that at some point, in fact, attention to teaching must suffer as staff flexibility approaches zero. In other words, so long as teaching staff are able to do so, so long as time for academic capitalism is not too obtrusive, they will continue to devote the necessary time to teaching matters; however, there must be a point at which one can do no more. Regardless of whether this point has been reached, it is clear that additional time devoted to commercial activities reduces the *share* of time and other resources committed to teaching.

16. In a survey of approximately one hundred universities Campbell (1995) found that faculty, whether involved or not with academic capitalism, found teaching to be a role they could not give up. Faculty believed that they must teach if they were professors.

Secretiveness/Confidentiality (Mean, −1.4) (Johnson 1984; Blumenthal et al. 1986a; Fairweather 1989; Anderson and Sugarman 1989)

In our interviews we mentioned the reports, in the literature, concerning commercial clients who sometimes required contractees to hold research results in confidence or delay scholarly publications. Interviewees were aware of the controversy surrounding this practice but denied any such personal experience. There was, however, strong agreement that any such restrictions would have very negative effects on academic values. Perhaps four or five respondents noted some personal, minor inconvenience with confidentiality agreements, whereas all of the few individuals who assigned high negative values to this item reported having had no personal experience with such problems. Their high negative ratings simply reflected strong personal values against confidentiality agreements. In the United States such agreements already are matters of some concern, and it may be that problems in this area are inevitable consequences of academic capitalism.

Departure of Faculty and Staff to Client Organizations (Mean, −0.7)
(Dimancescu and Botkin 1986; Matkin 1990)

This item was added in relation to the aforementioned concern that exposure to clients might result in employee proselytizing. The only reported direct losses were in the case of staff whom interviewees were "happy to see depart"— in other words, staff who were not highly regarded. A very few respondents indicated that there had been some loss of project personnel to clients after the project had ended, but the employment of redundant personnel was seen as positive. In a physics department it was reported that faculty who gained expertise through the projects sometimes left for industrial jobs, but not with former clients. In one unique case in which the university had set up its own company to develop a patent, several university departments were raided of top personnel; however, these individuals were merely transferred to another university enterprise. Although small, the problem of personnel loss to clients was significantly greater at Oceania than at Snowy Mountain.

One would expect this cost or problem to accelerate, although personnel losses may not necessarily be to client organizations. In the United States there appears to be substantial migration of successful academic entrepreneurs to business and industry. Some separate completely from universities, whereas others take part-time or even dual positions elsewhere. Perhaps this is most evident in the biotechnology field (Krimsky 1991).

Monetary Losses (Mean, −0.5)

Most commercial contracts and grants are structured in such a way as to prohibit losses to the university. One loss that did occur was in connection with the purchase of an expensive computer by a unit that was not legally separate from the university. The unit was required to make up the loss in subsequent fiscal years. This problem was viewed as almost nonexistent at Snowy Mountain and very small, although statistically greater, at Oceania, where the computer purchase was made. (For more monetary losses stemming from faculty and institutional efforts to develop products or processes for market, see Chapter Five.)

One would expect that as academic capitalism grows in scale, losses will increase and that both individual academics and universities will bear the consequences. For example, the prevailing view within many U.S. research universities is that it is unlikely that *technology transfer* revenues ever will equal costs. This is almost certainly true for most universities at present. Where this is true, already scarce resources are being taken from other functions, with an additional pressure being placed on academics for revenue self-generation.

Legal Fees (Mean, −0.5) (Blumenthal, Epstein, and Maxwell 1986; Weiner 1986; Geiger 1989; Rosenthal and Fung 1990)

Very few legal fees had been assessed in relation to the universities' commercial projects, in part because of the absence of significant patent activity. Most respondents indicated that legal fees were handled centrally, but if such costs were experienced they were held to be covered under the terms of contracts.

Recent experiences in the United States suggest that difficulties and costs in this area may increase in Australia, although making generalizations based on the highly litigious United States is risky.

Patent/Copyright Application Fees (Mean, −0.5) (Blumenthal, Epstein, and Maxwell 1986; Feller 1988b)

Again, there were very few such fees paid in connection with academic capitalism activities because patent activity is minimal, but increases may be expected as technology transfer increases in Australian universities.

Product or Process Liability (Mean, −0.2) (Anderson and Sugarman 1989)

A major concern expressed in the literature is that patented products or processes may lead to large legal liabilities on the part of universities. The notorious case of thalidomide is often cited. There were no such concerns among the Australian respondents in this study. The common response was that the university had insurance against such claims, and although insurance rates might increase if claims were filed, no such concerns were seen for the near to intermediate future.

Other Costs

Beyond those identified in the literature and the pilot study, several other costs were suggested. Among the more serious of these was increased stress experienced in units that had become heavily engaged in academic capitalism. This is precisely what Philpott (1994) found in the highly entrepreneurial university that he studied. There were other matters as well: promotions believed missed because of insufficient time for scholarly writing and basic research[17]; unit internal conflicts between the haves and have-nots; and perhaps most seriously, possible conflicts of interest. In two cases faculty members questioned their colleagues' ability to maintain proper scientific attitudes when continued or future funding might depend upon obtaining results favorable to the clients' interests. One individual questioned the propriety of competing with the private sector for contracts, and another cited the greatly increased tax-reporting requirements. Finally, several persons decried the loss of leisure time. Said one civil engineer, "I might as well have gone into business. The only difference would have been a higher salary!" (For a further examination of other costs in the case of faculty bringing products and processes to market, see Chapter Five.)

Institutional Financial Policies Influencing Academic Capitalism

Generally, the literature on the benefits and costs of commercialization of knowledge does not address institutional policies that deal with how academic capitalism is financed. Because the cost-benefit taxonomy was based on the literature, we did not raise questions about institutional financial policy with our respondents. However, a number of interviewees spontaneously addressed issues related to institutional financial policies.

Administrative or Management Fees Are Small

Not only are official assessment rates for academic capitalism projects small,[18] they are seldom collected in full, if at all. Official rates are as low as 5

---

17. One study that compared biotechnology faculty "with industry support" with those "without" found that the former published significantly *more* than the latter (Blumenthal et al. 1986a).

18. Charges assessed by administration for entrepreneurial projects, usually based upon the total value of the award.

percent of contract amounts at Snowy Mountain and are said to be collected only about 10 percent of the time. Total collections were only $176,000 in 1990, less than 0.8 percent of academic capitalism amounts. Although project directors occasionally complain about such charges, the level of complaint is relatively low, in our experience, as are the amounts collected. In Oceania in the unit where complaints are most serious, total management fees assessed are only about $35,000 of some $3 million in total research and development revenues (1990). Although the Oceania management fee or overhead rate is officially a high 35 percent, 57 percent of this amount is returned to the unit, about 21 percent is retained centrally, and 21 percent is allocated by a university-wide committee. At the same university, however, an engineering department head reports that all consulting activities "have been removed from the university" because management rates are too high. Here it may be that the university's problem is largely one of communicating its *effective* management fee rates. The alternative explanation is that effective rates vary by function— that rates for consulting are in fact so high as to be a disincentive. (If there is one characteristic of management fee policies in the two universities, it is that the policies are applied inconsistently, often being based upon what the client is willing to pay.) For academic capitalism on the whole, rather than management fees or overheads being too high, there appears to be considerable potential for the universities to charge more, thereby offsetting real university costs without importantly affecting incentives and disincentives for academic capitalism.

Interest Payments May Be a Lucrative Source of Revenue

At the university enjoying the greatest amount of patent success a major amount of associated revenue emanates from interest earned on lump sum patent payments. This is similar to the conclusion reached in an in-depth study of one of the most successful (patenting) universities in the United States, the University of Wisconsin, Madison (Wisconsin Alumni Research Foundation), where the investment of patent revenues has generated far more income for the university than have the royalties for the patents themselves (Blumenthal, Epstein, and Maxwell 1986).

The principle may apply equally for internal units and academic capitalism, broadly defined. Oceania permits units to capture the interest earned from certain large sum academic capitalism payments and from departmental operations accounts that are formally set aside for a minimum period of time and which are in excess of a stipulated amount. The interest earnings on the former can run into the hundreds of thousands of dollars per year and may serve as a primary unit revenue source. One unit is in the unusual position of operating entirely on the interest earned from a single multimillion dollar grant, which was paid in a single lump sum.

At Snowy Mountain independent research centers and institutes also are usually credited with interest payments, but interest earned on accounts held by academic departments is generally retained entirely at the central level. This is a policy that does not escape departmental academic capitalists. When confronted with claims that university central costs associated with academic capitalism projects are not recovered fully through overheads, the academic capitalists sometimes raise the issue of the interest earned on their academic capitalism accounts. As an agriculture staff member rejoined, "We would be happy to pay higher management fees; just ask them [central administration] to give us the interest earned on our money."

Personal Academic Accounts Are an Effective Incentive Instrument

Faculty and professional officers (non-tenure-track academic staff) are permitted to contribute certain academic capitalism earnings, particularly from consulting, to personal university accounts. This policy not only permits some university oversight of faculty activities, but faculty realize higher net earnings because income taxes are avoided so long as account expenditures are for university-related purposes. This is a win-win situation. In the end the personal accounts result in some substitution of faculty-earned moneys for university moneys because the accounts commonly are used for such items as faculty travel, computer software, and professional books.

Although institutional financial policies affecting academic capitalism have not been studied by scholars writing about commercialization, university-industry partnerships, and technology transfer, such policies may play an important role in creating incentives or disincentives for academic capitalism. If administrative or management fees are inconsistent, some faculty may be reluctant to engage in entrepreneurial activity, and others may be able to negotiate such low rates that the central administration must subsidize academic capitalism, perhaps creating hostility toward entrepreneurial faculty and units. Interest payments on lump sums brought in by faculty and units were important sources of revenue, but there was no consistent policy on who captured these. Oceania let units keep the moneys; Snowy Mountain did not. The sharing out of these moneys, whether to academic capitalists or to traditional faculty, would seem to provide a powerful incentive if central administrators want to encourage entrepreneurial activity. Personal staff accounts are an example of institutional incentives that create a win-win situation for central administrators and academic capitalists, but these incentives do not address the problems presented by units not engaged in academic capitalism.

Conclusions

The cost-benefit taxonomy reveals quite clearly what the faculty view as critical resources. The highest mean values assigned by faculty to academic capitalism were to prestige (mean, 7.0) and to relations with external bodies (mean, 7.0). These ratings suggested that faculty confronted with reduction in research moneys and increased competition for resources within the unified national system sought to alleviate resource dependence difficulties by winning external moneys—but not just any moneys. The funds they preferred were those that conferred status and prestige. Such moneys increased faculty, unit, and institutional prestige because they were earmarked for research, the function that distinguishes among universities. These funds were equally valued because they contributed to better relations with external bodies. By working on commercial projects, faculty strengthened their ties with government agencies and client groups, thereby enhancing their credibility as relevant social actors concerned with meeting national policy objectives aimed at benefitting the public. These faculty were eager to alleviate disruptions caused by changes in resource patterns, at least in part because they were able to do so while maximizing status and prestige.

Faculty were aware that their new focus on commercialized knowledge was somewhat at odds with the traditional status and prestige system of their research universities, which venerated basic or fundamental research. Faculty expressed concern over the shift in the sort of research in which they engaged by ranking spillovers to research (mean, 6.5) as a benefit just below prestige and relations with external bodies. They claimed that their applied efforts in academic capitalism spilled over to their basic research. In other words, they collapsed the differences between basic and applied research, legitimizing their work as academic capitalists without directly challenging the traditional status and prestige system. (We will explore faculty attitudes toward basic and applied research more fully in Chapter Six.)

Although the moneys generated by academic capitalism in our two cases are at most 12 percent of total institutional income, faculty spoke frequently about how the pursuit of competitive funding altered the ethos of departments and entire universities. The relatively small proportion of moneys needed to change faculty behavior points to the importance of *critical* resources. Faculty are willing to change behavior to pursue resources for research and development because these moneys fund discretionary activity and confer status and prestige both within the academic community and with external bodies. The willingness of faculty to pursue moneys that are viewed as critical resources, at the margin (additional), suggests that incentive programs that are not sharply at odds with faculty status and prestige systems might make change within segments of universities easier than is commonly thought.

Apparently, when resource dependence articulates with national policy—in Australia, targeted research for national economic goals—professors are eager to exploit the new opportunity structures. Indeed, pursuing commercial research, especially in technoscience fields valued by international markets, may be a way of furthering differentiation among faculty, upping the status stakes. As faculty noted in the cost-benefit taxonomy, becoming involved in commercial research sometimes creates haves and have-nots within units. As distribution across fields indicates (see Table 4.1), the division is not only within fields but also among fields. Although technoscience areas are not the only units engaged in commercialization of knowledge, they account for the great majority.

5

TECHNOLOGY TRANSFER STRATEGIES AS A RESPONSE TO RESOURCE DEPENDENCE

IN CHAPTER FOUR WE looked at academic capitalism without differentiating among faculty by rank, discipline, or types of market or marketlike activities. We found that faculty responded to conditions of resource dependence by pursuing academic capitalism, especially when such revenues involved research moneys for activities that did not conflict directly with the traditional status and prestige system. In this chapter we look at a somewhat different group of Australian university faculty: those involved in technology transfer. Technology transfer is the movement of products and processes from the university to the market. We decided to scrutinize technology transfer because it is one of the most direct forms of academic engagement with the market and, as such, a signifier of the issues that academic capitalism presents. Moreover, we disaggregated the faculty, studying different strata—central administrators, department heads, faculty at various ranks, and postgraduate students—separately. The questions we ask are: (1) How do central administrators respond to increased resource dependence, particularly with regard to technology transfer? Do they develop new organizational strategies and forms? (2) How do center heads involved in technology transfer respond to increased resource dependence? Do they develop new organizational strategies and forms? (3) How do academics other than central administrators and center heads respond to unit involvement in technology transfer?

We draw primarily on process theories of professionalization, but resource dependence theory sets the stage. Resource dependence theory led us to expect central administrators to develop strategies and organizational forms that would generate the greatest amount of resources for their institutions (Pfeffer and Salancik 1978; Pfeffer 1992). We expected central administrators to encourage faculty to pursue critical resources, not all resources. In other words, university administrators would look to maximize resources that contributed to their research profiles and met national economic priorities, given that these priorities to a degree shaped the government's willingness to fund research.[1] Because Australian central administrators are not highly professionalized, we did not expect a cohesive, organized response that inserted them in the policy making process at the national level.

Process theories of professionalization view professionalization as a process for which knowledge, theory, expertise, and altruism are not enough; organizational, political, and economic skills are equally, if not more, important. Process theories of professionalization look at professionals' active agency, particularly at their intervention in the political economy, to gain a greater degree of control over their work lives and income streams, through, for example, state licensure laws. Because process theories of professionalization emphasize the ways that professionals act in moments of great change in the political economy—for example, the rise of industrialization (Bledstein 1976; Haskell 1977) and the formation of the welfare state (Finegold and Skocpol 1995)— they should help us understand how Australian professors position themselves at the advent of global economy.

The center heads we studied were successful, experienced professionals. Process theories of professionalization suggested that they would react to resource dependence changes by treating technology transfer as a highly promising professional opportunity structure (Starr 1982; Freidson 1986; Abbott 1988; Perkin 1989; Brint 1994). We expected the destabilization of Australian science and technology policy to create a new set of conditions which would allow the heads to engage in market activity while still being shielded by their professional status. We thought they would move aggressively to exploit this opportunity, creating new professional organizations, securing new staff, and developing long-term strategies to safeguard their gains. Process theories of professionalization also suggested that center heads and faculty involved in technology transfer might begin to develop special organizations at the national or international level devoted to issues concerning marketization, or they might even begin to seek special legislation that privileged academics involved in the market. Guided by process theories of professionalization, we thought faculty would begin redefining technology transfer as a particularly

1. We believe that administrators' search for resources is also shaped by institutional resource conditions such as geographic location, investment portfolio, and the types of expertise which characterize the faculty. In other words, a university in a major metropolitan area which has a large endowment and faculty strength in science and technology might pursue a rather different strategy than a university in a rural area with a small endowment and faculty strength in professional schools designed to serve agriculture. However, if we explored these aspects of the universities we studied we would compromise confidentiality, since such details would reveal to readers the identity of the university.

privileged form of knowledge, a point to which we will return in the next chapter. Generally, we thought center heads would respond to shifts in national research and higher education policy and subsequent heightened resource dependence as professionalization theory would predict: they would treat destabilization as yet another professional opportunity structure.

We did not know how faculty and graduate students below the level of professor would respond. Usually process theories of professionalization focus on high status faculty at elite institutions, not on the rank-and-file (Larson 1977; Starr 1982; Freidson 1986; for exceptions, see Collins 1979; Abbott 1988; Slaughter 1994). When we disaggregated the faculty and studied faculty and students below the rank of professor separately, we saw consistent differences. Rather than seeing destabilization of higher education and science and technology policy as an opportunity structure, lower level faculty, postdoctoral fellows, and graduate students were confused and ambivalent; they were reluctant to participate in reshaping the traditional status and prestige system by embracing technology transfer. Degree of ambivalence increased the lower the respondent's rank. Gender, too, seemed to play a part, with the very few women in the study having responses somewhat different from those of the men. By disaggregating the data, then, we found variation in response. Faculty who were less well situated to take advantage of new opportunity structures presented by technology transfer were less willing to commit themselves to it.

Recently professionalization theorists have examined the way professionals intersect with the market (Abbott 1988; Bok 1993; Brint 1994). Very often they attempt to explain variation in prestige and salaries for different professional fields. We use this emerging theory to attempt to explain how fields and centers are valued within universities. Like Brint (1994), we see professors in fields close to the market as most able to accrue prestige and resources. As a result of the increasing intersection of professors in particular fields with the market, we see a new hierarchy of prestige and privilege emerging within universities.

We gathered the information presented in the remainder of this chapter through interviews with forty-seven persons in eight units in three universities between January and July 1991. We selected those units most deeply involved in technology transfer. Faculty in these units were turning academic knowledge into intellectual property, defined as patents and processes, trademarks or copyrights, and organized consultancies aimed at the commercial market. Of the forty-seven persons, thirty held academic track appointments (graduate students, research fellows, lecturers, senior lecturers, associate professors, and professors), nine were staff (professional officers in Australian parlance, academic professionals in American), and eight were administrators. With regard to rank, eight were professors, three with their own chairs. Three were associate professors, four were senior lecturers, six were lecturers, and nine were postdoctoral fellows or Ph.D. students.[2]

The forty-seven interviewees were located at three institutions. One was a well-established middle rank university that we renamed Outback University (OU) for purposes of this study. Another was a relatively new, somewhat experimental university, referred to as New Wave University (NWU). The third was a top ranked science and engineering university, which we called the University of Science and Industry (USAI).[3] At Outback University we identified a single unit and interviewed all unit faculty and professional staff as well as institutional administrators responsible for technology transfer—twenty persons in all. At New Wave University we identified two units. Again, we interviewed all unit faculty and professional staff and all administrators whose jobs touched on commercialization of science—fifteen persons in all. At the University of Science and Industry we interviewed only administrators concerned with commercialization of science and heads of departments or units that had developed intellectual property, for a total of twelve persons, five of whom were professors. We shifted emphasis at the University of Science and Industry, focusing on heads rather than whole units, because we wanted to speak with more faculty responsible for bringing ideas to the market, and faculty who were successful at technology transfer frequently became center heads. The interviews were semistructured and usually took an hour to an hour and a half to complete, although some interviews took two or three hours.[4] We supplemented

2. Six members of the sample were Asian men, one was a senior lecturer, two were lecturers, one was a postgraduate student, and one was a graduate student. One of the professional officers was Asian. There were five women in the sample. Three were on the academic side: one was an associate professor, one a lecturer, and one a graduate student. Two of the professional officers were women. In their interviews the Asian men responded in the same ways as did Caucasian men of similar rank, so we do not explore Asian men as a subgroup. However, the two of the three women on the academic side responded quite differently than men at the same rank, and we pursue these differences later in the chapter.

3. Because we guaranteed confidentiality to the persons we interviewed, we altered the names of the universities at which they were located, as the name of the university would have provided a strong clue as to the identity of the respondent. Thus, we used pseudonyms for all respondents and changed titles for administrators, who were the smallest group and the most well known, substituting more generic American titles for the Australian ones. For the same reasons that we changed university names, used pseudonyms, and altered titles, we also changed the technologies that the administrators and center heads discussed.

4. We took the interviews on a laptop computer, recording as the administrator or department or center head spoke. We were able to capture about 80 percent of the spoken responses. We regarded the laptop as a compromise between taking notes or tape recording and transcription. The interviews generated 275 pages of double-spaced, typed, transcripts and forty-four pages of field notes.

the interview material with a variety of materials (brochures, organizational flow charts, contracts, vitae, reports). Because the supplemental material was not available for all faculty and centers, we indicated when it was used and relied on it primarily for purposes of clarification.

The broad areas we covered were: (1) experience with academic capitalism, with special emphasis on how commercialization shaped policies, strategies, and plans for the future; (2) experience with institutional structures for the organization of commercial science; and (3) understandings about how academic capitalism shaped careers and resource flows.

Central Administrators

Central administrators were keenly aware of globalization and how it shaped national higher education and science and technology policy, creating conditions of resource dependence at the institutional level. For the most part they did not view these changes as creating new opportunities. Instead, they preferred the former binary system, which had accorded them markers of status and prestige: exclusive designation as universities and guaranteed government funding for faculty's curiosity-driven research. (For a discussion of these policy changes, see Chapter Two.)

All of the vice-presidents thought that the Australian economy was in dire straits and that universities had a role to play in improving it. As one said,

> I'm an intense nationalist, I believe that Australia has to do things for itself. I think we should pick what we do well and go out and do it. . . . We have to tell industry that the best horse is the local horse in the long run. . . . [Universities have] some very interesting industrial experience. . . . If we can pull it off, we can be a really powerful nation, small but fulfilling. We lost our way for thirty or forty years. I think in the postwar period we were very big on import replacement, but we got locked into an intense tariff protection scenario, and our industry lost its way from then on. (USAI)

Generally, they took the position that Australian universities should build technologies that lent value to Australian raw materials, contributing to the formation of processing industries in Australia rather than overseas. For example, they thought universities needed to participate in the development of food industry technology, which would allow Australians to do at least the preliminary processing steps in country, even though the final treatment—packaging, adjusting for particular styles of national preparation—might be performed elsewhere. Australia, then, could find a market niche in the secondary processing of raw materials.

Although the vice-presidents favored bringing universities closer to industry, for the most part they were not happy with the Dawkins (Minister, Department of Education, Employment, and Training) initiatives (for a description of the policy changes initiated by Dawkins, see Chapter Two.) They thought Dawkins had gone too far too fast and had undervalued and perhaps jeopardized the research infrastructure in place before he took office.

> So, even in the Dawkins setup, he's still providing money for research support via his formula. Where his system has been criticized and is deficient is infrastructure support, not connected to students but to staff . . . and then there's the questions of new staff and those changing their directions. (NWU)

They were particularly unhappy with the collapse of the binary divide. In the words of a dean,

> I think it's a disgrace to make them all equal. This world is not equal; it's not about equality. We should all compete at an equal level, but in the end, there will be differentiation by ability, otherwise we will have to go to the lowest common denominator. If we're looking from an educational point of view . . . who's going to do what the CAEs [colleges of advanced education] used to do? Technicians—who's going to train them? . . . Established universities keep saying this to Dawkins, but the new universities have a direct interest in becoming universities so they're into it, and they have more students, so they get better funding. (OU)

The attitude expressed by this administrator reflected the attitude of almost every study participant who addressed the new unified national system, whether administrators or faculty, with the exception of members of one unit, whom we will discuss later.

In sum, university administrators supported the movement of their faculty closer to the marketplace, and their support was undergirded by a belief that development of technology was necessary for economic growth. However, they were not happy with the Dawkins initiatives, particularly when these initiatives cut into the prerogatives of established research universities. They saw the unified national system as eroding infrastructure at established universities and as undermining the efficiency and economy of a tiered system that they thought, surveying the situation from the top, had worked well.

The common response made by university managers to the Dawkins initiatives was to move closer to the market, although the course they took varied with their histories and cultures. Outback University was well established, well funded, and highly regarded, and it did not perceive academic capitalism as a top priority. New Wave University was started in the 1960s, was located in a large city but not in one of the two major metropolitan areas, and was experimental in nature, placing special emphasis on developing innovative curricula. It was not as well funded as the other two universities. New Wave vigorously pursued external funds but remained somewhat sensitive to educational and organizational experimentation. The University of Science and Industry was established to develop technoscience fields and was located in one of Australia's two major metropolitan areas. It regarded the Dawkins initiatives as complementing its own mission, and it participated enthusiastically in the push to bring faculty and science closer to the market.

The research leaders at the three universities had quite different strategies for technology transfer. Outback University took a laissez-faire approach. New Wave University pursued a targeted commercialization strategy. The University of Science and Industry followed a corporatist course.

At Outback University the laissez-faire approach to the market meant there was little centralized control over commercial ventures. At one point, Outback University, like many universities, had started a university company to manage technology transfer. In the words of an Outback administrator,

> Five to seven years ago, many universities established university invention companies, but most of those flopped.

Another administrator explained that the Outback invention company

> was put in place to help the business community with consultancy projects and then broadened to the whole university. It tried to develop a product, an electronic device . . . but this failed. It had a full-time executive office on a rolling three-year contract, plus a staff of six or seven, and consultants. But the company was simply self-perpetuating, without any results. The staff got paid whether they brought in contracts, fees, or not, and soon it was losing $200,000 per year, with nonrigorous accounting.

The company was not successful, according to the central administrator quoted above,

> because the process of university administration was too different from that of the private sector, because universities were not willing to take risks, could not work on partial information, and were not fluid enough.

At Outback, faculty usually handled patents and relations with corporations or state agencies. There was no university company. Patent agreements were reviewed by a university attorney before faculty concluded any agreement, and there was a university patent committee through which all patents were supposed to be cleared. However, the administrator in charge of intellectual property said of the patent committee, "I've never used it once." The university had no plan to invest large amounts of university moneys in technology invented by faculty. Instead, Outback wanted equity positions and royalties from arm's-length companies started by faculty. The university, according to these administrators, took about 30 percent in overhead and about 50 percent of the royalties, although there was some disagreement about these figures, each case seemingly being negotiated on an individual basis. At Outback, faculty were free to act as independent entrepreneurs, subject to sharing their profits with the institution. They were supervised very loosely by the central administration and virtually not at all by their colleagues.

New Wave University took the position that it owned all faculty intellectual property. It had a strategy of developing this property by targeting particular areas and inventions and investing in them. This strategy was more focused on earning a return on faculty ingenuity and inventiveness than was the Outback approach, and it also involved a greater commitment of institutional funds than did the Outback strategy. The New Wave strategy was not without problems. New Wave administrators found it very difficult to identify what sorts of property in which to invest. Moreover, the administration had difficulty controlling and shaping faculty entrepreneurial energies so that the university reaped the profit it thought it should. The effort at centralized control via the university company contributed to conflict between the central administration and the faculty.

The New Wave administration did not want to prioritize ideas and inventions according to government initiatives. Rather, New Wave wanted to review ideas generated by faculty and select a few for investment and further development. As the administrator in charge of intellectual property said, "We direct what funds we have to the ideas that have the greatest potential, no matter where they come from."

New Wave was not notably successful in its investment in technologies. The Fission Energy Source System (FESS) typifies the problems of a targeted investment strategy. Initially FESS was supported by New Wave because outside financing was available, and the university had to contribute relatively little. When outside financing fell through, the project was at the prototype stage. New Wave put $11 million into bringing it from the prototype to the development stage, but the project was still far from the market. As a vice-president said,

> FESS . . . was a promising idea that came up from the academic areas, and the university saw a potential for commercializing. At the time the decision was taken to go commercial, the university was not looking to do it from its own resources, but with an outside financier. It's the only way a small to medium university can handle such a thing. Only since the financier got into difficulties has the university gotten into the

project from its own income . . . [if we had known how much it would cost] we couldn't have done it, wouldn't have done it. What's really required in Australia is a venture capital fund, if the government is really serious about the commercialization of ideas in the university. I can understand why the government doesn't want to get into it, but they could do policies that would encourage financial institutions and industry to get into it.

New Wave wanted to realize a big return on faculty ideas and was willing to invest modestly in them. However, New Wave was not happy with the risks that went with the possibilities of big returns.

Because New Wave was eager to realize a return on faculty ideas, the New Wave university company tried to monitor closely faculty involvements with corporations and government agencies that wanted to buy New Wave faculty products. However, unleashed entrepreneurial energy was difficult to contain. As the head of the university company said,

They [faculty] need to tell me [about their dealing with external organizations with regard to intellectual property], but nine times out of ten they do not, and I only find out after they've gone down a path and faltered. They only come to the university company when there's a problem, which means there's a fire to put out, such as [who's entitled to] ownership of intellectual property. There's no forethought or planning that's gone into the commercial avenue they've gone down. They'll talk to companies and promise them everything, and they have no authority.

The head of the university company gave chapter and verse on the number of contacts and contracts which faculty, whom he saw as acting irresponsibly, had initiated with outside organizations. He was very clear that legally the university had ultimate control over the entrepreneurial activity of faculty:

the fact is the university owns all the intellectual property here . . . it's automatically vested in the university company, and I can certainly force the issue on anything commercial.

But he did not force the issue, perhaps because he was uncertain as to how the faculty as a whole and the administration would respond, given that norms around ownership of intellectual property were unstable.

The vice-presidents, too, found themselves confronted by competing agendas held by entrepreneurial faculty. For example, the university planned to develop part of its acreage to generate an income stream, and several faculty members presented plans that were at odds with the mandate the faculty senate had given to the head of the university company. The head of the company and several faculty members were besieging the vice-president on this matter. For the moment the vice-president was backing the university company head, who had a very ambitious plan that included development of shops, a golf course, and a retirement village. The senate was not enthusiastic about these ventures, and the various faculty members continued to put alternative plans forward aggressively. The introduction of an entrepreneurial climate had unleashed a great deal of intraorganizational competitiveness that was not necessarily focused on shared institutional goals.

New Wave's emphasis on centrally controlling entrepreneurial activity and intellectual property heightened tensions between the central administration and faculty and exacerbated the conflicts between academic and commercial culture. When we asked the head of the university company if he had any problems with faculty, he responded,

> Problems with faculty? How long have you got? The different agendas . . . I have a commercial lien, I'm under pressure from the senate to—and I quote, "bring in millions of dollars to the university." So I'm under tremendous pressure to bring in money. But the agendas for the faculty are varied . . . there's tremendous jealousy. Another problem is the whole basis of promotion—they're promoted on research funds and papers published, and those two things don't assist me. First, you don't want to publish information, you want to protect it, and they apply for a whole load of research funds and don't look at commercialization or at what's going to happen at the end of a research project.

According to the company head, business and academe were two different cultures. He acted as the central administration's bridge between the two cultures, but, as he acknowledged freely, he was firmly committed to the business world. He viewed publishing and grant writing as thwarting his efforts to commercialize. Moreover, he saw most faculty as being inept at commercialization:

> A lot of academics are not commercial, and I wouldn't utilize them on any commercial project. I simply wouldn't use them on a commercial project. On the other hand, there are some who are champions, but the majority I wouldn't allow out in the real world. I wouldn't let them deal with business and industry, they're coming from a sheltered environment.

The head of the university company had little time available to educate faculty about the commercial world. As he said,

> Because of the pressure to bring in commercial return, we can't allow any project to slip by. We have to evaluate every opportunity, which means I'm spread too thin.

Unlike at Outback University, New Wave administrators tried to control faculty entrepreneurship centrally. New Wave thought it would obtain a higher return through active management of academic capitalism, through institutional investment in research directed by a university company. However, New Wave was unhappy with the degree of risk inherent in its strategy and was seeking ways to minimize those risks, primarily through government incentives or subsidies. New Wave's direct involvement in academic capitalism via the head of the university company created a fair amount of tension between the central administration and the faculty.

The University of Science and Industry had a corporatist strategy for commercialization of science. Administrators were not so much interested in developing specific pieces of intellectual property through their university company as they were concerned with constituting long-term relationships among members of the university community, business and industry, and various government agencies through cooperative research centers (CRCs). The CRCs were initiated by the federal government in 1990. They brought together university, government, and industry to fund commercial research and were scheduled to receive $100 million a year. They were modeled after the interdisciplinary research centers of the United Kingdom and the industry-university cooperative research programs funded by the National Science Foundation in the United States (Hill 1993). University of Science and Industry administrators considered CRCs to be a way of establishing stable and enduring relationships with external entities in order to develop predictable flows of resources. The CRCs were regarded as superior to other forms of commercialization because CRCs provided long-term funds for very large projects, covered patenting and patent costs, and ensured resources for bringing products and processes from an idea to the market, covering the costly development stages. Moreover, the risks were expected to be spread fairly evenly among the several parties to the CRCs.

According to a vice-president at the University of Science and Industry,

> The university company has a catalog of patents it tries to flog. There are some successes, but it's not a joy . . . we've only really made money on one big windfall. We organized a company that licensed the intellectual property and then converted the licensing to shares that went up by a factor of twenty. The money made by the company is on shares sold.

He noted that the university company did not have the large sums needed for investing in bringing an idea from bench science to demonstration prototype. He looked to the government for those moneys. He viewed the most difficult step in commercialization as the final step, from prototype to world market. "The $10–20 million that's needed to bring it to world product" was most difficult to secure. According to this administrator, the way to secure reliable resources for bringing inventions to the product stage was by developing CRCs:

> The corporations are willing to do it. Patents are useful to selling, but not worth all that much. The CRCs can be like agricultural research where they levy funds. It's a factor of four on ARC (Australian Research Council); it's big bananas.

This vice-president considered the most difficult aspect of creating CRCs to be selling them to industries. He relied on his former contacts with industry and the trust he had established with corporate leaders over the years to bring them to the point where they would commit to CRCs. Despite the difficulties he encountered in convincing corporate leaders to invest in CRCs, he envisioned fifty CRCs at his university in the near future.

Other administrators at the University of Science and Industry held similar views of CRCs. Even administrators of the university company realized that there was a need to move beyond "offering a piece of technology in a shoe box for a fee and royalties." They understood that intellectual property had to be tied to proposals for research and development programs and broader research packages.

Unlike those at New Wave University, administrators at the University of Science and Industry did not place great reliance on the university company as a mechanism for capturing the benefits of faculty invention. One administrator estimated that faculty ran only 50 percent of their intellectual property through the university. However, administrators were still interested in securing a share of the benefits from faculty intellectual property. In their view CRCs were a more effective way to capture those benefits than central monitoring schemes. CRCs committed disparate parties—universities, business and industry, and government—more wholeheartedly to commercializing innovative ideas than could a university company. University companies acted primarily as go-betweens, linking individual researchers and companies, usually at early and tenuous stages of product development. The CRCs were more likely to provide stable resources and predictable funding over the long term. The CRCs also brought a substantial government commitment of funds.

The several university administrations had different organizational structures and different strategies that informed their organizations. Outback University had a laissez-faire approach that involved no new organizational structures within the university. The only new structures were external to the university, in the form of arm's-length companies. The strategy employed by central administrators was to encourage faculty to act as individual entrepreneurs and hope that they would develop a substantial number of revenue-generating ventures. The strategy depended on the energy of faculty rather than that of administrators.

New Wave University established a university company to deal with the commercialization of faculty inventions. The company was a central organization responsible for inventorying and monitoring the development of faculty intellectual property. When a piece of intellectual property looked promising, New Wave was ready to invest some money, but not a great deal. The New Wave strategy depended on close monitoring of faculty, targeting certain pieces of intellectual property, and taking manageable risks to develop these.

The University of Science and Industry hoped for a high return on faculty invention and used the university company in some cases. The company was used to inventory and broker, but it did not do a great deal of monitoring. Faculty were not closely controlled by a central entity. Instead, the University of Science and Industry turned to CRCs to capture faculty entrepreneurial energies. As an organizational form, the CRCs called for long-term commitment on the part of faculty, business and industry, and an array of government agencies.

As resource dependence theory suggests, central administrators developed organizational strategies and organizational forms to generate resources for their institutions when national higher education and science and technology policy were destabilized. However, central administrators, with the exception of those at the University of Science and Industry, did not try to devise strategies and organizational forms that would generate the greatest amount of money for their institution. Only at the University of Science and Industry had central administrators moved beyond a focus on specific pieces of intellectual property to a broader strategy—CRCs—which minimized the capriciousness of the marketplace. The University of Science and Industry central administrators may have been able to devise a broader strategy than the others because their expertise in science and engineering complemented national policy emphasis on commercialization and globalization and was consistent with a new status and prestige system that put technoscience near the top of the hierarchy.

Center Heads and Professors

National policies developed in Australia in the late 1980s destabilized the academic research environment. (For a detailed discussion of these policy changes, see Chapter Two.) The unified national system created conditions in which a larger number of faculty and institutions competed with each other for research moneys that were often targeted to national priorities. By 1993, increased competition within the tertiary system meant that the ARC was able to fund only about 20 percent of grant applications (Hill 1993). Moreover, professors were no longer able to count on institutional research funds, once awarded as block grants to the relatively small numbers of institutions designated as universities.

In the mid 1980s, legislation supporting two kinds of centers was introduced. The first were special research centers "funded by ARC at approximately $500,000 to $600,00 per annum for six to nine years . . . [They] concentrate [on] strategic basic research in areas of national priority by groups with proven research records" (Hill 1993). The second were key centers for teaching and research which were developed to meet industrial training needs in areas of industrial demand. In 1990 these centers were augmented through legislation that allowed formation of CRCs[5] and several centers of engineering excellence.

The primary organizational response of faculty to the destabilization of the research environment was to create interdisciplinary centers. Sixty-five percent of Australian research centers were established after 1989, whereas only 12 percent were organized before the 1980s. More than nine hundred research centers were formed. Of these, 7 percent depended mainly on internal funding, and 55 percent were funded primarily by external grants and contracts. It is estimated that at least 50 percent of all academic research takes place within centers. The centers are usually interdisciplinary (Turpin and Hill 1991; Hill 1993; Hill and Turpin 1993).

All faculty and professional officers whose voices are heard in this chapter were in centers, all of which were formed after 1980, most in the mid 1980s and after. One center was a special research center, three were CRCs, and four were centers without a particular federal designation. All were interdisciplinary. Our sample differed from the general trends reported by Hill only in that all of our units were engaged or trying to engage with the market, and all had external funding, the bulk of which was provided by the state; in Hill's sample, only 50 percent had mainly external funding, and the source of funding (private or state) was not clear. We selected our sample to study commercialization of science and technology and faculty's market behaviors, not center formation.

According to the professors in our sample, a major factor in the formation

5. The CRCs were initiated by the federal government in 1990. They brought together academe, government, and industry to fund commercial research and were scheduled to receive $100 million each year. They were modeled after the interdisciplinary research centers of the United Kingdom and the industry-university cooperative research programs funded by the National Science Foundation in the United States (Hill 1993). University of Science and Industry administrators considered CRCs as a way to establish stable and enduring relationships with external entities in order to develop predictable flows of resources.

of almost all centers or institutes was the need to secure reliable resource streams in a period of research destabilization. As one professor said,

> In the current climate in Australia, it was becoming increasingly difficult to get long-term funding for anything. . . . We're accepted as an institute by the grant-awarding bodies and so on; it's important for raising money—the company in Sydney is dealing directly with the institute, which gives us a lot more credibility, rather than dealing with a handful of scattered academics. (NWU)

Center status also meant that the institutional administration viewed the unit favorably because the centers enhanced university profiles and indicated university compliance with federal goals. Institutional favor often meant seed money for various projects.

Centers were valued for the autonomy they conferred as much as they were appreciated for the resources they attracted. The two were closely related. Centers conferred autonomy that made it easier for members to enter the market with products and processes that garnered profits. Among the organizational privileges attached to centers or institutes was freedom from securing the consent of their departmental colleagues for their entrepreneurial endeavors:

> An institute was seen as autonomous, with commercial potential, where possible. When we initially proposed the institute, we got a lot of negative reaction from senior people because they thought we were empire building, and we weren't, in the sense that they thought. We just wanted to be autonomous so we could function. So now we're only responsible to the senate—it's much easier for us to work. (Professor, NWU)

Centers were often designed to engage in commercial work and had developed policies, approved by central administrators, which streamlined their entry into the marketplace. For example, heads of centers and senior faculty members were able to conduct wide-ranging negotiations with external entities, virtually concluding agreements before seeking approval from the central administration or the senate. Centers also were able to enter into contracts with external entities. These privileges stemmed from center autonomy and contributed to enhancing center resources.

Autonomous centers often enabled their members to transcend traditional disciplinary boundaries, a process that was valuable in several ways. Centers were able to pluck the outstanding people from within traditional departments; they were able to pursue avenues of research not approved by conventional disciplines; they were able to bring together a new mix of people whose synergy enabled them to solve new problems in unusual ways.

Heads of centers and senior faculty within the centers often had research goals that were impossible to realize in conventionally organized departments. For example, the organizational impetus for one center stemmed from the members' inability to change the direction of their department. They saw the future of their field in molecular rather than conventional biology. As the head of the center said,

> We . . . had a perceived need—the school as a school had to get involved in modern developments in molecular biology, and there wasn't much known about it, and there was a reluctance on the part of the senior members to think about taking on people in molecular biology. It would have involved changes of positions within the school which would have been difficult . . . there was very little enthusiasm, so we had to do it on our own. . . . That meant commercial projects. . . . We don't really see it [the center] as personal profit but fulfilling needs we have as researchers and dragging the school into biotechnology. It was a matter of necessity. (NWU)

In another instance the center head established his organization because he thought that his research area was disdained by his field. As he said,

> I took up an appointment here in 1971. Hearing aid research was considered to be cosmetic, like doing research in lipstick. Although there are sixty million hearing aid users, people didn't take the research seriously. It was considered something that serious people did not get involved in. (USAI)

The center organized by the just-quoted head quickly became one of the most successful centers in his university.

Heads argued that autonomous centers enabled them to bring together faculty in new configurations to create a synergy that made solving commercial problems easier than in conventional departments. They saw the freedom and independence of centers as creating the necessary conditions for entrepreneurship. The heads and senior faculty members thought that center members developed an élan and esprit de corps that enhanced their performance.

The center members saw faculty members in conventional departments as jealous. As one said,

> People on the outside looking in will feel that these groups [centers] are privileged and get more benefits than they do. . . . There are no major commercial organizations in Australia doing fundamental research as part of companies for the next twenty years, so it's this kind of place that will be doing the work. (OU)

The interdisciplinary centers conferred special privileges on their members. Center members were able to attract more resources, had greater autonomy, and were more easily able to enter the market. Center members could escape the confines of traditional departments, often taking other well-known, talented faculty with them, and pursued research directions that they defined as important. Center members, especially heads of centers, also had well thought out strategies for dealing with destabilization of the research environment.

Center Strategies

The strategies used by heads of centers usually focused on maintaining and improving the centers' resources and status. The strategies of the heads of centers usually took into account ways the centers could position themselves competitively in relationship to other academics and vis-à-vis the market; strategies involved plans for expansion and guidelines to use during expansion. The heads and senior center members were very consciously trying to position their units to transcend the destabilization of Australian research policy.

We outline two strategies that we take to be typical, one that we see as atypical, and one that we view as anomalous but very important to understand because the anomaly has bearing on the impact of centers on universities. The two heads who had typical strategies led the Center for Petroleum Research (CPR) and hearing aid CRC. The center head with an atypical strategy led a social science center closely linked to the Australian Labor Party and deeply concerned with social justice and the environment. The center head with an anomalous strategy supervised no academics. His center was directed and staffed by professional officers and was self-sufficient as a result of product sales.

The CPR, a special research center, was housed in a school with three large engineering departments. The head of the center, Robert Alexander, was aggressive and energetic, committed to developing an organizational structure for the CPR which would provide a revenue stream for his research interests in hard times. He did not see himself as turning to commercial work in response to federal initiatives; he took the position that as a professional engineer, he had always been concerned with application. He saw the global movement of capital and the Dawkins white paper as confirming the direction he was already inclined to take.

The organizational structure that Alexander developed was complex; it was designed to serve as the infrastructure that would sustain the center through any crisis. Alexander conceived of the organization as having an academic arm, a consulting arm, and a commercial arm. The academic arm was composed of four permanent faculty members, and the consulting and commercial arms at various times had six or more full-time employees. The academic arm served students at the undergraduate and graduate levels, and the consulting arm generated fairly routine projects that kept the faculty "in cash" for their research projects. All of the faculty were able to participate in consulting, even untenured lecturers whose future with the unit was uncertain. The commercial arm was more exclusive and consisted of the head of center and several professional officers (non-tenure-track academic staff) working full-time with external entities, government agencies, and a multinational company. Alexander planned to expand the commercial arm so that more faculty would be able to participate. He foresaw expansion as occurring as soon as his first product entered the international market. At the time of our study, he was negotiating an agreement with the multinational company.

He considered the commercial arm as most important for securing a reliable and predictable resource stream. His strategy in dealing with the private sector was threefold. First, he wanted to make sure that the individuals who conceived of and created products were rewarded. Second, he wanted to ensure that royalties would come to his unit to support future research for more sustained product development. Third, he wanted to play a part in commercialization, to ensure that the company made a quality product and that the product was marketed aggressively.

The head of the hearing aid CRC, Timothy Gill, had a similar strategy, although he placed much less emphasis on organizational structure and much more on market demand. He thought there was a virtually untapped demand for his products in Asia and India. He began to develop hearing aids for the Asian market and to create an educational infrastructure to inform Asians about hearing aids and how to use them. Sometimes he focused on specific problems such as hearing aids for use after the mastoid surgery so common in India. His staff regularly offered seminars and workshops in Asia, sometimes serving as many as 2,500 persons per year.

Initially Gill did not want to work through the university because he saw it as taking too great a share of his profits. Instead, he started his own foundation, which the hearing aid industry supported with several million dollars a year. He refrained from working with the university until he was forced to enter negotiations because he wanted a CRC and access to more students. As a tradeoff he pledged to the university the buildings his foundation had purchased for a new school of hearing science, and he agreed to work with the university company to protect his intellectual property. Because of his commercial successes, he did not have to abide by the usual formula for splitting royalties; he was able to secure an agreement more favorable to himself.

Gill saw his unit as expanding in terms of faculty, students, and staff. He thought he would be able to attain more industry support through his CRC and more government funds than he had thus far been able to attract. In the near future he thought he would have to develop a light manufacturing subsidiary. Like the head of the CPR, he saw himself as a successful entrepreneur but more as the head of a medium sized firm than a small one.

The head of the social science unit, Thomas Cobb, saw himself as concerned with community as well as government and industry. He wanted to rectify inequities in the social system and solve environmental problems. His unit was new and was composed primarily of lecturers who were charged with securing enough external contracts to support research with a social justice agenda. Cobb was linked closely to the Australian Labor Party. Indeed, he saw the center as a Labor think tank, offering a resource that the Labor government could use to free itself from dependence on the conservative civil servants who remained from the Menzies era and staffed so many state and federal bureaucracies. He saw his unit as a Labor analog to right wing think tanks such as the Institute for Public Affairs.

His center demonstrated its allegiance to the Labor Party through members' political affiliation and through their active commitment to Labor policy. This was the only center where faculty uniformly supported breaking down the binary divide and establishing a unified national system. The social science center faculty saw the binary system as conferring unwarranted privilege on faculty in universities, particularly pre–World War II universities, and thought that the unified national system remedied inequities suffered by their colleagues in CAEs and promoted access to universities for working class students.

Cobb wanted to develop projects that decentralized power. He worked with his faculty to create a technology park that dealt with low technology or appropriate technology—windmills, solar power packs, and alternative energy sources. He wanted to develop a demonstration area together with a training facility. The aim of the training facility was to encourage people who used the technology to learn how to assemble and operate it.

The social science center had been successful in attracting enough students to justify its small staff but had been relatively unsuccessful in securing the consultancies necessary to make the unit self-sustaining. The director was working on renegotiating and expanding the center's consulting contracts. To secure more resources, he hoped to work with industry to augment his contracts with state agencies and volunteer groups.

The social science center had been started with funds from the state Labor Party in the hopes that the center would work out the organizational and policy bases for technology development. However, in our sample, the faculty hired were among those most critical of market behavior. Cobb's unresolved strategic dilemma was how to establish lucrative industrial consultancies without compromising his faculty's values. His short-term strategy was to hire two new faculty members whom he thought were more attuned to the market.

Ronald Collins was head of the Water Systems Institute, the anomalous group that was self-sustaining and run by professional officers. His strategy was as sophisticated as the strategies articulated by the heads of other centers—perhaps more so. Collins used research grants, royalties, and direct product sales to support his group. His strategy was to use a diversified approach. He brought to market both low and high technology products, and he made sure that the group's products had a very high degree of integrity. At the low technology end, he focused on services and simple product development supplemented by consultancies, creating products that were made in small batches by local manufacturers and which were already generating royalties. At the high end, he tried to develop patents and intellectual property, sophisticated electronics produced for him in small quantities by a foreign manufacturer. The electronics depended on two chips that were used together in a system. Without both of the chips, the system could not operate. The chips themselves cost very little to manufacture, and the head was not interested in producing them for the world market. Instead, he used the chips in a complex system that he offered under certain circumstances to state agencies that needed the system. He was able to get hundreds of thousands of dollar for the system rather than several hundred for the chips.

Collins looked forward to the time when his several projects could be manufactured on the campus of the university where he worked. He thought his plan was feasible, especially given that his unit was self-supporting; indeed, he turned back tens of thousands of dollars a year to the university. He saw a future with manufacturing plants, more electronics systems, a technology park, and spinoff companies.

Unlike most other centers, the Water Systems Institute generated more money than the university or government agencies put into it. Although most centers sought to be self-sustaining, few had reached that goal, let alone arrived at a point where they contributed money to the university. The Water Systems Institute was anomalous in another regard: it had no students. The Water Systems Institute was concerned with making profits, not with educating students. Although most centers saw education as a primary mission, their entrepreneurial activity often called for the addition of more and more professional staff, who had greater technical capability than graduate students and who were more reliable, at least insofar as they did not depart after finishing degrees. Center heads had not consciously developed strategies that called for reducing the number of faculty or graduate students and adding professional staff, but that may be an inadvertent consequence of academic capitalism—one we discuss below.

Whether the heads of centers and senior members would realize their long-term strategies was not clear. Sometimes statements made by the center heads were contradicted by staff members. For example, a center head who saw himself as a successful leader was considered by most of his staff *not* to be "the crash-hot people manager" that he envisioned himself to be. Most of the staff hoped that he would move away from management. Similarly, university administrators were often not as sympathetic to centers' strategies as the heads and senior members thought they were. Most university administrators admired the center heads but regarded them as difficult, hard to manage, and overambitious. University administrators talked frequently about the need "to rein in" the heads of centers.

Whether the heads of center and the senior members would realize their long term strategies was to some degree unimportant. In the short term they had succeeded in building new organizational structures within the universities, were creating transdisciplinary knowledge, were engaged with external entities, and were differentiating themselves from their colleagues. In the process they were reshaping their universities and creating organizations like small firms that were always in the process of expansion, often in ways not particularly related to the educational process.

Professional Officers and Nonacademic Staff

Over the course of their existence, the centers hired more and more nonacademic personnel or professional officers. The smallest number of professional officers in a center was two, the largest was forty-seven, supporting a single faculty member who was the center director. We failed to establish the exact number of professional staff because we did not realize how large the numbers of nonacademic personnel were until we were well into our project. Initially we focused on center heads and central administrators, none of whom tended to report the number of staff, mentioning them only casually, if at all. After we realized the extent to which nonacademic staff were involved in the centers, we interviewed all professional staff above the secretarial level at a single center. We use the data from this case to suggest ways that nonacademic personnel fit into centers and center heads' policy and strategic initiatives.

Six professional staff were interviewed in the CPR. Their positions were coordinator of applied research, head of technology transfer, business manager, operations manager, public relations officer, and engineer. The staff had attitudes not necessarily shared by academic track personnel or students. The staff had loyalties only to the head of the center, subscribed to a business ideology, were not involved with students (and usually did not want to be involved), and were eager to expand their operations in a nonacademic direction.

The professional staff were loyal to the head of the center because he hired them, because they depended on him and his commercialization agenda for their jobs, and because they were relatively isolated from the academic side of the enterprise. As one staff member said, "I was lucky I got this position. It was because of Bob Alexander." Another expressed his dependence on the head of the center:

> If InGen [the corporation with which the CPR was negotiating] . . . looked at it logically, they'd get rid of me . . . but Bob Alexander is very fond of me, and he'd probably keep me on even though finance is a critical issue. There are not the funds for me.

Another professional officer, an engineer building a prototype, spoke about the relative isolation of the professional staff, articulating at the same time how isolation fostered his dependence on the head of the center.

> I have a relationship with only one academic, Bob Alexander. I would say that relationships with other academics are conspicuous by their absence. Alexander provides direction, and then I do the implementation. However, I also have to formulate the whole thing. The concept is provided by Bob, and I provide the reality . . . it's an interactive process between the two us. (OU)

The business ideology of the professional staff was manifested in several ways. The professional staff saw the work they were doing in the university as being similar to the work they had done in the private sector. They saw faculty as not interested in business, but only in fundamental research, and therefore as sometimes hampering the process of commercialization. Moreover, the professional staff saw the larger university environment as an impediment to their commercial goals. The business ideology of the professional staff was probably strengthened by their relative isolation from the academic side.

A number of the professional staff made statements like the following:

> I'm an electronic engineer, and I head up the electronics support section . . . to assist on the technical aspects of commercialization. . . . My previous jobs have been with commercial companies. Inevitably the job is, a contract comes in, we build it, whether government or private, we build, and it goes out to the company. It's the same here, exactly the same situation. (OU)

Another said,

> I think of it [his work at the center] as a business. (OU)

The professional staff were often somewhat hostile to the faculty. One professional staff member expressed this hostility when he said businesspersons were leery of working with academics because they thought they might "be confronted by a graying boffin who can't talk if he isn't smoking his pipe" (OU). He saw himself, and the commercial side of the CPR, as projecting an image opposite to the "graying boffin." Another staff member saw academics as resisting commercialization.

> A typical example [of resistance to commercialization] was the time sheet. Most of the people on this end [the nonacademic side], who've worked in production environments, have no trouble with the concept of a time sheet. But you try to get an academic to fill in a time sheet! You're just as likely to get a fifty-page dissertation on why you shouldn't. Bob Alexander got them to do it by saying they didn't have to, but he would like them to. (OU)

Another professional staff member put the problem of faculty resistance more positively.

> To get these academics to do work, you have to motivate them. The only way to motivate them is to give them a problem that's interesting from the research side. It puts me in a difficult situation. I have to keep manipulating the jobs that come so they can be termed *research*. (OU)

The professional staff saw faculty culture as inimical to business culture. They thought faculty were resistant to commercialization and to practices that they thought fostered commercialization, such as keeping time sheets. They tried to manipulate faculty to bring them closer to commercial culture.

The professional staff's attitude toward students was related to their attitude toward faculty. For the most part, they were not involved with students and did not want to have to deal with them, but were ready to work with them in relatively limited capacities if the students could be useful to commercialization. As one professional staff member said, "My interactions with students are virtually nil, no matter what level of students" (OU). Another professional officer worked with several postdoctoral fellows, all of whom did research in his operation. He supervised a number of other nonacademic professionals, and the university was considering assigning some of them teaching duties. He said, "I wouldn't really like that. Out of the eight [professional staff], maybe two or three would do something in teaching" (OU).

However, professional staff were willing to work with students when they were useful. One professional staff member indicated that he would be happy to take student ideas that lent themselves to commercialization and hire a postdoctoral student or lecturer with the right background to develop the idea. He gave no indication of how credit or compensation would be arranged for the student or faculty member whose idea might be utilized.

Although there was a fairly large contingent of professional staff at the CPR, a number of staff members wanted to expand. Like the center directors, they had plans of their own, and their strategies were directed toward expansion of the commercial side of the enterprise. The scope of professional staff ambition and strategy was perhaps best expressed by Harold Gordon, the coordinator of applied research. Bob Alexander, head of the CPR, had given him this title, but his funded position was as director of a government laboratory that was tied closely to the center. The government depended on the center to run the laboratory, so they put up the money to fund the staff member's position, allowing Gordon to do what he wanted so long as the laboratory kept operating. Alexander expanded and reshaped the government-funded position, using Gordon to oversee all applied work in the center. Gordon wanted to expand yet again. He was promoting and developing more work for the center. He saw a future in which the center would compete for tender documents (bids) in the international market. In other words, the CPR would try to win contracts with overseas public or government entities for very large jobs. Gordon knew this was an ambitious scheme with a number of problems, such as hiring more staff, some of whom would be out of the country for relatively long periods. However, this was his preferred direction of expansion. To move in this direction, he thought he would need his own staff.

Generally, the nonacademic professionals were loyal to the center heads. They did not interact much with faculty other than the head and were not very interested in teaching, with one or two exceptions. They were much more a part of commercial culture than academic culture, and they tended to bring commercial values to their work. In terms of strategy, they were concerned with making their centers more like small firms, expanding the commercial side and generating increased profits.

As Hill remarked, "The growth in number of centers [has] been quite sudden and [has] caught many university managers by surprise" (Hill 1993, 1). Center heads responded eagerly to the opportunity structures created by the Dawkins reforms, for the most part seeking to enhance the prestige and resources of their new organizations. They developed elaborate strategies for making products, entering the market, and carving out niches for themselves. These faculty thought and acted very much like the heads of small and medium sized firms, often using the language of CEOs with regard to market share, competitive position, and plans for expansion (Etzkowitz 1989, 1992; Louis et al. 1989). They very rarely used the language of professionals whose work related to broader national and international disciplinary or professional associations, nor did they use the language of tertiary educators who trained knowledge producers for the future. The heads of centers did, however, show great concern about the integrity of their products and the reputation of their centers. The professional officers carried the language of the firm to an extreme, often taking the position that the product development they were doing in the university was no different from that in the private sector. More new professional officers than faculty were added. The new centers, heavy with professional officers and oriented to the market, moved the university as a whole closer to the market, but not necessarily in a way that considered or accommodated the educational function of the institution.

The only exception to heads of centers seeing themselves as heads of small or medium sized firms was the social science center. According to Hill, social science centers constituted about 36 percent of all centers and 24 percent of the centers formed in the past four years. Social science centers were smallest in size and probably had the least resources, given the large amounts allocated to CRCs, which did not include social science in their purview (Hill 1993). The social science center in our study was formed in the mid 1980s, was organizationally sophisticated, and was able to attract students who brought with them state funds. However, the center was unclear as to whether it would be able to support its social justice agenda given the institutional and governmental pressures put on centers to generate external moneys. Whether the center would continue to operate if the social justice agenda was dropped or seriously constrained was not clear.

The social science center illustrates the problems faced by units without a clear market niche. The center knew it was vulnerable without external moneys, so it sought to find such moneys but had difficulties in working with external agencies committed more to profit than social justice or environmental protection. The rapid formation of social science centers in response to changes in national higher education and research policy may be a general indication of the vulnerability felt by the social sciences in the face of austerity. Many of these centers have been able to secure external moneys, although the type of work they are doing on their outside contracts is not clear. On the one hand, they may be pursing social justice agendas; on the other hand, austerity may be directing them toward developing the organizational infrastructures for university-industry-government market relations.

Center heads and senior faculty saw technology transfer as a professional opportunity structure. They responded by forming centers devoted to the pursuit of intellectual property and other commercial endeavors. Centers gave heads and senior faculty the opportunity to escape from the confines of traditional departments, drawing together like-minded faculty who shared a commitment to academic capitalism. Center heads and professors were able to enter national and international markets with the intellectual property they developed and to generate resources, many of which were discretionary. For example, center heads and professors were able to hire large numbers of academic officers (academic professionals), who were often highly trained researchers, to assist them in their work. Although center heads spoke of themselves as the CEOs of small or even medium sized firms, they did not take the risks associated with entrepreneurship. If their intellectual property or other commercial endeavor failed, they still held positions as professors.

Center heads and professors did not commit themselves mindlessly to seeking any and all external resources. Most very consciously pursued intellectual property and commercial endeavors that complemented their long-standing research agendas. The way they responded to resource dependence, then, was shaped by their understanding of, and adherence to, their fields of expertise. Although they sought to expand activities deemed appropriate for their professional fields, they did not see themselves as undercutting or challenging established status and prestige systems.

Although the entrepreneurial activity of center heads and professors was protected from the market because they were state-subsidized entrepreneurs—academic capitalists—they did not appear to seek additional protection through avenues historically followed by members of professional associations. They did not develop organizations of faculty concerned with intellectual property or with technology transfer or commercial issues at the national or international levels, nor did they create special sections in their professional associations. They did not press for special legislation that would give them unusual privilege.

With some exceptions center heads and professors responded to changes in national policy and increased resource dependence as process theories of professionalization suggest. They saw the destabilized research environment as an opportunity structure, but they were discriminating in their pursuit of resources. They devised sophisticated strategies that were somewhat congruent with established status and prestige systems, but they expanded the system in ways that conferred greater status and prestige on the activities in which they were engaged.

Other Faculty, Postdoctoral Fellows, and Graduate Students

Center heads and professors usually followed collective strategies that embraced their units as a whole. Faculty below the level of professor, as well as postdoctoral and graduate students, had developed individual strategies that were focused on how to ascend the career ladder. Unlike center heads and professors, they did not see technology transfer or academic capitalism as an opportunity structure. Instead, they were confused by the shift to entrepreneurial science and technology, ambivalent about how to position themselves, and reluctant to participate in reshaping traditional status and prestige systems.

Two of the three associate professors in the study were optimistic about their chances for promotion. As one said,

> It [commercial science] will enhance my career, it will make me appear more rounded. I'm not just into fundamental research, I've done commercial where appropriate. It should help for promotion, but the next thing for me would be a personal chair. (NWU)

He was so certain of his promotion to full professor that his sights were already set on the next prize, a personal chair. He saw fundamental research as the foundation of his career but thought that at his career stage commercial research was useful as well.

One of the associate professors thought his chances for promotion to full professor had been blocked because of his commercial work. We will discuss his case with that of the four senior lecturers, most of whom related negative consequences stemming from their commercial activity.

Like the professors and associate professors, three senior lecturers as well as the one associate professor became involved in the pursuit of intellectual property because it provided a way to fund interesting research. The three senior lecturers and the associate professor were more involved with the scientific laboratory work than the full professors and seemed to experience greater anxiety about securing results and funding. For example, one spoke of unremitting pressure from his sponsor, who monitored his work more and more closely.

> Essentially, I was told by funding bodies—the Wheat Board—that we should be looking toward more applied areas and that there are very few companies doing disease prevention through biotechnology. . . . They [Wheat Board] are my biggest source of funds, and they funded two big projects. . . . The executive director just visited today . . . informally, he said they're working for a more applied rapid return on their money. So having heard that, I thought I better start thinking about the biotechnology aspects. The visits are at set periods to review what we're doing. Pre-

viously, it was once a year. Now it's two times. They're monitoring us more closely. Generally, there's a feeling for more accountability everywhere, through universities and funding bodies, and a feeling you should do more applied work. I'm not particularly happy about it because essentially it's not our primary function. (NWU)

Two senior lecturers told lengthy tales of efforts on their part to find second and third commercial partners after their initial partner had gone bankrupt or changed ownership and direction while the researchers' projects were up and running. Neither of these senior lecturers was able to secure money to move from the prototype phase to component manufacturing and demonstration models. One of these senior lecturers said he spent many sleepless nights wondering if he would be able to secure grants to keep his project going until he was able to generate adequate industrial funding. The other senior lecturer, faced with lack of funds, had to lay off his six technical staff, an action for which he felt responsible and guilty.

The associate professor and all four of the senior lecturers felt blocked in their careers. The associate professor had been denied promotion to full, and the two senior lecturers had been turned down for promotion to associate. Those who had been turned down attributed their lack of success to their heavy commitment to commercial work.

> I was encouraged to apply. I've got so many Ph.D. students, so many international journal articles. But at the interview, they asked only about my intellectual property. My head of schools said I should have turned the discussion at the interview away from the intellectual property . . . the head of schools interpreted [my failure] as a result of my emphasis on intellectual property. (USAI)

Another was unable to publish articles because his patenting plans precluded publishing. Moreover, the need for secrecy meant that he could not talk about his research to prospective graduate students, a fact that impeded his research further.

> It's a little bit disappointing for an academic to do commercial research. When you are living in the university, your promotional aspects and acceptability by academics depend on how many publications you produce. It doesn't matter what they are, but how many. In the commercial world there are two problems. First, you can't do research in a systematic manner. The commercial world wants a quick fix. Second, most of the information that is gained becomes confidential property of someone else, and usually it never comes out, remains hidden. . . . That affects the professional development of academics. Even if the university allowed me to publish, it wouldn't be the kind of publications the academic world wants to get—it didn't follow a particular line of thought which assists you in publication. . . . I didn't have access to students because of secrecy and because the project was so big I couldn't take them. At

the height of the project, I had ten staff members working for me, engineers, chemists, technicians. It was a very heavy supervisory research role, so to supervise Ph.D. students was not easy. . . . I could have been associate professor instead of senior lecturer, but for this project. The fault lies in the criteria used for promotion. All the rewards and merits that we won on the project were not to be considered for promotion. (NWU)

Yet another told a similar story.

> In Australia we're run by academic purists. I was ranked first in my school [for promotion], but the deputy vice-chancellor turned me down. . . . [He said] we're not doing basic [in my unit], we're doing applied. (USAI)

The promotional stories of two of the aspiring professors shared a turn of plot in that the universities where they worked had invested heavily in their intellectual property. Whether their failure to be promoted was the result of the universities' unhappiness with the lack of return on investment was not clear. Neither of the senior lecturers accused the universities of prejudice on this point. But regardless of whether the university administrators made judgments on quantity of profits rather than quality of academic work, they were in a position to do so.

Of the two senior lecturers who had not yet come up for promotion, one was afraid he would not have the magic mix of basic and commercial work.

> I think in promotion that commercialization is important. I'll do a little bit and not too much. I tried to do a little commercial, some very applied for the Wheat people, and then ARC money, which is more fundamental—that's what's judged highly, it's quality research. But I do perceive it necessary to do some commercial because it's thought necessary to fit in. But ARC would still be most valued by the promotion committee. (NWU)

The other senior lecturer thought he would suffer when the time came for promotion because he was in an interdisciplinary unit and had concentrated on policy studies rather than commercial work.

> I've done what I wanted to do, so I'm happier. . . . But in terms of promotion, it's difficult, because of the disciplinary structure of the academic system. (OU)

At a more general level, he thought that the choice he had made to pursue his own line of inquiry regardless of the promotional consequences might become increasingly difficult as the university moved closer to the market.

> It's gotten to the point where you're supposed to be a saleable commodity. If Dawkins has his way, promotion will be dependent on what you've been doing out

there, for industry. I've been able to take the career track I have because I can rely on the academic structure; I didn't have to be saleable. (OU)

An alternative interpretation of experience of the one associate professor and several senior lecturers is that they were unsuccessful in gaining promotion because they had not done a sufficient amount of quality work. Even if this were the case, the senior lecturers' experience with commercial science nonetheless suggests that academics still climbing the promotion ladder had more rungs to pull themselves up than did academics concerned only with fundamental science. In the unified national system those aspiring to professorial rank thought they had to demonstrate their competence in the commercial as well as the fundamental arena; proficiency in only one or the other arena was not sufficient. Even if their assessments of their situation were wrong, their perceptions were still powerful and will probably make them discontented permanent employees of their respective institutions.

Untenured faculty—the lecturers—were uncertain about how commercial science would fit into a conventional career, and they did not know whether the university could accommodate career paths that deviated from the traditional. The lecturers, on the bottom rungs of their career ladders, generally experienced commercial science as a speedup of academic work. They thought they had to do both fundamental and commercial work to succeed, and even then, they were not sure that they were interpreting their seniors' messages correctly.

> You get your promotion more easily if you do commercial . . . most people have that feeling. They have to bring in money. . . . I tend to work in priority areas. When they have a priority area, then most of the people tailor their research to that area . . . [but] I got told you wouldn't get a promotion if you got commercial money but not ARC money. (OU)

Yet another lecturer developed a strategy to guide his selection of commercial products:

> I have to see a benefit more than actual dollars for me to take the work. My sort of general guideline is that if I can see a scientific paper that I can publish out of this, then I'll do it. (USAI)

Another lecturer, new to the Australian system, initially did not comprehend a system in which funding depended on contract research with very specific ends. He thought his state sponsor was supporting his general line of inquiry, not product development. He described his gradually dawning understanding that the money he received was tendered in return for a commodity:

There's a different perception of what people want out of it [research money]. I thought it was just money to do my own thing . . . on this problem . . . then the commercial people told me that they wanted a product that they could use. It took me a while to finally figure that out. It's not publications that they want—they wanted a product. We discussed what they wanted. It came gradually; they were not rude. It evolved. I came from a very theoretical background, so that it was hard for me to accept at first. (OU)

Although this lecturer was willing to do commercial work to sustain his career, he was very clear that it was not his first choice.

I prefer theoretical. There are no hassles. It's like math. Reality is always much more complicated. You have to know for sure that whatever you develop produces a result. In theoretical, I don't have to do that. To demonstrate that my [product] works is much more difficult. (OU)

Other lecturers, earlier on in their career and not closely associated with commercial work, were even less optimistic.

I think that tertiary education might expand but not create more positions. So I think that student-staff ratios will increase. The only way there'll be more opportunity is if the death rate goes up among older lecturers. . . . It's almost impossible to get permanent positions, you just roll onto one contract after another. This is not tenure track, it's contract. (OU)

The researchers and postdoctoral fellows were similar to the lecturers, although they were less able to imagine themselves as successful professors. They regarded themselves as being positioned on the bottom rungs of the academic career ladder, and they expressed uncertainty as to whether they would be able to climb it. Their greatest fear was that conditions had changed so greatly that they would never reach the tenure track. As one research fellow said,

Stability of career path—I don't perceive such a thing in Australia at the moment because all that seems to be available is short-term contracts, commonly three years, sometimes five . . . so we have a dichotomy between haves and have-nots. The haves have been at it for at least five years [longer than I have]. (OU)

Some came to blend their dedication to research with a soul-destroying fatalism.

I know a guy in London who's worked with [a research] organization for fifteen or twenty years, generating research contracts, and that's how I've survived the last eleven years, with no tenured position. There's no ultimate security in that, but I don't tend to think of security as being of primary concern compared with doing what I want to do, which is research. I don't have any superannuation, no annual leave or sick leave, it's all just—I submit hours every fortnight, and that's it. I don't have any firm long term aspirations at the moment. I've never found that works for me. I take things as they come. . . . Every time I have applied for any sort of position, it's always been unsuccessful, no matter how strong the application. So I believe you do what you're meant to be doing. I believe that our lives are beyond human control. (NWU)

Others came to think they did not have what it took.

It [a career in academe] . . . comes down to personal attributes, whether you see your-self as determined enough, good enough to demand of the world a particular career. It comes down to determination as well. I don't feel that I have thus far in any way proven myself able to take a sufficiently determined stance to force open a particular career. (OU)

The lecturers and postdoctoral fellows saw themselves as facing a situation where the rules of the game had changed. Academic careers were not what they had expected. There were few full-time positions, the competition for those positions was fierce, and the path to permanence was not marked clearly. The magic mix of basic, applied, and commercial was elusive. Some of the lecturers and postdoctoral fellows blamed the system, understood they were caught in a sea change in tertiary education, and were bitter. Others internalized failure, blaming themselves for being unable to wrest an academic career from a grudging system.

Although the junior faculty and graduate students were for the most part not very optimistic about their futures, they did not turn to collective solutions to overcome the obstacles they thought they faced. Very few of them saw FAUSA (Federation of Australian University Staff Association), the academic union, or the various associations of learned disciplines or professional associations as offering any possibility of intervening in the changes occurring in Australian academic career structures. When asked directly, most of them professed to have little knowledge of the union and even less information about their professional associations. The junior faculty, postdoctoral fellows, and graduate students reflected the positions of their seniors. With the exception of faculty at one of the three universities, senior faculty engaged in commercial science tended to be somewhat anti-union.

Professors at New Wave University, regardless of what unit they were in, were more pro-union. They saw FAUSA as a vehicle for combating the changes instituted by Dawkins. In the words of one of the New Wave professors,

In Australia the man in the street doesn't see us [professors] as anything special; he just sees us as another area of the work force, that's rather privileged, at that. So we have to see that's what we are, just another sector of the work force, and we have to have a strong union. The notion that we're gentlemen, not involved in the day-to-day fracas, not involved in the structure of the economy, is ridiculous. We have to be organized to combat what's going on. . . . I'm not suggesting we become a militant left wing organization, but we have to resist any effort to centralize and control, and we'll have to make that clear.

However, the professors' union activity was not mirrored by those at lower ranks at New Wave other than by faculty in the social science unit.

With the exception of the professors at New Wave the faculty engaged in technology transfer did not view collective activity as a way to assert professorial rights. They were privileged as a result of their commercial activities and wanted to maintain and augment that privilege. Special centers built on academic capitalism seemed to increase the differentiation of the center staff from other faculty and from organizations designed to foster faculty solidarity.

Three (10 percent) of the thirty persons on the academic track were women, and they were generally on the lower rungs of the promotion ladder. One was an associate professor, one was a untenured lecturer, and one a doctoral student. These numbers are not surprising, given the concentration of commercial science in male-dominated professional schools. Only one was involved in developing intellectual property.

The woman with the highest rank saw no difference between herself and her male colleagues; she thought they were treated similarly. The two other women thought academic careers in science were different for men and women. The doctoral student noted some differences, one of which was the lack of other women students.

> I'm the only Ph.D. student, and I'm the only one who's been here, and it's going on ten years . . . [my main experience was] just being isolated. . . . I have to put up with twenty-four-hour discussion on golf and how drunk they got on the weekend. (OU)

Her concern for the future was how to integrate marriage and children with career. She lived with a man who worked in a similar field. They were "prepared to be apart for various periods of time, for several years, and to see one another only once every three months or so" (OU). Her biggest concern was the children they were already planning. She thought she would take a few months after she had a child and return quickly to work.

> KI: We got a lot flack from our friends, mainly the women, who say they'll never put them [their children] in child care.

> SS: Do other women doctoral students say that?

KI: No, the two women I know with Ph.D.s went back fairly quickly. The others act like we'll be creating criminals if we put them in child care.

The lecturer had a more highly developed critique of the relations between gender and science.

By and large there's a perception of women in science which sees women as butch or asexual or unfeminine characters—having been a scientist, there's a lot of truth about this. Females are so concerned about making it in a male paradigm, they can't look at the issues of femininity and sexuality and at the implications of these things because they'd have to—that's why I left science, because it felt so alien to my femaleness. I had a breakdown, a burnout . . . because I was working across my intuitive grain. I was a Ph.D. student. I finished and decided not to go on, to go into something with more of a social context, more of community context . . . the scientific community tends to be very individualistic. . . . Most of the women I know who went through the physics degree with me, who got good degrees, left science and are working in areas of alternative healing and education. I can't prove my case, but I think that science alienates women, not because they can't do it, but because it doesn't value women's cultural identity. (NWU)

Her critique saw science itself as alienating women and did not examine the ways that male ambitions with regard to academic career intersected with science to construct a milieu that was uncomfortable for women.

The fields that generate technology transfer from university to industry are heavily male dominated, whether in Australia or in other English-speaking industrialized countries. Academic capitalism is a specialized activity within those fields, and only a select few are involved in technology transfer. The interdisciplinary groups or centers that accrue the most resources—through government targeting, government-industry partnerships, government grants, and industry funding—are most likely to draw their faculty from male-dominated professional schools and physical science departments. These groups are even less likely than the traditional disciplines to include women.

When we disaggregated faculty by rank and gender, we found differences among them. As indicated in Chapter Four and in the previous section, center heads and professors responded to changes in national higher education and science and technology policy which created increased resource dependence by treating destabilization of research funding as a professional opportunity structure. They had sophisticated, long-term strategies for developing entrepreneurial technoscience activity in their centers. They were enthusiastic academic capitalists. Those at lower ranks were less committed, even though they were often closer to the day-to-day science involved in commercialization. Their strategies were individual, geared toward moving up the career ladder. They were distressed that the rungs were no longer marked clearly: the lower the rank, the greater the uncertainty. Postdoctoral and graduate students seemed unable to foresee themselves reaching the career heights attained by center heads and professors. Women had difficulty envisioning themselves as part of academic science and technology, let alone as successful academic capitalists.

Conclusions

Process theories of professionalization view professionalization as an ongoing process. Professionals are not automatically accorded respect, deference, and decent salaries when they acquire credentials, a code of ethics, a body of knowledge, state licensure, or even theory (Collins 1979; Abbott 1988; Brint 1994). Instead, they are constantly engaged in struggles to establish and defend the salience of their degrees (O.D.s versus M.D.s), the value of their expertise (nurses versus doctors), the boundaries of their jurisdictions (psychologists versus psychiatrists), and the legal and economic arrangements that undergird their practice (third-party payments for medical services; student grants and loans for higher education). Professionals strategize individually and collectively about how to position themselves in changing environments. In this chapter we examined how faculty engaged in technology transfer developed strategies to respond to increased resource development. Their strategies have implications that occur at three levels: individual, intermediate (centers), and institutional (research universities).

At the individual level, senior faculty and the professional officers whom they hired were committed to their work as academic capitalists. As we noted, center heads developed strategies for their centers which went far beyond a single product. They were concerned with developing reliable and predictable resource streams to support their centers' work. The center heads often viewed themselves as managers of small or medium sized firms, as was the case with the head of the CPR, the head of the hearing aid CRC, and the head of the Water Systems Institute. The professional staff who worked in the centers often spoke as if they were part of commercial culture. (For treatment of entrepreneurial U.S. department heads and center heads, see Louis et al. 1989; Etzkowitz 1992.)

Unlike the senior faculty, academic track faculty on the lower rungs of the career ladder had difficulty conceiving of careers for themselves which merged academic capitalism and conventional academic endeavor. The expansion of the status and prestige system to include a wider array of activity, including certain forms of commercial science and technology, created ambiguity and confusion for persons in the lower ranks. Given that they had not yet attained the security of the senior faculty, they were uncertain about how to respond to the new demands being made on them. Their perceptions may change as they move up the career ladder or if career opportunities increase or career paths become clearer.

Centers are intermediate organizational forms that enable faculty to relate directly to external markets. Centers bring together faculty with technoscience expertise in high demand outside the university. These faculty are able to convert market demand into higher prestige and more resources for research from the university, from industry, and from the state. Although Australian university professors do not yet have extreme salary variation by field, national priorities now seem to privilege fields able to engage the market. This privileging of particular fields may contribute to the creation of new hierarchies of prestige which ultimately may be followed by establishment of new salary hierarchies.[6] Steven Brint's (1994) treatment of professional salaries helps us understand how the market interacts with valuation of professional fields within the university and gives us a glimpse of emerging hierarchies of status which may capture changes in Australia as well as in the United States.

When explaining variance in professional salaries in the United States, Brint sees salary differentials as best explained by professionals' relation to the market. Faculty in some professions and academic disciplines may have advantages in forming centers that relate to the market. Large private group practices usually command the highest profits and salaries (physicians, attorneys, and accountants [Brint 1994]). For salaried professionals, a key indicator of income is "the industrial location in which members of the profession are predominantly employed." Income is highest when professionals are located "in the 'industrial-corporate core' (or 'technostructure') within organizations" (67). Brint contends that "technostructure occupations can be described as having three specific sources of advantage: (1) high value-added organizational applications; (2) rigorous and demanding technical cultures; and (3) high levels of integration with management. By the term 'high value-added application,' I mean work that is closely related to profit potentials, critical environmental uncertainties, or managerial effectiveness" (73).[7] The professions and academic disciplines closest to the market are business services, followed by applied science, culture and communications (which includes higher education as a

6. Historically, the salaries of Australian professors were the same at each rank across all universities and were collectively bargained, with the exception of medicine. Recently, university and government leaders have been discussing extending differential salaries to fields other than medicine.

7. In other words, *technostructure* is a concept very close to *technoscience*, presented in Chapter Two.

whole), civic regulation (professions involved with maintaining and enhancing the quality of civic life, i.e., public works, mass transit, conflict resolution, planning), and finally by human services (professionals who work on problems so that "society's 'minimum standards'" (53) are met, i.e., schoolteachers, counselors, social workers). Although professionals in any of the five categories can work in the private or public sector, business services professionals and applied scientists are most likely to work in the private sector; the culture and communications category is very mixed, and civic regulation and human service professionals are most likely to work in the public. The professions and academic disciplines that interact with the private sector receive the highest remuneration. Thus, business service professionals, who interact primarily with the private sector, are at the high end, whereas human service professionals, who interact primarily with the public sector, are at the low end.[8]

Among the Australian centers we studied, the most successful were applied science centers.[9] Brint views the applied science sector as composed of "people who apply scientific knowledge to practical problems of production. The sphere includes nearly all engineers, chemists, geoscientists, biotechnology and product-related medical scientists, production-centered computer scientists, mathematicians, statisticians, and economists and organizational psychologists working on practical problems of production" (Brint 1994, 49). The applied science centers in our study had "rigorous and demanding technical cultures," and the products and processes they were developing were likely to have high "profit potential" (Brint 1994, 73). The center faculty in the applied sciences were in a position to act like scientists in small private sector consulting firms who articulate with the technostructure of corporations on the basis of technoscience. Like applied science private sector professional firms, center faculty competed for costly but discontinuous projects—in this case, development of innovative technology—which corporations often outsource (Brint 1994).[10]

8. In Chapter Two, Table 2.2, the information regarding average salaries of full professors by field, 1983–93, reveals that academic salaries are highest in fields that are closest to the market.

9. We did not study business or producer services fields. In retrospect, we wished we had studied at least one center in those areas so we could have compared it with the applied science fields.

10. Brint says that the work corporations contract out to professionals is usually discontinuous. In other words, the reason the corporations do not do the work themselves is that they do not have an ongoing need for expertise in the area. This may be the case, and university centers may compete for discontinuous projects, especially if they are multiyear contracts, but we think faculty in university centers and university administrators prefer arrangements such as CRCs, which offer predictable and continuous resource flows. We think arrangements like CRCs will flourish in the traditional industrialized countries, replacing industrial laboratories because they socialize the cost of production for industry and meet university needs for research funding. See Chapter Seven for further discussion on this point.

Resource dependence prompted applied science faculty to develop centers so they could augment their resources through academic capitalism. Although professors in our study valued basic or fundamental science, as noted in Chapter Four, they were willing to engage in commercial science and technology if the activity were prestigious, in that the commercial work utilized advanced science and led to highly innovative products, and if the external entities with which they worked were high in status—if they were, for example, well-known corporations or government bodies. (For a detailed account of faculty interactions with external groups, see Chapter Six.)

Not all fields may be able to develop centers that interact successfully with the market. As would be expected from Brint's work on professionals' relation to the market, centers in the fields of culture and communications, civic regulation, and human services may have difficulty finding clients with the resources to support their research and expertise. In our study the social science center did not fare as well as other centers. The difficulties encountered by the social science center raise the issue of how academic capitalism will shape opportunities for centers and departments.

At the level of the institution, the proliferation of centers raises a number of issues. Centers are changing the knowledge base of fields, the organizational structure of the disciplines, and institutional resource allocation patterns. Center formation draws off talented faculty from traditional departments, relocating them in transdisciplinary units that are as aligned with the market as with the professions or academic disciplines. Ultimately, the market may provide more cohesion for center faculty than the professions or academic disciplines, given the varied backgrounds of center faculty. Centers are well funded with government and private moneys. They were created to attract such resources. Centers are often units with few faculty and larger numbers of professional officers, geared to entrepreneurial aims. The role they play in the education of undergraduates is not clear. The centers show great variation in their emphasis on undergraduate education, ranging from the center in which no one taught to the social science center, where teaching was the most important activity.

As the creation of global markets pushes nations toward political choices that constrict government services in sectors such as human services, civic regulation, and perhaps even culture and communications, the market opportunities for faculty in those areas are reduced. They may form centers, but it is not clear that governments will buy their expertise. For faculty who form centers in fields close to the private sector market, such as applied science and business services, market opportunities may increase greatly. The implications of faculty market potential for research universities are great. Faculty in fields close to the market (e.g., applied science fields, as defined above) who have an entrepreneurial bent or who are strongly encouraged by universities in need of resources may form centers where they spend most of their time as academic capitalists. They may leave behind in traditional departments faculty who do not want to become academic capitalists as well as faculty who have no entrepreneurial talent. Eventually, the faculty who are left behind may bear the burden of undergraduate teaching. Faculty in fields with uncertain market potential (e.g., culture and communications, which would include the humanities) might be asked to teach greater numbers of service courses or perform more institutional maintenance work (committee work, student advising). Faculty in fields with diminishing market potential (e.g., civic regulation, which encompasses some of the social sciences, and human services, which includes education and social work) may be cut altogether, particularly if the numbers of students in their fields diminish. If academic capitalism restructures universities in this direction, research universities eventually would be aligned more closely with markets than with the professions.

6

ENTREPRENEURIAL
KNOWLEDGE

IN THIS CHAPTER we look more closely at faculty engagement with academic capitalism. Specifically, we analyze faculty accounts of how they invented products and processes in centers and how faculty and universities found corporate partners to participate in product development. In other words, we look at the process of technology transfer, the movement of knowledge from the university to the marketplace.

The research questions we asked were: (1) How do scientists and engineers conceptualize basic and applied research as the market becomes more central to public and private investment? (2) How is altruism, once viewed as a distinguishing characteristic of professional behavior, reconciled with academic capitalism? (3) How do scientists and engineers describe their market relations? (4) Is there an epistemology of academic capitalism?

Three quite distinct theoretical traditions deal with technology transfer: the sociology of science, process theories of professionalization, and theories that treat the role of science in product innovation and economic competitiveness. The sociology of science literature is built on Merton's (1942) conception of the norms of science as characterized by universalism, communalism, disinterestedness, and organized skepticism. These norms characterize basic, fundamental or academic science and are distinguished from applied or industrial science, which is characterized by specitivity, practicality, and proprietary potential. When university research became more commercial in the 1980s in response to pressures from globalization of the political economy, changes in national higher education policy, and resource dependence (see Chapters Two and Three), sociologists of science focused on whether basic research, the "seed corn" of science, was being plowed under, presumably damaging the future of science. Initially scholars found that academics were able to do basic and entrepreneurial research simultaneously (Peters and Fusfeld 1982; Blumenthal, Epstein, and Maxwell 1986; Blumenthal et al. 1986b). As pressures on the academy grew, case studies began to suggest that science was being "renormed"

(Etzkowitz 1989; Hackett 1990; Slaughter and Rhoades 1990; Rhoades and Slaughter 1991a, 1991b). In the 1990s a number of large surveys of scientists concluded that the distinctions between basic and applied research were no longer central, given the contradictory responses of scientists and engineers, who seemed to be moving toward entrepreneurial norms in complex ways not easily captured by surveys (Rahm 1994; Campbell 1995; Louis, Anderson, and Rosenberg 1995; Lee 1997). Our study of the technology transfer activity of faculty at Australian universities suggests that basic research may be as much a signifier of faculty control over the research process as a kind of science that precedes application, that basic and applied were never salient categories for the many professional school faculty (engineers, medical school faculty, veterinarians, agricultural researchers), and that basic and applied were as likely to designate levels of prestige and sources of funding as they were a fundamental distinction between two types of research.

Professionalization theory concentrates almost exclusively on professions *outside* the university, even though these theorists would certainly grant that university professors are professionals. Process theorists of professionalization do not speak to faculty located in nonprofit, usually public institutions who participate in academic capitalism. If we extrapolate from process theories of professionalization (Larson 1977; Collins 1979; Silva and Slaughter 1984; Freidson 1986; Brint 1994), we would expect that faculty as professionals participating in academic capitalism would begin to move away from values such as altruism and public service, toward market values. The faculty in our sample did this, but not by simply replacing altruism with a concern for profit. Rather, they elided altruism and profit, viewing profit making as a means to serve their unit, do science, and serve the common good. Again extrapolating from professionalization theory, we would expect faculty to strive to retain the greatest measures of autonomy and prestige possible. We found that as professors sought more applied funds as money for basic research was curtailed, they began to define themselves as inventors and entrepreneurs and sought to negotiate contracts for themselves, to understand patent law and markets for scientific products and processes. They knew that if they did not sit at the table with industry and government they would not be players. They developed extensive entrepreneurial knowledge to protect their autonomy, prestige, and expertise.

In the 1960s and 1970s, theories that dealt with the role of science in product innovation and economic competitiveness argued that serendipity was the key: basic research, allowing faculty to follow science where it led, laid the foundation for innovation, even though the possibilities for product development might not be obvious immediately. DNA and biotechnology provide an example (Wolfle 1972; Smith and Karlesky 1977; but see Slaughter 1993). As globalization put pressure on the economies of traditional industrialized countries, theorists began to be more concerned with expediting product innovation by managing more closely the movement of science from university to industry. From serendipity, theorists went to spinoff and somewhat linear concepts of the role of science in product innovation (Peters and Fusfeld 1982; Fairweather 1988). Currently, an emerging and somewhat contradictory body of theory makes the case that the movement of science from laboratory to industry is nonlinear and complex (Mowery 1994), on the one hand, seamless, the boundaries between basic and applied research collapsed to the point where knowledge is inherently entrepreneurial (Kennedy 1984; Gibbons et al. 1994), but on the other hand, that basic science is not necessarily related to innovation in industry (Gummett 1991; Leydesdorff 1994). The scientists and engineers we studied underline the complexity of the product innovation process, particularly at the point where intellectual property moves into the market.

None of these explanations—the sociology of science, process theory of professionalization, theories of the role of science and engineering in product innovation—is particularly concerned with the university as an organization. (For a partial exception, see Gibbons et al. 1994.) As students of higher education, we are. We will conclude this chapter by analyzing how academic capitalism affects not only colleges of science and engineering but the university as a whole.

The data from this chapter are the same as in Chapter Five: interviews with forty-seven persons in eight units in three universities transcribed between January and July 1991 (New Wave University, NWU; Outback University, OU; and the University of Science and Industry, USAI). However, we concentrate on a subset of twenty-three of the thirty tenure-track faculty. These twenty-three faculty were working on ten different pieces of intellectual property (products and processes that could be patented, copyrighted, and protected by trademark, and sold or licensed to corporations). The method is content analysis of interview transcripts.

Basic and Applied Research

Clear distinctions between basic and applied research emerged in the United States after World War II. The success of physicists and nuclear engineers with nuclear weaponry was presented to government and industry as a triumph of basic research. In their efforts to penetrate the mysteries of physical matter, academics developed quantum physics and atomic theory during the interwar period (Kevles 1978). Although physicists knew an atomic bomb was theoretically possible, weaponry was not part of their quest until the war was imminent. After the war the academic community, led by boundary elites such as Vannevar Bush, made the case for national funding of basic research, using the bomb as a symbol of the serendipity that led from basic research to practical discoveries of great import to industry, the state, and the citizenry (Herken 1992).

The post–World War II academic science and technology community drew sharp distinctions between basic and applied research for several reasons. In part, the distinction separated what academe and industry did. University researchers worked on basic science, industry on applied. Industrial leaders did not want universities to receive government funding for applied science and technology because it might interfere with corporate efforts to secure ownership of intellectual property and competitive advantages with regard to products and processes aimed at the market (Kleinman 1995).[1] In part, faculty pursued the distinction between basic and applied because they were able to assert more control over basic than applied research. In the system that evolved, scientists made decisions about who received government money through the peer review process when research was labeled as basic; there was little accountability in terms of directly meeting societal needs (Kevles 1978). Indeed, historians and sociologists of science are beginning to consider basic science as a social and economic construct through which university-based scientists have claimed autonomy and resources. Although there are undoubtedly differences between working on broad scientific problems as opposed to concrete applications, the barriers between basic or fundamental research and applied or entrepreneurial science were probably always highly permeable (Slaughter 1990, 1993).

Academic researchers in the United States were dependent on the mission agencies—the Department of Defense, Department of Energy, National Aeronautics and Space Agency, and National Institutes of Health—for the vast majority of their federal funds. The National Science Foundation, the only federal agency arguably dedicated to basic science, has never accounted for more than 20 percent of federal moneys for academic research and development in any

1. Industry's position about universities doing applied research began to change in the 1980s. Unlike Australia, Canada, and the United Kingdom, the United States has antitrust laws that prohibit cross-industry funding of research consortia. In the 1980s industry pushed very hard to have these laws changed (Fligstein 1990). There was some new legislation (see Chapter Two, Table 2.1), administrative law judges began to make more lenient interpretations, with the result that broad government-industry-university agreements such as the Microelectronics and Computer Technology Corporation were funded (see Chapter Two for details). As these changes occurred, industry began to look to partnerships with universities to realize its research aims.

given year since 1971. (Indeed, National Science Foundation moneys declined from a high of 19.5 percent in 1973 to 14.1 percent of all federal moneys for academic research and development in 1991 [National Science Foundation 1993].) The mission agencies supplied universities with 80 to 85 percent of their federal research and development money, of which approximately 65 to 75 percent was designated as basic (National Science Foundation 1993). The academic science and technology community always interpreted *basic* or *fundamental* to mean that university-based researchers, following the logical imperatives of their fields, set direction for their research programs independently of the mission agencies (Wolfle 1972; Smith and Karlesky 1977). However, even when moneys were tagged as basic, it was not clear how distinct basic was from applied. Accounts of scientists' and engineers' negotiations with the mission agencies suggest that the academic interpretation of *basic science* was only partially shared by mission agency bureaucrats, many of whom had a much more instrumental definition of it. Some historians of science argue that *basic science* merely meant unclassified science and that basic science was powerfully and directly shaped by mission agency goals (Forman 1987; Leslie 1993).

We asked everyone we interviewed which they considered more important, basic or applied research, and we questioned them about how entrepreneurial science was related to basic. When asked directly about the importance of the two types of science, everyone, with the exception of some professional officers, spoke positively about the importance of basic research. However, they found it difficult to draw firm dividing lines between basic and applied and did not make the two dichotomous.

> My real interest is in basic research, it's just that I've been lucky in that the diseases and disease agents I study have always been important medically so there's always an applied as well as basic aspect. (Associate professor, NWU)

> I think it's good for us academics to be exposed to industry needs. The challenges are very different. The CPR (Center for Petroleum Research) operates on the notion that the two—industry and science—should go together. . . . It's not degrading the quality of fundamental research at all. (Professor, OU)

> If you look at applications today, they usually stem from fundamental research. But others believe that the fundamental research from one stream should be applied to the other because funds are more available . . . it's money that makes the whole process . . . go. I believe that there should be a balance. . . . Then a person can move in whatever direction is required by society. Fundamental research should remain intact in the university, while industrial research mixes in as well. (Associate professor, NWU)

Other than the social scientists, most of the faculty and professional officers were members of professional schools. On a number of occasions they spontaneously offered the view that research in professional schools led directly to application, that there was not a firm distinction between applied and basic. Although these faculty spoke to the importance of fundamental research, they spoke as forcefully about the importance of the applied or entrepreneurial nature of their knowledge. As one put it, "I'm an engineer. To be a full fledged engineer, you have to apply your work" (Center head, OU). Or, as another said,

> I've always been aware of commercial possibilities. Logically, where there's a disease problem to solve, at end of day, if I understand what's going on, it leads to some sort of way of dealing with disease, and clearly to do that you have to get commercially involved if you want to deal with it on a large scale. . . . [With] pure science, it might be different, but in a medical area, you are much closer than if you were in a science, in a pure science area. (Professor, NWU)

When our interviewees were pressed, they often expressed a difference between basic and applied in terms of the prestige of the funding source and the review process rather than in terms of the nature of the work involved. Most faculty were clear that funding from the Australian Research Council (ARC), a body that functioned through peer review, was more highly valued in terms of prestige and promotion than was funding from the Swine Research Board or the Wheat Board. However, the ARC was changing. In addition to providing support for basic research, the ARC under Hawke and Dawkins was the agency through which the government set national research priorities aimed at making Australia more competitive internationally.[2]

Faculty did not think that creating knowledge for profit contradicted their commitment to altruism and public service. Instead they saw the market as a mechanism for distributing their discoveries to society.

> We would just like to find useful and practical solutions to the problems that people have . . . to ameliorate the condition of mankind, and we work on that principle, that we find solutions to problems that people have. At the end of the process, it has to bought and sold, that's the reality. (Center head, NWU)

---

2. As the ARC under Hawke and Dawkins became more concerned with competitiveness issues, so the National Science Foundation in the United States became more involved in university-industry relationships that contributed to the economy. This concern on the part of the NSF became especially apparent during the Reagan years. See Slaughter and Rhoades (1996).

> I see my work as part of the work that's necessary to save the environment, to create clean energy, and it will be profitable as well. (Associate professor, USAI)

The public good was not envisioned as being at cross-purposes with the market, partly because most faculty did not see science and markets as having histories that were part and parcel of power and social class relations. Generally, faculty did not ask questions about what a fair price was for their products, for example, whether price concessions should be built into products because the public had heavily, if not entirely, subsidized large portions of the research involved in the discovery of products for the market. Nor did they ask questions about the social utility of their knowledge. All assumed that what they did was beneficial, whether the institutional resources and faculty time expended were for research on cosmetics or on solar energy.

We found that faculty, professional officers, and administrators were reshaping their epistemology of science to accommodate professorial interactions with the market. They began to see commercial application as inevitable, sometimes as intrinsic, to their inquiry. Professional school faculty, always to some degree concerned with applied research, did not seem to see a clear difference between the kinds of science they did for the ARC and the work they did as entrepreneurs, other than viewing one as more general and the other as more specific. They did not see basic and applied as dichotomies or see a broad or deep chasm between the two. Their commitment to fundamental research seemed as much a commitment to a known career path and support and reward system as a commitment to a particular way of doing science. Although they still spoke about the importance of basic research, they did not dwell upon it.

Recognizing the Market Potential of Science

Faculty in Australian universities understood that if they were to reap the rewards from technology transfer they had to acquire market skills and business savvy. Specifically, faculty had to learn how to recognize the market potential of their science. They had to learn how to find funding for the product, process, or service they were trying to develop and promote. They had to learn how to apply for and prove patents. They had to acquire knowledge about how to develop market strategies and negotiate with corporations for research contracts and royalties. None of these activities overlapped greatly or was congruent with faculty expertise in acquiring university or government funds for science.

Twenty-one faculty were involved in commercial science, and two were in the process of searching for commercial opportunities. These twenty-three faculty were working on ten different pieces of intellectual property (products and processes that could be patented, copyrighted, and protected by trademark, and sold or licensed to corporations). All were engaged in developing market expertise with regard to commercial science, and the process of acquiring that knowledge was often very difficult.

Government agencies were a major market that Australian faculty sought to tap for sales of their intellectual property. Government procurement (government agency purchases of products, processes, and services necessary to outfit bureaucracies and accomplish organizational missions) strongly shapes commercial opportunities in Australia. When the commercial potential of intellectual property was client driven (four of ten products), the clients were government agencies with strong needs for particular products (three of the four products). In all three cases it was possible, although not proven, that the products also would have private sector demand. In one case the possibility was very clear. As the faculty member who developed the product said,

> We knew that we were making better [product] than anyone else. It's easy to quantify and attract funding with clear efficiency numbers. (Professor, USAI)

In the fourth case the client was industry, but the industry's primary market was government.

In the remaining six cases three products were discovered during scientific work which had been a government priority for about two decades. In the fourth case the commercial worth of the scientific work was discovered during a conversation between two men who had been graduate school friends, one of whom worked for a university and the other for a multinational corporation. In the fifth case the faculty member pursued his product because he saw a vast, almost unlimited Pacific Rim market for it. In the sixth case the path to recognition of the commercial value of research for the particular product was not clear.

Generally, the commercial value of products was recognized without faculty and professional staff giving much thought to the workings of the marketplace or paying much attention to the principles of marketing. As the chief administrator of one university company said about a product he inherited when he started his job,

> There was no business plan for FESS [Fission Energy Source System], to encourage the investor, no marketing plan, no export plan or manufacturing or feasibility study—what does it cost to manufacture? We have an idea, but we don't know specifically. (NWU)

For the most part, faculty approach to the market was energetic but haphazard. Faculty efforts were sometimes client driven, and frequently the client was government. When the client was not government, the general area in which commercial development took place had been suggested by government funding priorities. The market was not preceived solely in terms of demand; in fact, market demand played a major part in the thinking of only one faculty member.

Negotiations with Industry and Government over Intellectual Property

Regardless of the ways in which faculty and professional staffs recognized that their science had commercial value, all faculty had to find a commercial partner to bring their product to development. For the most part, faculty and professional staff, not university companies or offices of technology transfer, found commercial partners. This was the case for eight of the ten pieces of intellectual property. As a professor with a successful invention put it,

> researchers are likely to have better contacts than university companies. . . . I found the [partners]. When you're making [energy cells] that are better, people approach you after you can quantify that [yours] are better. Conferences were where I made initial contacts. Then you have to have a champion in the company to push your product through. (USAI)

However, researchers often had to move well beyond routine contacts. An associate professor gave the following account of finding a commercial partner:

> The first place that we were pointed toward [by local contacts] was a commercial foundation . . . associated with [another university], and it had a biotech orientation. It's now defunct. They gave us the run around for about eighteen months because the board consisted of academics without many commercial inputs. The second commercial entity was a local company that markets general lab equipment and disposables—they're only local. They said they saw potential but couldn't afford to fund, so they said they'd act as our manager, do all the donkey work, liaise with us and the university, for which they'd get a percentage. But it became clear quite quickly that they didn't have the experience and weren't moving fast enough. Fortuitously, I was speaking with a friend about this who worked for a Swiss company with an offshoot in Sydney. He worked for the firm, and I wasn't even thinking of it, and he said why didn't we work with them, and it just started to go from there. It [the slow start] was out of naiveté and inexperience [on our part] and the university as well. It could have started eighteen months earlier. (Professor, NWU)

In Australia the process of finding commercial partners was both more simple and more complicated than in the United States. The small relative size of the Australian professional and commercial communities meant that professors could easily approach companies directly or be approached by representatives of companies who had heard of their research. This happened to faculty involved with half of the ten pieces of intellectual property. However, the Australian business community very often was unwilling or unable to bring the intellectual property to development. The business community did not command the capital available in large industrialized countries. In some cases the Australian companies sold the rights to the product to international companies; in other cases the Australian companies went bankrupt. With regard to intellectual property that was at the production stage or aimed at international markets, all but one product was owned or produced by non-Australian companies.[3]

Generally, faculty saw Australian business as uncreative and as being centered on technologies aimed at extracting minerals from the earth or at agriculture, not at high technology. They thought Australian business was limited by its lack of vision and relatively small amounts of capital. Several professors and administrators commented on the difficulties of finding Australian commercial partners:

> In Australia the infrastructure is not well developed to look to commercialization easily. (Associate professor, NWU)

> Australian industry wants to buy only finished products and not take any risks. I don't think we'll get an Australian company as a full partner. (Associate professor, USAI)

> There's a lot of basic hostility among a lot of Australian businessmen. It's a generational issue—many Australian businessmen never went to university. (Professor, USAI)

Negotiations over ownership of intellectual property were complex and often difficult for the inexperienced faculty who carried them out. In the eight instances where property was advanced enough for negotiations, seven were carried out by the professors.

The accounts provided by professors varied according to the difficulties they encountered, although the further away from the negotiation they were, the fewer problems they seemed to recall. For example, a professor whose products were already being sold on world markets was quite casual:

---

3. Two pieces of intellectual property were produced in very small lots for Australian niche markets, with government as the buyer. Another two pieces had not yet found commercial partners, although one of these was geared primarily to international markets, and the faculty member in charge was looking exclusively at multinational partners.

> I've done a lot of quasi-legal work. If the patent attorneys did [all the negotiating], we would be bankrupt. Another professor with research contracts showed me what to look for. He was a university-industry appointment. (Professor, USAI)

However, even this professor conceded that the negotiation took a great deal of time and that he made a number of mistakes in the process.

The percentage of royalties that a patent would earn varied from contract to contract. Even after royalties and licensing agreements were reached between an industry and the professor, how the amount or share would be divided within the university remained unclear. If, for example, industry agreed to a 5 percent royalty rate for a particular invention, the way the 5 percent would be divided among the faculty member, the unit to which the faculty member belonged, and the university was uncertain. As one researcher said,

> There is no formula, but it's usually understood to be one third, one third, one third—although it's on a case-by-case basis (Professor, USAI)

Another researcher mentioned the same split but noted that in his case the university allowed him two thirds to support his work further because he was so active with regard to licensing. In other instances faculty who had already signed agreements with industry were not clear as to what would happen when university companies later altered contracts, making concessions to industry to increase the likelihood of product development. Nor were they clear as to when they would be able to take their third of the royalties—before or after concessions.

Another ownership area that remained unclear involved the government. It was uncertain to what degree various government agencies would share in royalties negotiated between industry and universities. Unlike in the United States, Australian government agencies did not give rights to intellectual property to universities.[4] In many cases if a government agency had funded the development of intellectual property, the agency or agencies expected a share of the royalties. In one instance CIRSO held title to a patent and was claiming the royalties to a product on which a university group continued to do research. As the faculty member said,

4. As noted in Chapter Two, the Bayh-Dole Act of 1980 allowed U.S. universities to patent intellectual property developed by faculty on federal grants and contracts. Currently, U.S. businesspersons are somewhat unhappy with this arrangement. The Advanced Technology Program, housed in the Department of Commerce, is the centerpiece of President Clinton's technology policy. Industry receives matching grants from government for research and development, frequently subcontracting to universities. In this program, industry, not universities, has patent rights, regardless of where the technology is discovered. Universities have objected vociferously, but to no avail.

We're negotiating. We're having a meeting soon. I think we'll share the intellectual property 50-50. But the other side [CIRSO] has counted up the hours they've worked on this over the last ten years, so now we have to do it as well. It's quite ridiculous. (Professor, USAI)

Federal agencies were not the only government agencies seeking a share of royalties on university patents. Any agency that contributed to research costs seemed to want a share.

The state government [as well as a federal agency] has put money in, but before doing more they want to work out the contribution for royalties. (Associate professor, USAI)

As the commercial value of government-funded scientific research became apparent, federal and state agencies made retrospective claims based on their contributions. Since almost all scientific research was funded by the government, whether out of block grants given by the federal government to universities, by state agencies, or by federal agencies, the potential for claims was great and the legitimacy of the claims uncertain. The governments' claims generally were not figured into the one third, one third, one third formulas, which had been established before the government push began for university researchers to exploit intellectual property.

When we spoke to faculty who had not yet finalized patents, they frequently did not know how to divide among themselves the one third to which scientists were entitled. This process involved negotiation within the research team and was fraught with tension. The researcher quoted below realized how difficult this decision would be and solved it by putting the problem off:

There's a split within the university—same as a consultancy—one third, one third, one third—so one third goes to the university, one third to individuals, one third to the institute. The third that goes to individuals, that will be divided among a number of us. We'll cross that bridge when we come to it. That hasn't been worked out yet. It's going to be a very difficult decision. Frank and I were the instigators of the project. We administer it. But then we have two key figures who are employed on the project, who work on the project. There would have to be a split to those other people as well. We haven't worked it out, we haven't worked it out. One is a postdoc, and one is a professional officer. It's a long way off because once we have something that's potentially useful . . . it's going to be at least six years before the money flows to the university. (Professor, NWU)

The decision about whom to include on a patent is complicated further by patent laws. Patent regulations give primacy to the person who conceptualizes the product. Inclusion or exclusion of persons not contributing to the product can invalidate the patent. Faculty always saw themselves as conceptualizing the product, but very few were engaged in the bench science. Their impulse, as indicated in the quotation above, was to include those who labored on the project, especially if they were colleagues or students. Faculty, however, were usually untutored in patent law and did not know the metes and bounds of inclusion and exclusion. In the following account attorneys representing the university company informed a faculty member of the conditions surrounding patent claims, instructing him that only the person who had a novel conception had a claim, that persons who simply executed the conception were not entitled, and if a novel idea had been presented in the literature its uniqueness was lost, and it could no longer be patented. The attorneys brought this faculty member to the realization that he should exclude some persons he initially thought deserved recognition and with whom he had discussed patenting:

> This was the first time I was involved, and I had a different concept of intellectual property. I thought the honors student should be involved because she did the work. I thought the postdoc who'd demonstrated the invention in a practical system should be involved too. Then we were advised by the attorneys not to do it. . . . It was unpleasant, tough—I had no idea what an inventor was. It took me a long time to understand. It was awkward for me to tell them. The postdoc was not happy but accepted the chain of events as the attorney suggested. When I filed three improvements, I was much more aware. If I thought it was novel, I told them. The honors student did the first experiment. I had the idea; she did the experiments, and then the postdoc demonstrated. . . . When I discussed with . . . the third person [a now retired staff member] his contribution—he suggested something significant, the use of [a particular substance], although I worked out how it worked. But in the literature people had suggested you could use [the substance]. I just couldn't go back and tell him [his contribution] wasn't novel. I didn't want to be seen to be trying to get him off the patent. But [finally I did], and the retired staff said then that no students or postdocs [should be on the patent], and then the student and postdoc said not each other. No one understood. It took many hours with the university company and the university attorneys. (Associate professor, USAI)

A central point that emerged from the accounts of faculty members who were in the process of determining ownership of the researchers' one third of intellectual property was their confusion and uncertainty. They did not know whom to include, found the determination of whom to include very difficult, and often waited until the work was fairly advanced before making a firm determination, exacerbating the difficulties.

Although patent law is fairly specific as to who has legal claim, definitions of centrality to discovery are socially constructed in the laboratory, a setting skewed toward those faculty who direct student work and see themselves as the fountainhead of student creativity. Faculty were likely to view themselves always as the author of novel ideas. Regardless of whether students were included on patents, the determination of whom to put on a patent was difficult to make, in part because it brought market conceptions such as ownership and profits from ownership into relations that were not previously dominated by market considerations.

Another faculty member had a different set of difficulties which stemmed from his lack of familiarity with the patent process. He was unsure of the commercial value of his research and as a result,

> We almost fell into the trap of publication. Earlier, I took the project to the university company, but they said unless I had a company to develop fully, to license in twelve months, they wouldn't go forward. So, for [product], I didn't think of it, and I published two papers. [As a result] I lost the European rights. (Associate professor, USAI)

Because the scientific research was published, it became part of the public domain, and patenting was not possible.

Faculty had difficulty with patenting in part because they lacked patent experience. Of the twenty-three faculty involved in commercial work, only four held patents. According to an administrator responsible for commercial research, patents had become important only during the past two or three years as part of the government push to bring universities and industry closer together. Before that time, most research funding in Australian universities was public, and patents were not an issue. As a researcher and administrator said,

> Patents are useful with regard to selling [an invention to industry] but not worth all that much in themselves (Vice-president, USAI).[5]

Faculty with intellectual property often thought they did not need patents for protection, at least at the current stage of their research. These faculty thought it would be too difficult for a competitor to replicate the work they had done, reducing the invention to practice. For example, a professional officer said,

> We don't have a patent on the hydrology system. . . . We took a different approach. We decided that it wasn't in our interest to patent. What we did instead was take all the key electronic circuitry and reduce it to miniature and produced a special electronic chip through Kruger, a big German company, which contains all the intelligence of the system, and at the same time we developed a software package that goes

5. The situation is very different in the litigious United States, where patents are regarded as necessary to protect intellectual property.

in the microprocessor, so it communicates with our chip. All the innovation is in those two chips. Kruger will produce the special chip for us, and only us, under a confidentiality agreement. (Professor, NWU)

This researcher, like one or two others, was confident that he had sufficient protection because of the congealed labor embodied in the product, which would be difficult for a competitor to duplicate before the product entered the public domain through publication. The two-chip arrangement, which required both chips for the system to function, was an added protection.

All of the negotiations surrounding intellectual property were complex and nonroutine. Even the university formulas—one third, one third, one third—provided only a very rough guide, perhaps because they were developed for consultancies, not intellectual property. In many cases negotiations over ownership were not step-by-step, linear, moving from discovery to recognition of commercial worth to discussions with the university to searching for commercial partners. Negotiations were complex, fluid, rapid, and involved simultaneous decision making among a variety of partners. We had a unique opportunity to gain some understanding of the complexity of the negotiation process, especially negotiations over ownership, because we interviewed several people in a unit that was undertaking negotiations during the period of our interviews. We spoke with professor and CPR head Robert Alexander after his first round of negotiations. He was very optimistic, very positive, very certain of the outcome:

> We're just entering a phase where we are going to do a joint venture with InGen. . . . There are three components to the agreement. After stage one, there will be an intellectual property payout for this first item, $500,000 for four individuals within the CPR. The second point, 5 percent royalty off the retail price, comes to the CPR for as long as the product sells, and four years down the track we estimate that will bring in revenues of $400,000 per year. The third key point was that I would be appointed head of the board of InGen Instruments, which will do the production. Fourth was that we would form an organization within the CPR called Environmental Products, or some such name, where InGen would invest $100,000 a year and in return would get the first shot at any intellectual property. Basically, it will pay Ray's [head of the commercial side of the CPR] salary. The $100,000 is only the start. It pays his salary to bring new products to their attention, and then they have to bring it up to par, invest lots of money. (OU)

Alexander then turned the remainder of the negotiation over to Ray Dickinson, the head of the commercial side of his unit. When we interviewed him, Dickinson had just faxed his response to InGen's counteroffer to the professor's first statement of terms and conditions:

Everything [about the deal with InGen] is in a constant state of flux. They don't want to do a joint venture, it's not their philosophy. It will be a buyout, and we won't have a significant role. There is a philosophy [on the part of the company] of ongoing involvement with the CPR, and for a retainer. There will be intellectual property rights, and Bob [Alexander] will have a position on the board. But a joint venture just won't work. Bob was certainly thinking that I would be the executive [of a company created by a joint venture], but I will remain a facilitator. . . the lump sum payout [should be] equivalent to the development costs. I think they'll quibble about the magnitude. The government partners will agree, or not. . . . . Because there is no share holding any more [as there would have been in a joint venture], the government group—five departments—technically we're seeking their approval . . . may ask for a share of our royalties, but I doubt it, and they wouldn't get it. Only one group could justifiably ask for it, the local power authority, they were in on conception . . . we have acknowledged that [they have a right] to royalties . . . that come to the CPR, and they will have joint administration of these areas of . . . ongoing research. . . . All our legal and management costs will be paid by the company. They'll object to that as well, all that cost, which is substantial. They'll have to invest $500,000 to get to the next phase and $130,000 to $150,000 will have to come back to the CPR [for costs]. But they may want [to take it] from royalties, or the lump sum, but we're going to insist otherwise. . . . At the moment, the CPR gets 5 percent of the royalty on the instrument . . . we don't know what proportion the university will get, but Bob will argue that it all goes to the center. All the work was done without university funding, all done on contract funding, so that minimizes their claim. (OU)

Dickinson thought he would have a copy of a draft agreement in the hands of all parties (the company, five government departments, the university, the CPR) by the end of the week, and then he would wait for objections. In a very short time the deal had become quite different from that initially envisioned by Alexander. There was no joint venture and therefore no position for the head of the commercial side; the lump sum payout was undecided; the faculty member had a seat on the board rather than being head of the board; the amount of costs that would be paid for was unclear; and a number of other claimants— several state agencies and the university—to the 5 percent royalties had emerged. The negotiations were complex, fast moving but time consuming, and lacked any clear format. Alexander had an advantage many lacked in that he had his own head of commercial operations, Ray Dickinson, to negotiate for him; but even then he was far from realizing the terms for which he had hoped.

Vagaries of the Marketplace

Even when an agreement was concluded, it was not clear that products leading to royalty payouts would result. Indeed, three of the products were already experiencing difficulties. The difficulties were of two very different kinds. First, there were problems in completing the science and developing a prototype. Second, companies sometimes failed or sold intellectual property, either of which left agreements in limbo.

Companies were very concerned with time lines and bench marks. As part of their agreements with university researchers, they expected the science to be developed to specific points at certain times; if university researchers were unable to meet time lines and bench marks, there was a strong possibility of agreement cancellation. An associate professor talked about his negotiations with the company and what he had done with regard to the bench marks:

> We left all the legal negotiations, the contractual, to the legal people from the university and the company. We were involved in negotiating the grant, how much money we wanted, and the bench marks. . . . In retrospect, I think we'd probably be more assertive about the bench marks. We were sitting around the conference table drinking their coffee, being taken out for dinner, and we were overoptimistic, and then you get back to the lab, and the teaching and everything, and it goes slower than expected. (NWU)

The postdoctoral fellow doing the bench science to reach the bench mark had a different take on where the project was:

> They gave us what we wanted for the budget . . . but not for the time period we wanted. It ended up as a compromise. They only funded for six months, with a clause that we had to meet certain bench marks before they would continue funding for another year. I don't know if we'll meet them. It's still in balance if we'll meet them by the end of March. It's a matter of luck if we'll come up with the goods. If we don't get it, the funding will cease. We could try to renegotiate, but . . . unfortunately what's happened is because I came in at a late stage. They're getting impatient. Some of the deadlines have been unrealistic from my point of view, but overall they should have been meetable. . . . It would be ironic if they stopped funding just as we were about to get what they wanted. But you never know with these private companies. They may decide to pull the pin after having gone three years down the track. It's very stressful at the moment. Some people complain about one- or two-year grants, but we're on at six months at a time. (NWU)

Although the professor who signed the contract thought the bench marks might be difficult to meet, he did not seem to think the project as a whole was in jeopardy. The postdoc doing the science was not sure he would be able to finish, saw completion as a matter of luck, and was contemplating the possibility of the project losing its funding. The time lines, as he noted, were very different for private companies in comparison with government agencies.

Two other projects were unable to move from the prototype stage to the development stage because the companies to which they had licensed their intellectual property had encountered financial difficulties. One project involved a joint agreement with American and Australian companies

> to codevelop the technology and to take it to commercialization. That collaboration worked very well. We had a free exchange of information. We have been to the United States a number of times, and the U.S. companies have been here. We have been working well, until 1989. The Australian company . . . had raised $3 million from the public, and that money was spent in Australia for this research. But in 1989 the funds of the Australian company were lost in the failure of Duke Securities. That was a merchant bank. Because of the loss of money the Australian company was unable to continue. So we basically had to lay our staff off in 1989. But luckily we had produced a demonstration prototype at that stage. Then it was the university's responsibility to look for funds to continue because after doing so much and bringing the technology so far, it wasn't worth it just to dump it. But so far, we have not got any funds from anywhere. (Associate professor, NWU)

Faculty turned to commercial partners because the risks of taking products to market on their own were great. Estimates of success rates of start-up companies are one in ten. But even working with well-established commercial partners had risks. Carefully negotiated contracts with beneficial licensing and royalty agreements could end up running aground during financial downturns or bankruptcy, leaving the researchers and the university with enormous costs that might not be recouped. In the case just described the university had spent $11 million of its own funds trying to rescue the project. The faculty member had to disband his team, and his own future was unclear. Another project had come to a halt when the commercial partner had become part of a takeover, and the merged company had displayed no interest in the project. Still other commercial partners had bought licenses to intellectual property but had not developed it aggressively.

Faculty attempted to control the vagaries of the marketplace through political work.[6] Since the federal government rather than industry was the leader and in many cases a major funder in the push toward academic capitalism in Australia, academics had to develop expertise about how to influence the state with regard to the flow of resources for commercial science. A handful of academics drew on public relations knowledge, but most relied on close connec-

---

6. Randall Collins (1979) elaborates on the concept of *political work* as work professionals do in organizations to maintain their positions and prerogatives. We use the term in a slightly different way, in that we are speaking about work professors do to secure and maintain streams of external resources.

tions they had with representatives of the federal government. Senior faculty, especially heads of centers, increasingly had to develop political skills to advance their commercial endeavors, even if these skills were not recognized by faculty as such.

The CPR worked hardest and longest in the political realm, engaging a public relations officer whose primary task was government relations. As part of their job, faculty were expected to participate in visits of state dignitaries. The head and public relations officer arranged these visits, and faculty acted as hosts to a steady stream of very high level politicians. In the words of one full professor,

> When we have any visitor at all, we like to show and tell. Visually impressive science—that means lab experiments. You can't just show them oil pumps. [You need] colorful experiments, videos, movies. I'm involved in coordinating as well as actually running experiments. I'm always present on tour and get to meet them, have lunch, shake hands . . . four federal cabinet members, the premier of the state, state education minister, and the vice-chancellor, in tow, all came through in two weeks. So, at least on a limited time basis, I have contact with the high level—Dawkins, Michael Baldwin, the junior minister for higher education, in particular, special research center grants. . . . The only two who haven't come through are Bob Hawke and Simon Creane . . . it's long term selling. It's a long term and continuing exercise. We don't invite someone over the month before a grant is up. We don't fall in the trap of not selling ourselves to our political masters. (Professor, OU)

Many professors were not as conscious as those at the CPR of the importance of political work in securing commercial success. Nevertheless, most of the more senior professors were involved regularly in pressing their requests on government and industry acquaintances.

> We're a small community, even nationally. I can ring up federal cabinet members and say what I think is a problem and what I think should be done. I know them personally, I went to the university with them. I have a network that's very useful. (Center head, NWU)

Political work, especially when cooperative research centers (CRCs) were involved, meant putting in long hours with industrial leaders and government leaders, trying to build the coalitions needed for funding.

> I really tried to talk to a lot of people to string it [CRC] all together. It was a hard sell job. It was getting into the boardrooms of companies and saying, we should try this. I've spent a lot of time networking . . . making contacts, making groups of colleagues, who now have senior positions, old loyalties, friends I went back with. It's more than friendship, it's trust. People make a judgment about you, and then if you're promoting something, they're likely to listen. (Professor, USAI)

Only the faculty at the CPR self-consciously saw their work as political in the sense that their efforts to secure funds were as much based on promotional skills as on the merit, usefulness, or competitiveness of their products. Senior faculty at all three institutions were engaged in similar, though less obvious, promotional work, but they did not see this effort as political or as calling for any expertise. Even so, they were all highly skilled at using their professional and institutional positions to influence state and federal politicians as well as businesspersons.

Consultancies

Most of these faculty and professional officers also did consulting work. Almost all faculty did individual consulting, using the one day a week they were traditionally allowed. In contrast with the situation in the United States, funds from individual consultancies did not belong solely to the persons who did the work. Instead, consultancy moneys were divided in thirds, one third going to the university, one third to the department or center, one third to the professor or professional officer who did the work. These moneys could be pocketed or put in a "private" university account. The Australian income tax rate was about 50 percent, and as a result professors often preferred to keep their moneys in untaxed university accounts. Moneys in university accounts could be spent on a wide variety of academic related activities and equipment. The other thirds went to the unit and to the university, respectively. Although the individual profited, so did the units, most of which were organized around commercial science. Personal or individual consulting, then, was another form of market behavior used to defray the units' costs for commercial science.

One unit engaged in a somewhat different practice. This group or unit was organized to exploit its faculty and professional officers' consultancies to finance other university-based research and teaching endeavors. In other words, as originally conceived, a combination of student fees and consultancies was supposed to support this relatively new social science unit.

These faculty, put in a position where they had no choice but to enter the market, had a somewhat different set of entrepreneurial problems than did those with intellectual property. First, the unit had been established with substantial seed moneys from state government, and that same state government was their most likely source of consultancies. The state government expected some consideration with regard to fees in recompense for the seed money, leaving the unit without a rich source of income. Second, the faculty in the unit

were uncertain what their posture should be with regard to the organizations
with which they did consulting:

> I don't see myself as a consultant hack, who will say anything to please anybody. I
> think it's very important as an academic consultancy unit that we retain our credi-
> bility and integrity, and I am concerned that this being bullied into saying something,
> especially by a powerful client like the government, is an asset-stripping exercise for
> us. So, the government comes to academic institutions to be able to say, here we have
> an independent, reliable, objective organization with scientific rigor, and some de-
> gree of depth of analysis—but then as soon as they bully you into saying what they
> want, you don't get any more consultancies, you've been written off from that cate-
> gory. . . . They want you to be independent, but they want you to say what they want.
> (Lecturer, NWU)

The problem for an academic consultancy unit, according to this faculty member, was that you were damned if you gave the politically correct advice and
damned if you did not.

A third problem faced by academic consultancy units was conflict of interest. Most universities had regulations against conflict of interest with private
business, regulations that academics took to mean that they could not enter
into open competition with private groups. As one professor said,

> The competition [private business] on the commercial side is very ambivalent—
> we're taking a lot of business away from people, and they're not satisfied that it's fair
> trade. They say a lot of our hidden costs are unfairly borne by the government.
> There's a lot of suspicion. There's conflict-of-interest laws—but we're talking about
> a financial conflict. They say you're being paid by the federal government and un-
> derpricing yourself. . . . People in the private sector complain about it bitterly—they
> say we can underbid them, we have equipment, students, all free. (Center head, OU)

Academic consultancy units were not supposed to engage in routine consulting because they were regarded as having an unfair advantage, given that they
received basic salaries from the government as well as equipment, space, and
relatively cheap student labor. Academic consultancies were supposed to focus
on tasks that drew on staff research skills and were nonroutine, thereby differentiating this academic labor from that of commercial groups. One professor
tried to solve his problem with the commercial sector by including costs and
overheads in salary rates so his unit ended up with almost the same rates as the
private sector, blunting what the private sector thought was the unit's competitive edge. However, this professor's solution did not address the difference
between routine and nonroutine consulting, and the line between the two
was very thin. When pushed to raise money to support their research and

sustain their units, professors and professional officers had trouble with the distinction.

> We're governed by a university rule that says we're not supposed to do standard consulting; they [consultancies] should be research oriented, not ones that should be taken on by standard . . . practice . . . that ruling . . . is lapsing because the government is pushing universities into doing applied research. . . . In the future we'll be looking [at] much bigger jobs and broader in scope. . . . That will cause me something of a dilemma because there's going to be a certain amount of standard [work] in larger type jobs, and whether we should take this on—because it hasn't got a scientific component—that's a dilemma. (Associate professor, OU)

Consulting presented faculty with several problems. If faculty attempted to sustain their units through consulting, they put their scholarly reputations at risk if they too often produced information that pleased their sponsors; but they risked future commissions if they too often displeased their sponsors. Like other faculty, these individuals also faced of conflict-of-interest allegations. By increasing their activity in the market they entered into competition with private firms engaged in similar activities. Ironically, by acting as state-subsidized entrepreneurs, faculty were in a position to push small private sector firms out of the way, impeding the development of a broad culture of entrepreneurship.

Commercial Expertise

Faculty and professional officers participating in commercial science developed an entrepreneurial expertise important to their endeavors. This expertise consisted of the ability to recognize the commercial value of their science, to protect that science, to locate commercial partners, and to negotiate for intellectual property rights and research contracts with a variety of parties, including students and colleagues, their academic institutions, various state agencies, and industrial partners. Almost all of these negotiations were nonroutine, a characteristic of professional expertise (Abbott 1988). The time spent acquiring this expertise took professors away from their laboratories, their students, and university service, as traditionally construed.

There are several possible ways to reduce the need for professors to acquire commercial expertise, freeing them up to give more time to science and students and less time to the market. Some of these negotiations could be more highly routinized so that professors' and universities' negotiations with the market would mirror the relations they have with government granting agencies, with fixed overheads and standard formulas. However, the competitive nature of the market makes a high degree of routinization unlikely. In contrast to government agencies, business strives to have universities bear the largest share of research costs possible, making agreements more beneficial to the profit-maximizing sector than to universities.[7] Another way to minimize the amount of entrepreneurial expertise which professors need to develop is to assign negotiations with external entities to specialists. Indeed, a host of specialists has already emerged—managers and staff in university companies, technology transfer officers, research managers—ready to participate in the new opportunity structures offered by university involvement in the market. However, professors resist efforts to shift entrepreneurial expertise away from them. Faculty claim that they are better positioned to negotiate with external groups because they best understand the problems and possibilities of the science involved. They see themselves as better able to make contact with business representatives interested in their work than are specialists in intellectual property management.

More importantly, faculty understand that they will be able to negotiate the best deal for themselves and their units only if they are major players in the process. If they routinize negotiations or turn them over to special agents, they forfeit control over a mechanism that allows them to claim more resources and to differentiate themselves from other faculty. In short, faculty comprehend intuitively that turning negotiations over to specialized groups will weaken their professional authority and undercut their market position. Because faculty realize that entrepreneurship is the key to present and future institutional and cultural preference, approval, and legitimacy, they cultivate this new form of market expertise extensively.

Although the national government took the lead in redefining commercial science as the most important form of scientific labor, in this period faculty too began to redefine entrepreneurial science as a high prestige activity. As one faculty member said,

> It's a tough world outside. It's a completely different world compared with what we are [in the university]. But you start enjoying it after a while, come to see that there is some money to be made. (Associate professor, NWU)

Or, in the words of another,

7. In the United States, for example, researchers and policy makers expected the contributions that business made to higher education research to go up in the 1980s, as business drew more heavily on university research. However, business contributions only rose slightly throughout the 1980s, going from 8 to 9 percent of the share of academic research and development costs (National Science Foundation 1993, Appendix Table 5.2).

The only thing that's rewarding is to make scientific discoveries and then apply them—to make things work, that's my only motivation, to make something better than what's available. (Center head, OU)

Almost all faculty justified entrepreneurial work on the grounds of necessity. They saw current economic conditions and government mandates as driving them toward entrepreneurial work. Although entering the market was difficult, painful, even perilous, for the most part senior faculty seemed to find it exciting and stimulating. They were entrepreneurs in a culture that valued entrepreneurship (Etzkowitz 1989; Louis et al. 1989; but see also Rhoades and Slaughter 1991a, 1991b). Through their science and skills in negotiation, they were working to overcome the financial straits threatening universities and academic researchers. All faculty deeply engaged in entrepreneurial work had hopes of "the big hit," a discovery that would yield an endless and bountiful stream of resources. They justified their emerging commitment to entrepreneurship in terms of saving their units and finding the resources necessary to advance science. They seldom spoke about students, undergraduate education, education in general, or the institution as a whole.

Conclusions

When faculty engage in academic capitalism they move outside the treatment of professionals' market relations encountered in process theories of professionalization. Process theorists treat professionals' market relations in terms of market monopolies obtained through various forms of state licensure and accreditation. They take the position that professions as occupational structures predate market formation. When professionals were confronted with the rise of mass markets in the last quarter of the nineteenth century, they tried to escape the harsh discipline of these markets. Process theorists argue that professionals think they should be granted monopolies of knowledge because they use their expertise altruistically to serve the public good rather than special interests or self-interest. In return for state-enforced control over licensing and accreditation, professionals attempted to guarantee their integrity. Process theorists believe the professions became enmeshed in mass markets after World War II, compromising their claims to altruism and to state protection from the market (Larson 1977; Starr 1982; Freidson 1986). Brint conceptualizes professionals as moving from social trustee professionalism, characterized by "civic minded *moral* appeals and circumscribed *technical* knowledge" and alliance with the regulatory state to expert professionalism, which "emphasized the instrumental effectiveness of specialized, theoretically grounded knowledge, but included comparatively little concern with collegial organization, ethical standards, or service in the public interest" and intersected with the market (Brint 1994, 36–37; italics in original). Process theorists have started to consider the effects of the market on professions but do not speak to the consequences of academic capitalism for faculty as a professional group or for universities as organizations.

On the basis of our case studies in Australia, we think that the sociology of science literature has concentrated too much on norms of science, particularly on distinctions between basic and applied research, and not enough on resource dependence theory and on globalization conditions and forces that are changing intra- and interinstitutional relations and are renorming science and technology (Rhoades and Slaughter 1991a, 1991b; Slaughter and Rhoades 1990, 1993; Gibbons et al. 1994). Nor does the sociology of science literature look far beyond colleges of science and engineering, an oversight we view as problematic because we think the well-being of professional work depends on the health of the university as a whole, not only on science and engineering.

We think that academic capitalism creates substantial risks for professors, administrators, and public universities. Although only some professors, academic professionals, and administrators are engaged in academic capitalism, the risks they incur are probably faced by their entire units and by their institutions as a whole. These risks are several: business failure, product liability, failure to meet societal expectations of economic improvement and job creation, and above all, neglect of students.

Academic capitalists run the risk of failing to recoup the moneys their institution, government, or industry has invested in them. Capitalism entails risk; profit is the reward. In our intellectual property sample only one product was generating profits, and only one had failed, costing the institution millions of dollars. The remaining eight pieces of intellectual property were still in the development process. The business innovation literature suggests that only one start-up company in ten is successful.

In the United States, where intellectual property has been pursued by academic capitalists since the early 1980s, a small but growing number of institutions generates significant income from licensing and royalties. However, even those institutions often incur as much in legal and other costs as they gain in income. Moreover, published statistics that report annual income from intellectual property give no indication of the costs to the university—technology transfer offices, university foundations, university companies, direct monetary contributions. If Australian universities' intellectual property follows the American pattern to date, more institutions will lose revenues than gain them.

As in the United States, Australian administrators and faculty entrepreneurs saw product liability as a potential risk. They raised the problem of what might happen if intellectual property licensed by a university were implicated in consumer injuries such as those caused by thalidomide and breast implants. Although product liability is a real possibility, there have been no legal cases in Australia as yet, and the complex legal issues surrounding the responsibility of the university as a licensing agent for intellectual property have not yet been clarified.

To our knowledge, failed academic capitalists do not incur obvious penalties for losing institutional funds. Although several associate professors thought they had not been promoted because their intellectual property had not been successful, we had no way to confirm their suspicions, and the alternative interpretation, that their academic work was not sufficiently meritorious, was equally possible. The faculty member whose intellectual property had cost his institution A$12 million was not asked to make any restitution, nor was it clear that his institution would refuse further moneys for his project or decline to invest in another promising project put forward by him. In many regards academic capitalists are state-subsidized entrepreneurs, cushioned from the market by their salaries and institutional resources. As we noted in Chapter One, their position is somewhat analogous to that of researchers and entrepreneurs in primary sector industries that are cushioned from the market by government funds because the industries are perceived as meeting national needs in critical areas such as defense, food supply, and health. Like their counterparts in government-supported industry, state-subsidized academic capitalists do not want to face the market without government funds. In the United States we discovered that faculty had little interest in leaving the university to form start-up companies, that a number of faculty participating in technology transfer had moved from industry to the university, and that they were not particularly interested in the routine of maintaining a business (Slaughter and Rhoades 1990; Rhoades and Slaughter 1991a, 1991b).

There is another set of risks if universities fail to realize the promises inherent in national science and technology policy. Governments, whether state or federal, have provided the lion's share of funds for academic capitalism, supplying moneys in hopes of improving national economies and creating jobs. If academic capitalism does not contribute to prosperity or contributes to economic growth without generating high paying jobs, governments may shift spending priorities, curtailing moneys for university research. (Alternatively, faculty success in raising institutional revenues through intellectual property might result or may have resulted in revenue substitution, whereby governments curtail funding because institutions generate their own resources. For an elaboration of this point, see Chapters Three and Four.)

Although the consequences of failure on the part of academic capitalists are not clear in all of their particulars, it is likely that the institution would bear the burden of failure, making fewer resources available for education and nonentrepreneurial faculty research. Failure could also result in loss of public confidence and litigation, both of which might prompt greater state regulation or oversight of faculty and institutional activity. Whether the return on academic capitalism is worth the risks remains to be seen, as do the consequences of academic capitalism for the institution as a whole.

The science policy innovation literature that looks closely at the relationship between academic science and entrepreneurism generally examines neither the risks entailed nor the broad consequences for institutions of higher learning as a whole. On the one hand, this literature, in part developed by academic administrators promoting academic capitalism and in part by science and technology policy units initiated in the 1980s to study how technoscience can make greater contributions to national prosperity, argues that the very nature of science has changed, impelling academics toward the market. For example, Donald Kennedy, when he was president of Stanford University, argued that the trajectory of innovation collapsed as disciplines matured, "accelerating" the movement between basic and applied:

> A number of scientific disciplines are now being recognized as "ready" for accelerated application. Our perceptions of what is possible are sharpened in such fields; as a discipline matures in power and confidence, leaps from the laboratories to applications that once seemed intimidating become commonplace. That now appears to be the case, for example, in immunology and "genetic engineering" as well as in microelectronics (Kennedy 1984).

Similarly, Michael Gibbons of SPRUE, a prominent U.K. science and technology policy unit, describes the emergence of "Mode 2" science—science that is transdisciplinary, transinstitutional, and transnational, shaped by the drive to reach the new level to which science has risen, where there is no longer any distance between discovery and application. Science and product are one. There is no longer a gap between discovery and application, between laboratory and market. Science and technology are project specific, not located permanently in units within universities. In other words, scientists and engineers are part of the postmodern economy, members of the flexible labor force, signing on to just-in-time production teams, ready to move anywhere in the world as the demands of the project and the market determine (Gibbons et al. 1994).

On the other hand, evolutionary theorists argue that basic science is not necessarily related to industrial innovation and application. In contrast to Kennedy (1984) and Gibbons et al. (1994), who view the gap between basic research and product development as diminishing, these theorists think that discoveries leading to innovation are often developed in the manufacturing divisions of businesses rather than from basic research in the academy (Gummett 1991; Leydesdorff 1994). In the United States, industries are disbanding central laboratories that work on general problems and are moving research into the business divisions (Varma 1995).[8]

Although these two lines of argument developed in the science policy literature are somewhat contradictory, both undercut the primacy of basic research. The Mode 2 argument makes the case that there is little difference between basic and applied and that neither need be done in the university. The evolutionists see applied research as more important to innovation than basic, and they do not perceive a clear relationship between the two. In other words, increased funding of basic research will not necessarily lead to business innovations that will bring economic prosperity. The logical conclusion of both of these arguments, if applied to science and technology policy decisions, would undermine the need for government funding of autonomous or independent academic science and technology. If there is no difference between basic and applied, and if the new research is transdisciplinary and transnational, then there is no compelling policy argument for investing in particular fields or in institutions of higher education other than for their training functions. Contrarily, if basic research does not lead to innovation and application, the same conclusion follows: there is no compelling policy argument for investing in particular fields or institutions. In these arguments research funding serves the economy directly and is not mediated by professional scientists and engineers, who are housed in universities. Instead, researchers trained in tertiary institutions become part of the postmodern, flexible labor force, working intermittently on industry- or government-led technoscience projects, perhaps training graduate students when they are not engaged in projects, perhaps not. Our cases point to professors whom resource dependence pushed toward academic capitalism but who strenuously try to avert becoming project workers of the Mode 2 type or joining an industrial firm. Instead, they seek the advantages of professionals —protection from the market, state subsidy of infrastructure, and control over

---

8. It is not clear how much this movement stems from a need for greater economy and how much from a desire to alter the place of research in the innovation cycle. Nor is it clear whether industry envisions university research as replacing the functions once performed by industrial laboratories.

their own work. They seek to acquire the entrepreneurial expertise that allows them to act as academic capitalists: finding funding for the products, processes, or services they are trying to develop and promote; applying for and proving patents; developing market strategies and negotiating with corporations for research contracts and royalties. They have no intention of leaving the academy. They relish being state-subsidized entrepreneurs.

However, faculty might not be able to have their cake and eat it too. When faculty in public research universities engage in academic capitalism or Mode 2 production of science they probably raise questions about the nature of their implicit contract with society. The social contract between professors and society suggests that if professors altruistically serve the public good rather than their own special interests, then in return they receive a monopoly of practice which ensures them a decent livelihood as well as societal respect. As professors, stimulated by international economic competition, national policy emphases, and resource dependence, become more entrepreneurial, they may lose their monopoly on conferring academic credentials. More options for degree-granting agencies may become available, for example, proprietary colleges and universities or colleges and research groups located in corporations may rise to compete with established colleges and universities; state and national legislators may not limit that competition.

As universities develop hybrid research entities that span the boundaries between private and public sectors, governments may cut back on overhead for university research. Cuts to overhead would reduce funding in the sciences and engineering, but also in a variety of other departments. Loss of overhead funds would also reduce seriously the amount of money research administrators have at their discretion. Alternatively, as academic capitalism becomes more established, the several states and federal governments may deregulate the operation of centers so that centers and institutions bear more fully the risks associated with entrepreneurism. Forfeiting altruism may mean facing the strictures of the market.

Perhaps the most likely future of sponsored academic research is the development of corporatist (industry, government, university) funding arrangements, the priorities of which are determined by national technology policies. In some countries such as Australia, these would be government led in terms of priorities; in others such as the United States, they would be led by industry, even though it is likely that government would bear the greatest cost burden (Slaughter 1990). In essence, universities would take over the functions performed previously by industrial laboratories. Although such an arrangement would undercut faculty emphasis on autonomy, it would provide reliable and predictable, if somewhat reduced, resources for universities. Even if faculty are reluctant to allow external entities to determine their research direction, university officials usually place a high priority on stable resource arrangements. The Australian cooperative research centers were a move in this direction, as were the centers on which they were modeled—the interdisciplinary research centers of the United Kingdom and the industry-university cooperative programs in the United States (Hill 1993). The U.S. Department of Commerce Advanced Technology Program perhaps points out our future most clearly. Government works with industry to clarify the areas of research which companies in a particular field deem important to the midterm future; government and industry together fund that research, some of which is subcontracted to universities, with the proviso that ownership belongs to the companies (U.S. Department of Commerce 1995).

None of these explanations—sociology of science, process theories of professionalization, theories of the role of science and engineering in product innovation—is particularly concerned with the university as an organization. As students of higher education we have tried to understand how academic capitalism affects not only colleges of science and engineering, but the university as a whole. We see academic capitalism in general, and science and technology in particular, as bringing about broad change in higher education to the point where the center of the academy has shifted from a liberal arts core to an entrepreneurial periphery (see Clark 1993).

7

REPRISE:
ACADEMIC CAPITALISM

THIS BOOK EXAMINED ongoing changes in the nature of academic labor in the period 1970–95, with an emphasis on the 1980s and 1990s. We have argued that the changes currently taking place are as great as the changes in academic labor which occurred during the last quarter of the nineteenth century. Just as the industrial revolution at the end of the nineteenth century created the wealth that provided the base for postsecondary education and attendant professionalization, the globalization of the political economy at the end of the twentieth century is destabilizing patterns of university professional work developed over the past hundred years.

Many of our colleagues have also made the case that higher education as an institution and faculty as its labor force face change unprecedented in this century. Henry Etzkowitz (1983, 1989), David Breneman (1993), James Fairweather (1988), Patricia Gumport and Brian Pusser (1995), William Massy and Robert Zemsky (1990), William Massy (1994), and Gary Rhoades (1997) are some of the U.S. scholars exploring the dramatic changes in academic work and institutional and system management. In other countries other scholars are addressing similar change in higher education, for example, Burton Clark (1993), Guy Neave (1988), and Guy Neave and Frans Vught (1991); in the United Kingdom, Gareth Williams (1992, 1995) and Michael Gibbons et al. (1994); in Australia, John Smyth (1995) and Simon Marginson (1993, 1995); in Canada, Howard Buchbinder and Janice Newson (1990) and Buchbinder and Rajagopal (1993, 1995). These scholars, too, describe broad changes in higher education, often focusing on how the center of the academy has shifted from a liberal arts core to an entrepreneurial periphery, describing the increasing "marketization" of the academy and detailing the rise of research and development (R&D) with commercial purpose.

Our book drew heavily on the work of these scholars and the many others cited in the preceding chapters, enabling us to paint a broad picture of the changes faced by faculty and by institutions of higher education. However, our book expanded the work of these scholars in several ways. We began our analysis by looking outside higher education at global political economic change so that we could gauge the scope of change facing faculty and institutions. Because we saw change as precipitated by shifts in global political economic conditions, we included change in higher education in several nations through our study of the development of national higher education and R&D policies in four countries—Australia, Canada, the United States, and the United Kingdom. We followed up our analysis of national policy changes with an examination of shifts in financial patterns in higher education in all four countries over a twenty-year period, approximately 1970–90. To see the impact of global economic changes, national policy changes, and changed higher education finance patterns on faculty in research universities, we conducted case studies of Australian institutions which explored the effect of academic capitalism on faculty work lives and the creative ways in which faculty responded to new entrepreneurial opportunities. From our point of view the greatest weakness of our book is the lack of comparable case studies in Canada, the United Kingdom, and the United States. Some scholars, primarily in the United States, have developed case studies around what we call *academic capitalism*—Henry Etzkowitz (1983, 1989, 1992), Karen Seashore Louis et al. (1989), Gary Rhoades and Sheila Slaughter (1991a, 1991b), Sheila Slaughter and Gary Rhoades (1990), but more are needed to assess fully the changes that research universities are undergoing. (We have such a project now underway.)

The central argument of our book is that the structure of academic work is changing in response to the emergence of global markets. As national competition for global market shares increased, Australia, the United Kingdom, and the United States developed national higher education and R&D policies that in the end reshaped faculty work and both undergraduate and graduate education. Increased global competition interacted with national and state/provincial spending priorities so that less money was available from government, when measured as a share of higher education revenue or in constant dollars per student. This precipitated campus reactions of a resource-dependent nature. In all four countries the block grant as a source of funding for higher education diminished as a share of higher education revenues, with the result that faculty and institutions began to compete or increased their competition for external funds.

We called institutional and professorial market or marketlike efforts to secure external funds *academic capitalism*. These external dollars usually were tied to market-related research, which was referred to variously as applied, commercial, strategic, and targeted research, whether these moneys were in the form of research grants and contracts, service contracts, partnerships with industry and government, or technology transfer. Institutions also began to compete in the recruitment of students paying more and higher fees. Although *academic capitalism* may seem to many to be an oxymoron, we thought the concept captured dramatically the changes facing universities. More than alternatives such as *academic entrepreneurism, academic capitalism* seemed to grasp the encroachment of the profit motive into the academy. By using *academic capitalism* as our central concept we defined the reality of the nascent environment of research universities, an environment full of contradictions, an environment in which faculty and professional staff expend their human capital stocks increasingly in competitive situations. In this environment university employees are simultaneously employed by the public sector and increasingly autonomous from the public, corporate body. They are academics who act as capitalists from within the public sector; they are state-subsidized entrepreneurs.

In terms of practical implications, we hope that the concept of academic capitalism will enable faculty, other academic personnel, and administrators to make sense of their daily lives. When faculty find themselves spending increasing amounts of time in the pursuit of external funds or in external relationships that might yield more students, contracts, or partnership arrangements, thus increasing unit revenue, the concept of academic capitalism may help them put their activities in a meaningful context. Faculty and administrators may begin to view the rapid rise of costs for academic professionals as a way of funding academic capitalism and may begin to wonder when entrepreneurial activity on the periphery will begin to reshape the academic core definitively. The concept of academic capitalism may help administrators, who attempt to enhance faculty productivity, assist faculty to tap external resources and develop their own market schemes, and begin to think broadly about how to deploy institutional resources in the changed environment of higher education.

Global Political Economic Change, National Higher Education, and R&D Policies

The emergence of a global political economy has caused structural alterations in national economies. The rise of multipolar global competition destabilized the economies of established industrial nations. In three of the countries we studied—Australia, the United Kingdom, and the United States—national policy makers responded to increased competition for shares of global markets by reducing overall rates of growth in state expenditures and reallocating money among government functions. Generally, funds were taken away from discretionary programs—that is, those not of an entitlement nature. Further, within discretionary categories funds were reallocated to programs thought likely to contribute in a direct way to technological innovation and economic competitiveness.

The national policies of these three countries promoted academic capitalism—market and marketlike behaviors—on the part of faculty and institutions.[1] In terms of enrollments, institutions in Australia and the United Kingdom began to tender competitive bids for student places, contracting with the government to educate students for a fixed cost. In the United States, institutions competed increasingly to attract students who would pay high tuition and fees, especially nonresident and overseas students. In all three countries state support varies by curricula. The United Kingdom has moved furthest in this direction, providing differential state support per student, with the highest amount for students in technoscience fields. All four countries have instituted policies that treat R&D as a source of national wealth creation, although Canadian faculty and institutions in particular are resisting this change. Faculty and institutions lost autonomy as higher education was integrated more closely with the market. The freedom of professors to pursue curiosity-driven research was curtailed by withdrawal of more or less automatic funding to support this activity and by the increased targeting of R&D funds for commercial research. Faculty and institutions were pushed and pulled toward academic capitalism by policy directives and by shifts in the resource mix.

These national policy changes had tangible consequences for tertiary education in the four countries. Policies for academic R&D, the lifeblood of graduate education, became science and technology policies, more concerned with technoscience innovation and building links with the private sector than with basic or fundamental research that articulated more with learned and professional associations and less with the economy. For the most part, technoscience fields gained resource shares while fields that were not close to the market, such as philosophy and religion, foreign languages, letters and performing arts, or fields that served the social welfare functions of the state, such as education and home economics, lost shares. Measured by positions for faculty, places for students, and research money, technoscience fields became the growth area in tertiary education.

The immediate implications of national policy changes are several. At the

1. We simply do not possess the information necessary to reach a definitive conclusion on the fourth, Canada, but we believe the changes occurring there are not as fully advanced as changes in the other three.

institutional level, national policies that fund technoscience are likely to increase differentiation among fields within research universities. Government funding is likely to tilt fields and disciplines toward entrepreneurial research. Although faculty in all fields can engage in academic capitalism, fields and academic disciplines best suited for academic capitalism are more likely to receive greater government funding and be better positioned to win business and industry funds as well. The amount of external funding faculty are able to generate through entrepreneurial activity depends to some degree on markets for professional labor (Bok 1993; Brint 1994). Those professions and academic disciplines close to the market—for example, business services and applied sciences—are likely to gain; communications and cultural fields are likely to gain unevenly; and civic regulation as well as human services professions and disciplines may not fare well (Brint 1994). In the United States and Canada, where the several states and provinces play an important role in funding, in order to remain competitive public research universities are likely to deploy state funds in such a way as to strengthen fields with potential for academic capitalism (Volk 1995).

Although technoscience areas generally received more money over recent decades as policy makers took the position that postindustrial economies called for more highly educated workers, policy makers in all four countries sought to expand student participation without comparably augmenting resources for tertiary education. The increase in student numbers together with the slowing in the rate of growth in state spending began to change the conditions of faculty labor in contradictory ways. On the one hand, faculty were encouraged to engage in a wide variety of entrepreneurial activities. On the other hand, faculty became responsible for larger numbers of students and were surveilled more closely with regard to the instructional aspects of their work.

The implications of these changes for the ranking of institutions in national systems are not yet clear. If evolutionary science and technology theorists, who argue that basic science does not necessarily result in technoscience suitable for product development for the global economy, are correct, universities that do very well at basic research may not necessarily do as well at academic capitalism (Gummett 1991). In all likelihood those universities in all four countries which are at the pinnacle of their systems in terms of prestige and resources—for example, the pre–World War II universities in Australia, "Oxbridge" and the University of London in the United Kingdom—will probably have the resources and thus the flexibility to convert successfully to accommodate academic capitalism. However, in the short term in the United States, the elite research institutions lost shares of federal science funding. (See Geiger and Feller

[1993] on the dispersion of research funds in the 1980s.) Competition among the many universities in the second tier of research universities will probably increase, ultimately resulting in a shakedown in this group of institutions. Those institutions that engage successfully in academic capitalism will probably hold their positions in ratings schemes, but many will not. In the United States the public Research I Universities,[2] a group that increased dramatically in the post–World War II period, will probably be most vulnerable to increased differentiation. Those public Research I Universities outside the top ten have always been volatile with regard to rankings as well as the amount of R&D dollars they are awarded, and some will probably suffer severely in terms of status and prestige.

Australia, Canada, the United Kingdom, and the United States promoted academic capitalism as a means of stimulating national economic growth— that is, productivity and GDP—and increasing high paying jobs. Productivity and GDP increased somewhat in the four countries in the 1990s, but income inequality increased in all of the countries but Canada, with the increases being greatest in the United Kingdom and the United States (Atkinson, Rainwater, and Smeeding 1995). Businesses are making greater profits, but recovery is not generating high paying jobs (Rifkin 1995). Even those with "some college and more" are sometimes unemployed and often have difficulty securing high paying jobs (Harrison and Bluestone 1990). (However, young workers entering the job market *without* some college or more are *very* likely to fare less well than their college-educated counterparts.) Paradoxically, national policies that promote technoscience, its attendant automation, and corporate restructuring may play into the elimination of professional positions formerly filled by college-educated workers (Abbott 1988).

Even if national higher education and R&D policies do not deliver all that they promise, the several nations are unlikely to return to the status quo ante. In the immediate future, if income inequality increases and the number of high paying jobs decreases, national higher education policies are likely to promote training that directly meets business and industry needs. Training programs that prepare students for immediate entry into the world of work would cut costs for corporations, perhaps stimulating job creation. Training programs

2. According to the Carnegie classification of institutions of higher education, a Research I University is committed to graduate education, gives high priority to research, and is distinguished from other universities involved in research and graduate education (e.g., Research II Universities, Doctorate-granting I Universities) by the amount of federal research support per year (at least $33.5 million) and the number of Ph.D. degrees granted each year (at least fifty). For further discussion, see *Carnegie Foundation for the Advancement of Teaching*, 1987 edition.

would very likely be concentrated in the less costly sectors of the postsecondary system—community colleges, TAFEs (technical and further education), and technical schools. This may create difficulties in competition for students among four-year colleges, comprehensive colleges and universities, and some research universities, although the degree of difficulty will depend on student aid polices. To retain a competitive edge, four-year colleges, comprehensive colleges and universities, and some research universities may also begin to move toward training students directly for the world of work.

However, training for direct entry into the world of work may be difficult in a postindustrial economy. Technoscience and automation may eliminate positions in some professional fields, especially as sophisticated computer software is developed—for example, in accounting, medical diagnostics, legal research, and a variety of social science statistical applications—although new professions may arise to serve technoscience with a global reach—for example, producer services professionals, telecommunications managers, and administrators of academic capitalism. The crucial and thus far unanswered question is whether new professional positions will increase as quickly as old professional positions are lost and whether the new positions will have high salaries, status, and prestige attached to them.

Only three of the four countries successfully developed national higher education and R&D policies that promoted academic capitalism. The exception was Canada. Although there was a decline in real operating funding per student and some targeted funding for high technology research and for collaborations with industry, Canadian higher education did not undergo the same degree of change as the other countries. Even though the conservative Mulroney government tried to initiate a rapproachment among universities, industry, and government, for the most part there was little structural change. Canada, then, offers an alternative to the higher education policies developed by the other countries. The Canadian case suggests that changes stemming from the emergence of a global economy do not have to be met by changes in national higher education policy which promote academic capitalism. The crucial question in the immediate future is whether Canada can maintain a system committed to high student subsidy, basic or "curiosity-driven" research, and faculty and institutional autonomy, given the size of Canada's national debt. If Canada is able to maintain its system despite pressures for economic rationalization, the Canadian case should be studied in much greater depth.

Resource Dependence and Changing Patterns of National Higher Education Finance

Global political economic changes prompted national higher education and R&D policies that resulted in changes in patterns of national higher education finance. Although there was some variation by country and postsecondary sector (research universities, polytechnics, community colleges), in general the data were in the expected direction. At the very least, the rate of growth in percentage of GNP (gross national product) devoted to postsecondary education declined consistently. Further, revenue shifts were away from block grant funding sources to those that reflected a competition or market base. Overall, general public funds for higher education declined, when considered in constant dollars per student. However, revenue shares from other sources such as sales and services increased, as did shares from tuition. Private gifts, grants, and contracts, and sales and services also were up. Expenditure patterns directly reflected the changes in revenues. As government block grants declined as a revenue share, instruction declined too; as private and government gifts, grants, and contracts expanded shares expended on research, public service, and administration increased also. Shares of relatively discretionary funding categories such as operations and maintenance of plant and libraries experienced large decreases, whereas the student aid share increased sharply in correspondence with tuition increases. Very generally, universities and colleges in all four countries seemed to be changing their revenue-generating patterns, moving from funding by general public means toward higher tuition and competitive grants and contracts, private gifts, and other competitive sources of moneys, while expenditure patterns changed.

Research universities now face increased problems of a resource-dependent nature. The cause of these difficulties involves a shifting of the responsibility for higher education support from governments to other resource providers and modifications in the form of government support which is retained, specifically a decline in block grant funding and an increase in the use of market funding mechanisms (Wasser 1990; OECD 1990a; Neave and Vught 1991; Williams 1992, 1995; Gellert 1993). Simply put, major changes in resource dependence relationships have occurred; universities have been pushed and pulled in the direction of competing in a quasi-market arena for more and more of their operating funds.

The practical implications for research universities are many. Faculty will have to pursue competitive funding more actively, but competition for these funds will be fierce. In Australia after the unified national system was inaugurated, creating organizational turbulence and heightening problems of resource dependence, the Australian Research Council was able to fund a much smaller number of grant applications, only about 20 percent (Hill 1993). In the United States, case studies of research universities indicated that faculty now spend more time on grant applications, with less success (Slaughter 1987). Administrators may expend extra effort to target and support faculty, most probably gathered in centers, who will spend increased time on applications for external funds. Institutional resources very likely will be committed to support academic personnel or professional officers (non-tenure-track, noninstructional academic professionals) who will help faculty apply for and execute grants, contracts, partnerships, technology transfer, and other entrepreneurial activity. Also, more institutional funds will be expended on managing entrepreneurial endeavor (offices for patenting and licensing, technology transfer, arm's-length foundations, spinoffs, research parks). The loss in instructional productivity for entrepreneurial faculty will most likely be compensated for by hiring more part-timers, to keep labor costs down. Indeed, in the United States recently corrected Department of Education data "reveal that nearly 45 percent of all faculty held part-time appointments in 1992, up from 38 percent in 1987 and more than double the 22 percent in 1970" (Benjamin 1996). Because academic capitalism will come to permeate institutions as a whole, not just the units where instruction and R&D are carried out, administration will expand the university's sales and services functions, stocking university shops with products bearing logos and mascots, privatizing food services by licensing concessions to fast food chains such as McDonald's, Pizza Hut, and Burger King. Another area of ever-increasing activity will be institutional advancement. And, of course, tuitions will go up, a point we will address at the conclusion of this chapter.

Incidence of Academic Capitalism in Universities

Although there are a number of case studies of departments, centers, and institutes involved in a particular form of academic capitalism—development of intellectual property (Etzkowitz 1983; Weiner 1987; Slaughter and Rhoades 1990; Rhoades and Slaughter 1991a, 1991b)—there are no studies having either broad or in-depth analysis of a financial nature. In other words, there are no studies that examine entrepreneurial activity across all academic units within a university and none that concentrates on the financial costs and benefits of these endeavors. We thought such an accounting critical to understanding the incidence and impacts of academic capitalism within research universities.

At two research universities we examined those units that derived at least 1 percent of their budgets or roughly $20,000 from entrepreneurial activity. The unit budgets and related documents yielded information as to the sources of revenues and how the entrepreneurial funds were expended. The unit head and the unit financial officer (usually a department staff member) helped identify the departmental activities that met our operational definition of *academic capitalism:* "Activities undertaken with a view to capitalizing on university research or academic expertise through contracts or grants with business or with government agencies seeking solutions to specific public or commercial concerns." Activities such as consulting were included so long as the associated revenues entered university accounts, university expertise was involved directly, and the activities were applied or developmental in nature (excluding basic research).

At the two universities we found that, respectively, 10 and 12 percent of total university operating revenues were generated through academic capitalism; these amounts were 18 and 19 percent, respectively, as large as the recurrent or base funding provided by the commonwealth. Clearly, these were significant amounts. Indeed, the importance of these activities no doubt has grown since our work there, as Australian research universities had only recently encountered reductions in revenue shares provided by the state, thus pushing them more deeply into entrepreneurial activity.

By no means were the respective $16.3 and $12.3 million distributed evenly across the departments of the universities. Fewer than half of the university departments self-generated significant revenues, and such activity was highly concentrated in a few departments. The humanities and social sciences were unlikely to have received more than a few thousand dollars in such funding, although there were important exceptions. The same was true of most professional fields related to the social sciences, although a few notable exceptions existed; and the more basic natural science disciplines such as chemistry, physics, botany, and zoology tended to generate fairly modest sums, too (even for basic research, which was excluded from our analysis). It was in the applied science fields and professional schools—applied natural sciences, agricultural sciences, and engineering—where revenues from contracts and grants with businesses and governments were substantial.

A similar pattern was observed in the United States by Fairweather (1988) and was confirmed by Levin et al. (1987) from a survey of businesses regarding the relevance of various scientific fields to technical advances. Moreover, the distribution of funds from academic capitalism in Australian universities follows Brint's taxonomy of the relation of professions and academic disciplines to the market, discussed in Chapter Five, with the exception of business-related services. Again, with the exception of business services, the incidence of academic capitalism mirrors differences in salaries by professional field and academic discipline in the United States, suggesting that commercial markets and academic markets are interpenetrating on a global scale. (Given the different cultures, histories, and traditions of the several countries, we expect the incidence of academic capitalism to vary somewhat. For example, we were not surprised that Australia, which did not have an aggressive business class [Marshall 1995], at least in the early 1990s, exhibited little entrepreneurial activity in business services. We would expect a higher incidence of academic capitalism in business services in the United States.)

The location of academic capitalism in departments, centers, and institutes close to the market strengthens our previous arguments about the likelihood of internal differentiation within universities. As a result of the emergence of a global economy and the development of national higher education policy aimed at stimulating economic growth and innovation in business and industry, fields close to the market gain power and influence within the university. As organizational turbulence develops in response to changing revenue streams, faculty in fields close to the market are able to take advantage of competitive opportunities provided by changes in government policy as well as opportunities offered by business and industry. Faculty participation in academic capitalism is likely to increase differentiation among professions and academic disciplines within universities, since the generation of substantial revenues seems to be concentrated in the relatively small number of fields close to the market.

The relatively rapid involvement of Australian academics with the market suggests that universities and faculty stand ready to compete—engage in market and marketlike behavior—for critical resources. Those resources usually are for research, a fact that fits nicely with the university orientation toward prestige maximization; since relatively few faculty win competitive research funds from government or industry, research is the activity that differentiates among universities. Further, faculty are selective in their pursuit of external research money. They compete for basic or fundamental research funds with the same vigor as always and look for commercial research funding that draws on frontier science and engineering tied to national policy initiatives and partnered by prestigious firms, usually national or multinational in scope.[3]

The practical implications of Australian faculty's move toward the market are several. Faculty behavior may not be as difficult to change as scholars of higher education have thought. If resources do not undermine faculty status and prestige systems, a relatively small amount of money at the margins can alter faculty activity substantially. In other words, as state block grants decline, faculty in fields able to intersect with the market may move swiftly toward academic capitalism. However, change within public research universities will be uneven because the opportunities for developing market relations are uneven; nevertheless, there is abundant evidence of academic capitalism in units ranging from archaeology and poetry to criminology and physical education. Within such units, however, there is wide variation in the number of individuals who interact with the market. Moreover, faculty in such units are less able to develop research-related market relations and are more likely to sell services. How universities might manage the increasing differentiation stemming from academic capitalism is a question we turn to in the final section of this chapter.

Academic Capitalism Strategies of Institutional Leaders and Center and Department Heads

Generally we found that Australian faculty and institutional leaders were extremely sensitive to changes in the resource mix at the level of the institution and the field. In terms of technology transfer, their hope was to develop products and services that would generate resources through for-profit activity such as licensing and royalties, direct sales, or shares of faculty consulting.

The approaches administrators used to promote academic capitalism were various, but encouragement of academic capitalism was widespread. Some administrators let faculty take the initiative. These administrators provided broad policy guidelines and offered incentives to encourage faculty to develop products and processes for the market, but they did not otherwise participate. Other administrators targeted particular products and processes and regulated their development closely. Yet other administrators worked with the business community and government leaders to create a large resource pool to support the development of complex technologies. In the last case, faculty were en-

3. In the United States, big companies are the only ones with the resources to sustain multiyear funding of large research projects. For example, in biotechnology, large pharmaceutical firms initially funded buildings, research staff, and multiyear contracts in biotechnology (Slaughter 1990). Although a number of small spinoff biotechnology firms were developed by university professors, they very often were purchased by large corporations (Kenney 1986).

couraged to band together in interdisciplinary arrangements, to act as partners in relatively stable, ongoing enterprises.

Overall, we believe that administrators in all four countries will seek to develop strategies for academic capitalism which stabilize and make more predictable the resource flows to institutions. Unfettered competition (laissez-faire academic capitalism) is too risky. In the United States as early as the 1910s, The Massachusetts Institute of Technology developed the industrial liaison program to routinize market relations with corporations. Rather than working with a corporation on a single contract, MIT organized programs in areas of interest to business and industry and persuaded corporations to pay them a yearly membership fee for updates on research in science and technology (Noble 1976). Decades later, many research universities strong in the applied sciences followed suit, particularly in the 1980s.

Centers that form government-industry-university partnerships serve a similar function. They routinize support for R&D in much the same way the mission agencies did, making available large, predictable pools of funds for which faculty compete. This funding pattern provides some stability in the funding environment for research universities even though competition for the moneys is fierce.

In Australia, administrators worked with groups of faculty to develop centers that had government and industrial partners—special research centers, key centers for teaching and research, and cooperative research centers. Guaranteed government funding for multiyear contracts that ranged from A$500,000 to A$100 million per annum made resources more predictable and reliable. The Australian centers were modeled on the interdisciplinary research centers of the United Kingdom and the industry-university cooperative research programs of the United States (Hill 1993), indicating that this is a strategy common to the three countries.

Consultancy programs are another way to make resource flows from academic capitalism more predictable. In Australia, faculty and professional officers are permitted to contribute certain extramural earnings, particularly from consulting, to personal accounts. This policy not only permits some university oversight of faculty consulting activities, but allows faculty to realize higher net earnings because income taxes are avoided so long as account expenditures are for university-related purposes. In public research universities in the United States, medical schools that have clinical practice plans are the only units that operate in a somewhat similar fashion. As problems of resource dependence increase, universities in all four nations may inaugurate organized consultancies and professional practice plans, making academics' use of expertise more like that of professional consulting firms outside the university.

The heads of departments or heads of centers whom we studied were as or more active than university central administrators in aggressively developing procedures for generating revenues from entrepreneurial faculty activity, including income from technology transfer activities that provided intellectual property and shares of faculty consulting. They used new organizational structures to create interdisciplinary knowledge that tapped fresh revenue flows, and their tactics looked more like business plans than professionalization strategies. Very often the new units added large numbers of professional officers and nonacademic staff, who were fiercely loyal to center or institute heads, did not engage much with faculty, and were not very interested in teaching. They were much more a part of the commercial than the academic culture and tended to bring commercial values to their work, concentrating on making their centers more like small firms, expanding commercial activity, and generating increased profits.

Centers and institutes are the organizational vehicles for academic capitalism in Australia. They are intermediate units, positioned between departments and the central administration. As they gain power and become responsible for their own financial well-being, the likelihood is that such units will increase at an accelerating rate, given the new financial environment. If the number of such units increases, academic life within the university and among individuals in centers and institutes will change. The most fundamental change of this kind, we believe, is in the associations among members of the production unit. Some of this effect may be negative, but our evidence suggests that the outcomes are largely positive for most intraunit relationships. As units become more responsible for self-financing, their members become more interdependent. Competition for resources requires that they collaborate with each other, that they capitalize on each other's strengths while holding each other accountable for the production and quality efforts that are essential to the collective well-being.

There can also be competition within units, and the results can be either positive or negative. Whereas competition can encourage greater efforts by individuals, our interviews suggested that for the unit, the yield from cooperation was substantially greater than from internal competition, indeed, that unit members often were compelled to cooperate. Interviewees regularly referred to their determination to avoid the debilitating effects of internal rivalry.

As we noted in Chapter Five, there can also be internal unit divisiveness of another form—between full professors eager to act as entrepreneurs and junior faculty less ready to pursue academic capitalism. Junior faculty thought performance expectations had doubled; they felt they were required to demonstrate excellence in basic as well as entrepreneurial science and technology. Perhaps they will become as committed to academic capitalism as their seniors as they move up the career ladder or as career routes clarify.

There are several implications of the various administrative or leadership strategies—whether central administrators or center heads—for the university. In whatever form, these strategies direct increasing amounts of faculty and administrative time toward activities other than instruction, with no clear indication of how resources from these activities might contribute to instruction. These strategies increasingly integrate academic, commercial, and bureaucratic cultures, decreasing the distance between universities and business and industry, and between universities and government. As centers and universities increase participation in the market, the contract between faculty and society, an implicit contract that grants faculty and universities a measure of autonomy in return for disinterested knowledge that serves the public welfare, may be undermined. To some degree, academic capitalism undermines the *raison d'être* for special treatment for universities and faculty, increasing the likelihood that universities will be treated more like all other organizations and professionals more like all other intellectual workers.

Faculty as Market Actors

The tendency for faculty to act more like their counterparts in commercial organizations was apparent in our examination of faculty engaged in technology transfer, which was perhaps the most direct form of academic capitalism. Faculty developed innovative products and processes and tried to find corporate buyers for licenses to produce and market their work. With regard to altruism, professors engaged in technology transfer were ambivalent. Although they still hoped their research would benefit humankind, they began to speak about research paying its own way. If they were able to support their research with funds aimed at commercial targets, they saw no reason why other researchers could not do the same. This pattern also held true in terms of basic versus applied research. Faculty still considered basic research as the bedrock of science, but they saw entrepreneurial research as folded into that strata, forming a new composite. Merit was no longer defined as being acquired primarily through publication; instead, it was defined at least in part by success with market and marketlike activities. (For confirmation of marketlike activities figuring in merit reviews and promotion and tenure processes in the United States, see Rahm 1994; Campbell 1995; Lee 1997.) For faculty in high technology fields close to the market, knowledge was being integrated with the market and was being valued as much for its commercial potential and resource-generating capability as for the power of discovery. And discovery was being redefined to include products and processes. In each of these regards faculty were changing their conceptions of knowledge more rapidly than administrators.

Unlike the partnerships and organized consultancy arrangements discussed above, technology transfer remains relatively risky. As our Australian findings indicate, securing commercial buyers is often difficult. Even large corporations encounter economic difficulties; all too often they are purchased by or merged with other corporations. Any of these conditions may result in canceled contracts. Establishing a small firm or start-up company also may pose problems. In the United States only one in ten start-up companies is successful. Although some universities in the United States make money from patents, copyrights, and trademarks, most do not, even though the majority of Research I Universities now support offices of technology transfer.

In the future, we think technology transfer initiated by faculty will diminish as an activity. The United States is the only country in which universities hold title to intellectual property developed by faculty with federal research grants. In the other countries the patent is applied for by the faculty member who makes the discovery, but royalties are split by the various agencies that contributed to funding the work, usually involving a split among universities and various government agencies. For all countries but the United States, the partnership and consultancy arrangements discussed above are likely to result in more reliable and predictable resource streams than does technology transfer.

Conditions in the United States are in the process of changing. Historically, business and industry in the United States did not want to support research in universities because they could not capture competitive advantage, given antitrust laws that prohibited business and industry funding of generic research from which a pool of corporations could benefit (Fligstein 1990; Kleinman 1995). However, new antitrust laws in the 1980s made it possible for a group of corporations to fund precompetitive or generic research (Slaughter and Rhoades 1996). As corporations reduce their investment in their own industrial R&D laboratories or disband their industrial laboratories altogether—as was the case with Bell Laboratories—and move their R&D dollars into short-term efforts in their business divisions, they are likely to turn to universities for more of the R&D once performed in industrial laboratories. In this new environment U.S. corporations will probably discourage university ownership of patents. Instead, corporations and government very likely will promote partnerships that supply predictable resources for commercial R&D in universities, but corporations will probably own the intellectual property produced, in much the same way that they own intellectual property produced by their employees.

Whether working in university-industry-government partnerships or independently, faculty will still strive to negotiate with the party or parties involved in these market relationships. Only by mastering the intricacies of markets, in much the same way that they mastered the complexities of mission agencies' agendas and program goals, will faculty be able to retain a measure of autonomy over their work. Since faculty in fields close to the market still possess a scarce commodity—the expertise needed for product and process innovation—they are likely to retain a strong role in shaping the conditions of their work. However, business is likely to play a greater role as well, beginning, for example, to participate in the peer review process, judging the merits of the business plans attached to projects that involve commercial research, as is already the case in the Advanced Technology Program in the United States (U.S. Department of Commerce 1995).

Our central thesis at the institutional level is that organizational relationships are determined or are affected importantly by the changing financial environment. These changes have numerous implications for the individual faculty or staff members. In reverse, personal implications may affect the organization importantly. Among the implications are effects on personal autonomy, power, prestige, and personal wealth. Of course, individuals may be affected negatively or positively, depending upon their relative success.

From the viewpoint of the corporate body, internal units that generate revenues and profits for the larger organization, conceptually, are little different from resource providers. To a considerable degree, they enjoy the same kinds of powers and expect the same kinds of perquisites as do external resource providers. Academics have become important resource providers for the university and as such they possess powers and expect perquisites either individually or as collectives. In fact, the informal operating procedures of universities, their formal rules and regulations, may grant the individual considerably more privileges than are realized by successful private sector employees.

The academic staff who generate millions of dollars for universities contribute critically to the financing of the university and thus to the institutional mission, broadly defined. They make important additions to the prestige of the university. They are highly valued and in demand, and their value can only increase as third-stream revenues continue to grow in importance. "If these million-dollar-a-year staff ever realize how much they are worth to us, we are in a lot of trouble," ventured an Australian pro–vice-chancellor. In the United States the eventuality has occurred already. As economist Gordon Winston (1994, 10) writes, "What's going on appears, in significant measure, to be the working of an active market for faculty—a national market—in which prestige-seeking colleges and universities compete with each other to build institutional excellence. They do it, in important part, through the faculty they hire. Institutions vie for both faculty superstars . . . and the best of the new Ph.D.s. They bid with money but more importantly . . . [with] discretionary time."

If one is successful the rewards may be great; but if one is not, the market may not be forgiving. Some journalistic reports of the early 1990s lend interesting insights. In letters sent to forty-eight of its tenured faculty, one U.S. university (admittedly, a medical school with fewer than four hundred students) threatened to fire faculty who failed to attract research grants that would provide from 50 to 100 percent of their salaries. The university went so far as to specify the journals in which faculty should publish and the areas of research in which they should concentrate (Mangan 1994). Reporting on the current environment in the United Kingdom, Bollag (1994) quotes David Smith, president of Wolfson College at Oxford, as saying, "If you have a post open these days, you say: 'Let's find someone who can build a good research center and hope he can teach well, too.' Since research brings in the money, teaching is losing out."

In Chapter Four we reported that Philpott (1994) found a high level of stress among the staff of a highly entrepreneurial Australian university and that this was in contrast with our own findings from interviews in Oceania and Snowy Mountain Universities, which were less entrepreneurial universities, but it was similar to our interviews at Outback and New Wave Universities, as well as at the University of Science and Industry, where we only interviewed faculty involved in technology transfer. In the United States a contemporary survey (Dey 1994) confirmed earlier research establishing that time pressures and lack of personal time were by far the most common sources of faculty stress. Following were teaching loads, research or publication demands, and concerns about (job retention) reviews and about promotion. Another study (Wilger and Massy 1993, 4B), which reflected interviews with faculty at twenty U.S. higher education institutions, again found that time was the critical factor. The heading for the section labeled *Time* was *They* [the faculty] *work like dogs*.

Australian faculty complained vociferously about the increasing use of formal competition for allocating resources internally. The additional work and related stress were considerable and were particularly resented because these were funds that formerly had been distributed *pro forma* and because these additional demands were on top of already overwhelming requirements for obtaining extramural funds. Whether to regain lost funds clawed back from operating units by central administration, for teaching or graduate assistants, or even five hundred or a thousand dollars for a small research grant, virtually every little extra now was said to require a proposal.

With the growing importance of individual ability to attract third-stream revenues, personnel decisions take on added importance. This places stress not only on those who must render decisions in an increasingly litigious environment, but of course on those being reviewed as well. Tenure is becoming increasingly stressful, in part because the standards are being raised constantly (Kennedy 1993).

We were left to wonder whether all of this was manageable in the long run, whether the amount of stress upon successful entrepreneurs was sustainable. Philpott thought that the system might be near the breaking point.

Academic Capitalism and Distribution of Power within Research Universities

Alterations in patterns of resource dependence lead to changes in power relationships. Paradoxically, we see central administrators as gaining power even as they lose power. On the one hand, central administrators may lose power to centers, institutes, and departments successful at academic capitalism. In the for-profit sector internal organizational differentiation is required so that firms can interact efficiently with their resource providers; that is, differentiation results in specialized internal units being organized to deal with subsegments of the external environment (Thompson 1967). For the sake of effective and efficient overall operation, the firms' central managers may require that these units be granted considerable autonomy (Pfeffer and Salancik 1978). In short, the specialized units that are granted significant autonomy possess important authority to act independently of the larger organization and, as a result, may possess considerable power within the organization. On the other hand, central administrators may gain power because they are able to use block grants and discretionary funds to reward and build up those production units most likely to secure large amounts of external revenues through academic capitalism.

We argue that a robust test of movements of power is to trace the flow of resources. If central administrators are becoming more powerful, this will be revealed by changes in internal allocations to related expenditure functions (in accounting parlance). In fact, budget shares to administration have increased substantially in recent years, as shown in Chapter Three and in many other studies and publications of the 1980s and 1990s, although such shares now appear to have stabilized. (For a review of these developments, see Leslie and Rhoades 1995.) These increases are support for the notion that the roles and tasks of central administration are growing and that central administrators are winning out in an increasingly competitive internal struggle for scarce resources. As discussed in Chapter Three, a greater expenditure share means relatively greater activity in that expenditure category.

It follows that university governance structures will change, and that is the expectation (State Higher Education Executive Officers 1994). A decline in collegial governance appears inevitable. The role of the market in this decline appears clear. In writing on the implications of the new environment, Breneman (1993) emphasizes the role of finances. He sees administrators becoming more technocratic than academic leaders, the process becoming more management than governance. As seen by two Canadian academics, "The role of the professorate shifted with the development of entrepreneurial professors, the creation of spinoff companies, the diminution of any force at the department level, and the marginalization of academics and academic work. These developments diminished academic autonomy and altered even further the role of democratic process in the universities as they chased after the establishment of a corporate model" (Buchbinder and Rajagopal 1993, 273).

In a 1994 essay Clark Kerr wrote about the paradigm shift in academic life whereby faculty members have become committed less to the academic community and more to economic factors, the allegiance being to funding agents and outside employers. He has written of reduced willingness to serve on committees and to accept campus responsibilities. He has blamed the reward structure that emphasizes individual and group advantage over the university welfare. However, the shift may be even more pervasive. As departments and centers are reconfigured to match market opportunities, academics may find their corporate and government counterparts a more meaningful reference group than their professions or academic disciplines.

Increasingly, universities compete in complex environments. Not only is the environment characterized by many potential resource providers, often there are numerous more or less autonomous resource-providing units within government agencies or companies, each with one or more counterparts in a given university. In the United States the state governments, the federal government, alumni, students, and business firms provide resources; within the federal government the National Science Foundation, the National Endowment for the Humanities, the Department of Health and Human Services, and many others provide research and training grants and contracts; and companies have special units to deal with grant and contract work with universities. Even if potential funding agencies are not complex, they may rely upon review panels composed of specialists so that success in gaining contracts and grants is highly specialized—that is, biochemists relate to biochemists, molecular biologists to molecular biologists, economists to economists, and so forth. Individual units (such as departments) and individual academics engage in the critical interactions that affect the success or failure of these resource exchanges. In contrast, the central administrators of the university are seldom involved in the vital aspects of the contract work, nor are they usually engaged in the substantive work or even have any expert knowledge of the work. However, if universities participate regularly in university-industry-government research projects, such as the Australian cooperative research centers and the U.S. Advanced Technology Program projects, administrators may retain a powerful voice in shaping and approving these large projects.

The contrast between monopoly or monopsony (single supplier) and a competitive environment is substantial. In the traditional public university environment, where the government provides the bulk of resources in largely unstipulated fashion, and internal allocations are made by central administrators based upon collegial or political considerations, internal power is centralized. In the competitive market those who generate the resources possesses the lion's share of internal power. Yet, much power (the ability to force compliance) that affects university actions lies outside the organization. In the traditional scenario, government exercises substantial control over the university through regulation; in the competitive case, more varied resource providers exercise power over the university through market forces.

Devolution of budgets stimulates units to increase competitive revenues and to control their expenditures. This devolution is an integral part of marketization (Williams 1995). Budget devolution may serve little purpose when block grants are the overwhelmingly dominant funding mode and when resources are abundant, but devolution is almost inevitable under conditions of resource scarcity and competition.

Empirically, evidence already exists in support of this generalization. In most universities, budget authority and responsibility for more and more functions are transferred increasingly from central to operating units as fiscal stress increases. Wholesale devolution of budgets, however, is a relatively recent phenomenon, and the connections to market competition are now more clear. In the United Kingdom the major changes in financing already experienced have resulted in extensive devolution of most university budgets (Williams 1992).[4] In the United States, where changes have been more gradual,[5] several private universities have employed devolved budgets for some time, and a few public universities have begun experimenting with the technique. The functional term commonly employed to reflect budget devolution is *responsibility-centered budgeting*. That responsibility-centered budgeting is an outgrowth of the increasing role of the market is attested to by the fact that U.S. private universities are dependent upon their successful competitiveness for most of their revenues, whether from students, government, or industry.

The implications of devolution of financial authority for academic labor are large. Paramount among these are the implications for the *university as community*—an organization in which the members act in harmony for the good of the corporate body—which many believe is what the university is all about (Massy 1994; Massy and Zemsky 1994). Under devolution, or responsibility-centered budgeting, the operating unit is allocated the revenues it has earned, minus any taxes imposed by the university, and it is responsible for meeting its financial obligations from those revenues alone. The taxes or assessments are to pay for support costs, such as administration, and for cross-subsidies of units presumably having little or lesser capacity for revenue self-generation.

Financial assessments for central administration have never been well accepted by faculty—overhead costs for research grants being the best-known example—and subsidization of other units often is not well received either. Further, with devolution, central administration attempts to pass on more and more administrative responsibilities to operating units, often keeping the associated resources at the central level. We can anticipate an exacerbation of these and other problems in the United States as the move in the market direction accelerates, as has been the case in the United Kingdom.

Budget devolution is the primary vehicle for the decentralization of power and authority. Some of the implications for staff of greater power being captured at the operating unit level are direct and apparent; others, which will be discussed below, are more indirect. Major changes have occurred, and more are on the way.

In seeming contradiction, greater centralization of power is both predicted

4. Williams (1992, 29) reports that of fourteen universities studied, four had devolved budgets entirely to departments or similar cost centers; three had devolved everything save academic salaries; four had partially devolved their budgets; and three had not gone very far in this direction.

5. A U.S. professor of engineering observed that although he had never heard of devolution, and the concept had never been discussed by his administration, it was a "done deal" in his university.

theoretically and evident in public universities in this period of financial stress. While important budgetary authority and responsibility are being delegated to operating units, authority also is being transferred to central administrators along with the financial means to exercise that authority.

Tensions between academic staff and central administrators are likely to grow. Many central administrators oppose budget devolution even when market intrusion in the university is broad and deep (Williams 1995); no doubt the loss of financial authority and the accompanying negative effects on community help explain this reaction. Nevertheless, operating units are in a strong position to press their claims for autonomy. The costing and pricing of services and products that are necessary in a quasi-market system are other sources of open conflict (Williams 1995). Subsidization of university support costs is put under increasing pressure when those costs are specified in contractual agreements and when those costs increase routinely.

From both theoretical and empirical bases it is evident that in a stressful financial environment there is greater willingness by organizational stakeholders to vest in central management the power to deal with external agents. The demand is for increased central coordination of efforts and reporting mechanisms—in short, greater centralization of efforts to manage the environment on behalf of the larger organization, because, as Pfeffer and Salancik put it, "solutions . . . require the concentration of power" (1978, 284).

In the competitive environment, staff perceive that the university is at risk and that resources are inadequate to maintain existing functions. The perception is that the government philosophical support of the university is less, even if the university is not actually under government attack. Institutional preservation requires that central administration be granted authority to deal with the external environment. The university must speak with one voice, and the central administration must be able to coordinate the university response. This empowerment of administration requires that traditional shared governance procedures be modified, at least temporarily.

Another factor contributing to this centralization of power is that as operating units generate more and more of their own resources, their staff members become aware that most events of importance to them occur at the unit level. There is much to do if the unit is to survive and excel. There is less time or inclination to be involved in general university affairs, such as serving on universitywide committees; besides, staff may perceive that in the new financial environment the central administration must have greater freedom to act, anyhow. Once again, the impact on the idea of community is evident.

At the outset of this section we asserted that power is becoming both more and less centralized. How is this possible? The seeming paradox can be explained in at least two ways. Part of the answer is that although unit personnel are gaining greater power to decide matters of immediate and direct importance to them (e.g., the authority to deal directly with those who provide resources for research projects), they are surrendering power for general university governance. In turn, central administrators are relinquishing some power for resource allocation (budget devolution) while gaining greater authority in other areas. Another possibility may be a diminution of power at middle organizational levels so that the distribution takes on an hourglass shape. This answer seems logical. If the operating units have the power to make most of their own decisions about their own activities while coordinating and reporting functions are the domain of the central administration, what is left for the level of the college dean or division head? We wonder about the functional utility of these offices in the new environment, where operating units in effect generate the resources and central administration coordinates and reports. In this environment is their any need for an intermediate administrative unit?

Perhaps intermediate administrative units—large departments, colleges—will be important as differentiation increases between units involved in academic capitalism and all other units. Presumably, centers engaged with the market will interact directly with central administrators, who are deeply concerned about generating external resources. Department heads not engaged in academic capitalism as well as deans of colleges that are far from the market will very likely have to manage faculty closely, including large numbers of part-timers, who bear an ever greater share of the instructional burden. Indeed, faculty in departments and colleges far from the market may have double the teaching load that faculty engaged in academic capitalism have, requiring greater oversight at the intermediate level.

In our four nations this may be far more a speculation about future events than a statement of present reality, however. In the United States, for example, middle level administrators, such as deans, probably have lost little power or few resources (assuming there is a difference) to date; indeed, although the hard evidence is meager, the general perception is that deans are growing more powerful, not less. (One such piece of evidence is a U.S. university case study showing that over a recent five-year period, administrative expenditures at the college dean level exceeded such increases at the central administration level [Rhoades 1997].) Leslie and Rhoades (1995) reason that patterns of resource allocation within universities reflect unit organizational distance from budgetary authority: the resources one receives are in part a function of the number of levels one's unit is removed from the resource allocator. Middle managers such as deans are higher in the allocation scheme than are the production units. Further, middle managers are highly useful to central administration; for instance, the elimination of deans would greatly broaden central administrators' tasks and responsibilities. Perhaps the determining factor is that in the end it is administrators who possess the authority to reallocate resources.

In the present environment the issue is whether resource dependence pressures will increase to the point where market considerations overwhelm convenience and tradition; that is, on a cost-benefit basis, many middle level university administrators may not be justified. The recent experience regarding middle managers in the U.S. private sector, where financial pressures have already resulted in massive layoffs, illustrates what may occur in public universities. As U.S. productivity declined relative to other nations prior to the early 1990s, many middle level personnel were dismissed, sometimes ruthlessly, as pressures on profits increased. Simply put, functionally, many middle managers were found to be expendable. It may be that many middle managers in public research universities similarly may be found to be expendable, that in time resource dependence pressures will marginalize these positions. Whether this occurs will depend upon the degree to which public universities successfully resist many of the growing, natural pressures brought on by revenue declines from traditional sources, in particular growing resistance to tuition increases and increasing competition for grant and contract revenues.

In their award winning book *In Search of Excellence* (1982) Peters and Waterman included in their list of the important characteristics of America's best-run corporations the internal presence of "small, fluid organizations." Since then, in his weekly newspaper columns Peters often has reflected back on this principle, going so far as to conclude that he now believes it is the only principle of any consequence for long-term organizational vitality. The idea of the small, fluid organization is that company employees are organized or organize themselves to pursue a particular idea or area of strategic promise to the firm. Within universities, centers and institutes would seem to be the embodiment of the Peters and Waterman idea. In contrast, academic departments often are criticized for their resistance to change, for example, standing in the way of interdisciplinarity. In some cases academic departments have been notorious for their degree of internal acrimony over the direction the unit should follow.

Of course, the obstacles to reorganizing faculty and staff into new units are massive. In the absence of departmental restructuring, what occurs is the informal, but real, internal division of labor, in particular between instruction and research (Barnett and Middlehurst 1993). One means by which this occurs is the buying out of teaching and service responsibilities by those able to secure extramural funding and the assumption of those responsibilities by other unit members. Breneman (1993) sees this division of labor as desirable; he observes that academic departments could be assigned output goals and be left to work out the details. In the new environment we would expect to see the tendency toward greater division of labor to be expanded. Of course, such divisions already exist, de facto, in many if not most academic units; however, the increasingly competitive environment promises even greater demand for efficiency in the use of human resources.

In our mainstream Australian universities, under university policy, buyouts were not an option, nor did faculty entrepreneurs seem inclined to question the policy. In the United States a recent survey of faculty participating in collaborative activities with industry revealed that faculty were unwilling to consider giving up teaching to engage in academic capitalism. For these faculty, teaching was what made them different from professionals working for business and industry (Campbell 1995). However, as Campbell noted when comparing faculty attitudes toward teaching with faculty reports of responsibilities for collaborative research, faculty were probably unrealistic in their beliefs that they could continue to pursue both activities; that is, they were spending approximately three quarters of their time on academic capitalism.

Academic Capitalism and Undergraduate Education in U.S. Public Research Universities

In the United States, where public university autonomy in the internal allocation of block grant and tuition revenues is considered virtually a right, the congruence of internal university allocations with the (enrollment) bases of government appropriations often is lacking.[6] The result is that there actually may be a *disincentive* for individual internal units to enroll additional students; more students can mean nothing more than an increased workload. Operating units often promulgate regulations such as higher admission standards in order to limit student enrollments, knowing that internal allocation shares are unlikely to decline accordingly. This tendency is particularly characteristic of the professional schools, most of which are primarily upper division, or graduate schools. If resources do not follow the students the result may be an excellent educational environment for the fortunate departments and their gradu-

---

6. In more than half of the states, enrollment-based formulas drive allocations to universities; in the remaining states, enrollments implicitly serve as a primary base.

ate or upper division students but a poor environment for lower division students and less favored upper division students, for example those majoring in the humanities and social sciences. In short, deterioration in the *overall* quality of undergraduate education may result because resources are denied to units that educate the masses of students, resulting in widespread disaffections among students, the electorate, and government officials. The political pressures mount; faculty are urged to teach more. Meanwhile, the market mitigates for more functional resource allocation methods.

When universities must turn to other resource providers, they must redirect their efforts. This is nothing more than the accounting identity from Chapter Three. If revenues for a particular function decline as a share of all revenues, the expenditure share for that function will decline, too. If government, the primary provider of resources for instruction, appropriates proportionately less for universities, there will be proportionately less university attention paid to instruction, all else equal. Universities may attempt to redirect their resources, but in the end human resources can be stretched only so far. Our interviews suggest that something will give and that the breaking point may not be far off. In the end the choice is clear: less money for instruction means less instruction.

The general pattern we find with regard to institutional expenditures on the traditional tripartite faculty role—teaching, research, and service—is that less money is spent on teaching, more on research and service. The U.S. case is illustrative. Within public sector institutions between 1982–83 and 1990–91 instructional expenditures increased least, whereas the increase for research was 40 percent greater than for instruction, and the increase for public service was 30 percent greater. We argue that this change reflects the following causal sequence: a decline in block grants to higher education results in heightened organizational turbulence, which prompts faculty and administrators to seek external funding from research and service activities.[7] An alternative explanation for the alleged decreased attention to teaching focuses on faculty time allocations rather than dollars and sees the faculty reward system as the culprit (e.g., Massy and Zemsky 1994). According to this view, faculty enjoy research more than teaching, prefer to spend time on research rather than teaching, and, through control of institutional evaluation processes such as merit review and

7. Historically, public service was faculty and university pro bono work for various institutional communities. The classic example was the expertise schools of agriculture offered to farmers. However, public service is being recast. Much technology transfer and commercial science and technology are being represented as a public service even though this faculty work brings in outside grants and contracts. See Slaughter and Rhoades (1993).

promotion and tenure, shape the faculty reward system to honor research above all other activities.

As we note elsewhere, although the faculty reward system no doubt plays an important role in determining faculty behaviors, we believe that this alternative view is shortsighted and that focusing on the reward system, in the end, acts to prevent desirable changes from occurring. For decades critics of higher education, both internal and external to universities, have decried the so-called *publish or perish* syndrome. Faculty have been threatened, cajoled, implored, coaxed, and even bribed—to no apparent effect. We would argue that the explanation for this failure is that the reward system is an outgrowth of, rather than the root cause of, the problem—if in fact faculty *do* fail to give adequate attention to teaching. The *root* cause, as we see it, is resource dependence. The faculty reward system is no more than a rational response to a very mixed and constantly changing university revenue pattern. Members of the university community—faculty, administrators, staff—are rational actors who perceive correctly that they must optimize revenues from various sources and respond to those resource providers as required under the terms of the associated implicit and explicit agreements.

Admittedly, the relationships among faculty rewards and resource dependence are complex, and disentangling the causes of any changes in the allocation of faculty time and quality of effort is a difficult task. If we argue that the faculty reward system is the major cause, we should be able to document marked recent changes in that system because institutional expenditure allocations *have* changed importantly and fairly recently. Although we know of no such documentation of changes in the system, our own perceptions are that faculty incentives (salaries, tenure, promotion) increasingly do include the ability to secure grants; however, if this perception is correct, we would see this increase as a direct outgrowth of changes in resource dependence—the need to replace lost revenues. Regarding attention to teaching and research in the faculty incentive system, our vicarious observations suggest clearly that there is increasing, not reduced, attention to documenting good teaching, whereas the importance of research, though great, does not appear to us to be accelerating other than in regard to grantsmanship. *If correct, these observations would argue that the faculty incentive system is a major mechanism through which resource dependence adjustments are made by universities rather than being an independent, causal explanation for the expenditure shifts.* In other words, in response to revenue declines, university agents (e.g., administrators and the collective faculty themselves) signal individual faculty members that they should increase their efforts to secure grants, which typically are closely related to research.

Those "signals" are encompassed in changing reward systems that compensate faculty both financially and by granting to successful faculty relative power and prestige on campus.

Put another way, in responding to external forces, faculty and administrators jointly construct reward systems. Historically, administrators have been as eager as "star" faculty to push professors toward research (Caplow and McGee 1958; Jencks and Riesman 1968). Administrators provided the moneys to recruit and make offers and counteroffers to faculty who would contribute to institutional financial ledgers and prestige as manifest in national prestige ratings such as R&D Expenditures rankings. Through the mid 1970s most faculty indicated that they preferred teaching to research. From this we might speculate that the role of administrators in promoting the research emphasis was considerable.

Although we agree that the current faculty reward system—which we prefer to call an institutional reward system—privileges research, we do not think that all research is rewarded equally. It is by disaggregating fields, faculty groups, and rewards that we see the unequal return to faculty investments in research and begin to appreciate the power of resource dependence.

As we demonstrated in Chapter Two (see Table 2.2), faculty are rewarded most highly in fields close to the market. Salary differentials reflect labor markets for professionals outside the university as well as faculty potential to win external revenues for the university. The faculty in fields that command the highest salaries are those with the greatest potential for academic capitalism. Differential salaries are reinforced by institutional practices. In a study that used state dollars for research as the dependent variable, departmental ability to secure external grants and contracts was cited as the strongest predictor of institutional resource allocation (Volk 1995).

It might be argued that if the collective faculty indeed controlled the reward system they would reward basic, curiosity-driven research most highly. As we have shown through our analysis, in most countries research having economic potential is preferred to basic or curiosity-driven research. At the institutional level this preference is reflected increasingly by differentiated salaries favoring faculty in fields close to the market. More faculty may engage in research, but not all are rewarded equally.

In sum, those critics who limit their critiques to the faculty reward system disingenuously blame only the faculty for perceived lack of attention to teaching. They consider neither changes in external agencies that provide funds for higher education nor the role that administrators and others such as government agents, university trustees, and corporate leaders play in shaping institutional rewards systems. By singling out faculty in a period of fiscal duress and university destabilization, these critics, unwittingly, very likely reduce the likelihood of change in that faculty defensiveness and solidarity are thereby enhanced.

In many countries the most important source of new or additional income is in the form of tuition payments from students. The significance of tuition as a revenue source has increased as its share of university total revenues has grown. With these increases, student power to affect university decision making has grown, although student power remains relatively limited in most settings. Significant student power is already evident in Australia and the United Kingdom, where overseas students now pay (at least) full fees, and in the private institutions in the United States, where most students have long paid a large share of their educational costs. In Australia and the United Kingdom overseas students are recruited widely and vigorously; within the universities they are treated with respect if not solicitude, in particular where a substantial share of their (full) fees follows them to their units. For example, in Australia the enrolling universities receive all of the fees collected from overseas students, and the majority of these revenues are passed on to the units that enroll them. In the three universities where we conducted most of our interviews, this share averaged 60–70 percent. In the United States the income from students in most private colleges and universities (particularly the former) has composed a large share of institutional revenues for many years. The result is that students are treated as important clients, particularly in research universities in which budgets are devolved—that is, where internal units largely are responsible for generating their own revenues and for making their own spending decisions. The contrast with student treatment in public universities is often stark. Although student power within U.S. public universities presently is modest, this will change as the share of institutional revenues from tuition increases and as inevitable adjustments are made in internal resource allocation procedures.

Experiences with the full fees paid by overseas students in Australia and the United Kingdom and with the high fees paid by students in U.S. private universities having devolved budgets tell us that ongoing evolution of financial authority extends to student-based revenues. The large sums involved usually cause these universities to develop strategies to recruit these students. Because the departments of these universities possess the best information about their own programs and staff and because the recruiting task is so large, eventually recruitment incentives are established in the form of tuition profit sharing with departments.

The sharing of other tuition or other enrollment-based revenues may not automatically follow, however. In Australia block grant appropriations are allocated internally in only general conformance with enrollment distributions, although pressure is growing for greater enrollment-budget connectedness. Faced with the greatly increased demand for higher education places among native Australians who do not qualify for government financial sponsorship while ever increasing numbers of full-fee-paying overseas students are being admitted, the Australian Vice-chancellors Committee (AVCC) has urged the government to grant permission to enroll the former students at the full fee rate. The interaction of market forces and political realities may lead to approval of the AVCC request. If this occurs, one wonders whether the nation and its universities will be willing merely to substitute domestic tuition revenues for those from the overseas students or rather may choose to expand enrollments further and thus capture more tuition dollars.

Within U.S. universities, academic capitalism creates two different pressures. On the one hand, academic capitalism presses for decentralization of power to the operating units. On the other hand, it presses for differentiation among units. Centers, institutes, and departments involved in academic capitalism and bringing in substantial amounts of external revenues successfully press central administrators for decentralization of power and devolution of budgets and often for institutional funds for start-up costs for more entrepreneurial work. Central administers are generally responsive. Because central administrators use institutional funds for centers, institutes, and departments in technoscience fields likely to bring in large amounts of external funding, they have fewer funds to reward units in the communications and culture fields or in the civic regulation and human services fields, even though centers and departments in these fields raise some external revenues, recruit large numbers of students, and teach service courses for the technoscience and business services fields. Thus, academic capitalism that brings in substantial and prestigious revenues is preferred over academic capitalism that brings in fewer revenues, revenues in less prestigious areas, or increased tuition revenues.

U.S. public research universities are attempting to maximize revenues from external sources as the several state governments decrease their shares of support. U.S. public research universities have tried to attract high prestige research dollars for research and academic capitalism, particularly advanced technoscience research for government-university-industry partnerships. To do this, university central administrators use their power to make internal allocations of (marginal or incremental) block grants or unstipulated funds in accordance with their own perceptions of needs.

The power of universities to allocate block grant funds internally is the very essence of why these revenues are so important. In our lifetime the orthodoxy, to which we ourselves have subscribed strongly, has been that government should appropriate revenues and leave the internal allocations to the universities. Government may use whatever bases it desires to determine appropriations, but once the money arrives on the campus those bases can be completely ignored. Decisions about the spending of the money must be left to the institutions. Anything less is mixing policy making with administration; it is micromanagement. With great reluctance we assert that now may be time for a change.

Initially we thought public research universities should move to state-related or independent status. Elsewhere we have raised the question as to what separates a public from a private university and whether there may not now or soon be an advantage for public universities that attain quasi-public or even independent status (Leslie 1995). Most public U.S. research universities receive about 30 or 40 percent of their resources from state governments; yet, the states consider public universities to be little different from any other state institutions, and they regulate them essentially as though they were 100 percent state funded. While lecturing at Harvard, Bruce Johnstone, then chancellor of the State University of New York, observed that he received 30 percent of his money and 90 percent of his headaches from the State of New York. He seemed to argue for a new relationship. Adjoining New York, the Commonwealth (state) of Pennsylvania contains a mix of state-owned, state-related, and state-aided public universities, each experiencing varying degrees of state financial support and control. The State of Colorado operates state universities through a memorandum of understanding whereby relatively modest support is provided the universities, and relatively few constraints are imposed. In Maryland, Oregon, Virginia, and Washington, trends are in the direction of state relatedness rather than state ownership.

If the state share of public university funding continues to decline, at some point the universities will become de facto independent or private, if they are not already. Breneman (1993) believes that as student charges continue to increase, the body politic may cease to view state universities as public, causing state support to decline even more, the political bases for state oversight to diminish further, and stronger universities and colleges to seek independent status. An *Economist* article, "Universities: Towers of Babble," notes that U.S. universities have raised student fees dramatically and that quasi-market disciplines are being applied in public universities. The *Economist* wonders why "universities are still mired in the public sector," forced to tolerate governments "bent on university reform."

But the move to state-related or independent status will not solve the problem of administrative reallocation of block grants unless research universities raise tuition by extraordinary levels, which would price many students out of the market for public research institutions. The fact is that university resource allocators acted too rationally. They shifted substantial amounts of those largely unstipulated resources provided by government and students to other purposes, which often were at some odds with state government and student interests. They used significant shares of the public and student moneys to leverage additional revenues in the more competitive areas. They diverted money into research, research equipment and facilities, university companies, intellectual property offices, university foundations—all for the purpose of increasing supplementary revenues.

Some of the largest amounts were maneuvered within the instructional budget. Money was allocated less on the basis of student demand than on the basis of leveraging extramural revenues, by diverting funds to areas where the greatest potential for grants and contracts existed. At the margin, money was moved to the natural sciences and engineering and away from the social sciences, the humanities, and most of the professional schools. The primary object was to recruit faculty who would attract large sums and prestige to the university through grant and contract work, faculty who were paid relatively handsomely (Slaughter and Rhoades 1996). The net effect was to strip high enrollment units of resources needed to meet student demand and to create unit disincentives for student enrollments. Some units accomplished this by limiting class and section offerings; others raised their admissions standards.

The legacy of this era was wide public dissatisfaction with public universities. Faculty workloads, especially hours taught, came under closer scrutiny. Faculty were seen as self-indulgent and unresponsive to students (see, e.g., Massy and Zemsky 1994). Students complained to the university, to university governing boards, to their parents, and to their elected officials. University administrators were charged with correcting the problem, and when that was perceived to have failed to achieve results they were subjected to regulation and even legislation.[8]

A system that is a mixture of unstipulated and stipulated funding may be unworkable in the long run. It is to be expected that universities will move discretionary money around internally to maximize revenues from nondiscretionary sources. Although public universities probably would solve the problem for themselves eventually, the loss of public confidence in the interim may

8. For example, in the United States, two states set limits on university administrative costs.

make it unwise to wait for university action. The need for remedies in university undergraduate instruction and the regaining of public confidence is too urgent.

Thus, in what may appear to be a contradiction, *we call for state action to ensure that universities permit market principles to operate internally.* Very few, if any, university administrators or policy analysts are likely to agree with us; this is a revolutionary recommendation, which we offer with great reservation. We conclude reluctantly that to regain public confidence in public universities, government action may be required to free up internal university procedures, not to regulate them. Specifically, we urge that governments providing block grants act like any other resource provider, that they take actions to ensure *generally* that their moneys be spent for the purposes intended. We believe that to increase allocative efficiency within universities, government should provide incentives for public universities to disburse state-provided resources in *closer* concordance with student demand. *In effect we are calling for incentives for budget devolution, the allocation of state block grant money in some correspondence with student enrollment patterns and the provision for sanctions if the principles are ignored.*

Some readers will observe that governments are already actively seeking greater instructional accountability. To us these efforts are having little effect on internal university operations. The sanctions imposed are sporadic and feeble. They are no more than attempts to *regulate* the way out of the difficulty, an approach that probably has little chance for success in the face of more powerful market forces being imposed by other resource providers. We wish to emphasize that we are *not* calling for government regulation of how government money is spent; rather we are calling for getting the incentives right.

Gaining responsiveness to students for their tuition money also bears consideration. Although responsiveness to students probably is improving as tuition charges increase, students still possess relatively little consumer power in most public universities. The reason is that public higher education is monopolistic, or at best oligopolistic, chiefly because of large public subsidies. The majority of students are unwilling or unable to pay the substantially higher prices associated with private education or nonresidence status. Just as administrators and academics mediate the wishes of the state, so they do also the desires of student (Williams 1995). Simply put, student fees are collected by universities and distributed internally as universities see fit.

What is the solution? We favor devolution of tuition money, but we recognize that if government block grant providers begin to take on the characteristics of clients, alterations in the present university resource allocation ethos—

including that for tuition revenues—will occur anyhow. For this reason we favor using government aid rather than student tuition revenue as the vehicle for change. This approach will be less obtrusive politically than using tuition money as the principal mechanism because the latter funds are often paid directly to the universities. In short, universities frequently view tuition income as their own money, not the state's.

In sum, we see universities facing great changes. As the economy is making structural adjustments in response to globalization, so public research universities are trying to accommodate changes in national higher education policies and resource dependence.

Last Words

We conclude our book by looking at the implications of our data and theory for the future of public research universities. Because we are most familiar with the United States, we will concentrate on U.S. public research universities. Given the risks of prediction, we draw a worst case and best case scenario. We understand that predictions often are little more than expressions of hopes and fears, fantasies of the future as much as scientific forecasting. We start with the worst case so we can end on a more positive note, with the best case.

Under the worst case scenario, we see greater globalization of the political economy, less discretionary funding available at the national (federal) and/or state/provincial level, and continued acute institutional destabilization in higher education systems. If these conditions obtain, we think there will be greater differentiation among research universities, with a number of them being downgraded to a status more like that of comprehensive universities, offering undergraduate education, an array of master's programs, and very few doctoral degrees. We would not expect to see reduction to a single public research university per state, but we think that private universities might absorb more research functions, with students paying very high tuition to attend graduate school in all fields, as is now the case with medicine and increasingly with law. Major public research universities probably will be concentrated in those states without a strong private sector and with a high population. Those public research universities that survive will in effect be privatized, given the high tuition students will be expected to pay.

Research funds will remain approximately the same or decrease slightly but will be concentrated even more heavily on commercial science. Federal funds will be concentrated in university-industry-government partnerships in areas deemed central to national technology policy, determined largely by industry.

Industry will be heavily represented by multinational corporations delivering products, processes, and producer services to a global market. Overhead payments to universities will decrease, and universities will by and large perform the sorts of research once done by industrial laboratories. Private funds will be of the venture capital variety, and university centers, acting like small to medium sized firms, will employ high risk, high technology entrepreneurs to develop innovative products and processes with high returns. Fields far from the market will receive little in the way of federal or private funding for research.

At the same time that differentiation among public and private research universities occurs, differentiation within public research universities will become much greater. Faculty able to organize themselves in centers and become successful academic capitalists will do so, and the remaining faculty will teach more. Even in the sciences and engineering, some faculty will teach more than others, given that not all specialties have the same potential for academic capitalism—for example, physics departments may teach undergraduates whereas materials sciences centers become heavily involved in academic capitalism. And of course, some faculty in fields not commonly thought to have opportunities for academic capitalism will create them—for example, sociologists might undertake survey research projects for university-government-industry projects.

Generally, faculty in fields close to the market will teach less; those far from the market, more. Greater numbers of part-timers will be hired, until teaching departments have small cores of full-time faculty and large contingents of part time faculty, graduate assistants, and technical staff. The full-time faculty in fields far from the market will have little time for research and scholarship.

Because of the disparities among faculty, the concept of the university as a community of scholars will disintegrate further, and management will replace governance. Administrators will be most responsive to those elements of the institution which bring in increased revenues—academic capitalists and students. Faculty in centers involved in academic capitalism will continue to have considerable autonomy, although they will be monitored closely by central administration because these faculty increasingly will be critical to institutional revenues. As part-timers replace full-timers to keep costs down, administrators will assert greater control over departments, beginning by managing the large contingents of part-timers. Regents and trustees concerned with rising institutional costs will encourage administrators to take over more and more planning, until administrators rather than faculty decide which fields will grow and which will not.

Tuition will increase, and grants and subsidized loans for all but the very needy will decrease. Parents and students paying high tuition will complain about the high numbers of part-time faculty, and the pressure will build for more teaching by full-time faculty. Over time, research universities will hire more and more full-timers on a contractual basis, redeploying them as they once did part-timers. Faculty not participating in academic capitalism will become teachers rather than teacher-researchers, work on rolling contracts rather than having tenure, and will have less to say in terms of the curriculum or the direction of research universities.

The best case scenario is that the globalization process stabilizes, nations bring their budget deficits and debts under control, and funding remains steady or increases modestly at the federal and state levels for public research universities. Differentiation occurs among institutions, and some downgrading takes place, but every state has a least one relatively high quality public research university. Graduate education becomes a statewide enterprise, with particular fields and schools housed at a single campus, eliminating duplication. In some cases graduate students may have to move to the designated campus, but in many cases graduate education is conducted through advanced telecommunications systems that link campuses in a state system.

The majority of research money continues to be for university-industry-government partnerships directed toward successful competition in global markets, but some state and federal funds are set aside for regional development of small and middle sized firms that the community has a voice in shaping. A significant portion of these funds is directed toward companies that meet public service needs—for example, environmental clean-up companies, home health care service firms, and educational tutoring services. Universities form consortia with corporations, consumers, and local or regional governments to perform the research necessary for these endeavors. Public service research universities collect a modest overhead, contribute to local and regional job creation, and build companies that make reasonable profits.

Differentiation continues within universities but is somewhat different than in the worst case scenario. If policy changes permit institutional revenues to follow students, then departments and centers have broad scope in planning. They sustain themselves by recruiting and graduating students, by competing for commercial research funds or public service research funds, or by some combination of the two. Given that a relatively small number of faculty bring in large grants and contracts, most departments devote more time to teaching, or, more likely, to developing a mixed portfolio, where faculty are involved in teaching and research, probably with a heavier emphasis on teaching. To deal with fluctuation in demand and faculty concern with research, greater variation in workloads occurs. For example, in some years faculty teach three courses each term, followed by a semester in residence for research and writing. Although the research component of faculty work is preserved, more time and attention are devoted to teaching.

In this best case scenario, faculty have a greater role in governance, perhaps replacing middle level management. They capitalize on faculty initiative and develop small, fluid interdisciplinary units that are matched more closely with student demand and the external world. These units develop strategies for recruiting students and the dollars that follow them by creating programs that provide teaching, research opportunities for students, and research time for faculty to stay abreast of their fields, varying faculty work load across all members of a unit to meet overall needs.

The best case and worst case scenarios posit the two extremes. Undoubtedly, the development of the public research university of the future will be uneven, sometimes more nearly approximating the worst case, sometimes the best. In the end, developments probably will fall somewhere in between the two extremes.

CHANGES IN FINANCING
HIGHER EDUCATION IN
OECD COUNTRIES AND THE
FOUR NATIONS

THE ORGANIZATION FOR ECONOMIC COOPERATION and Development (OECD) data are available for varying time periods and are of varying currency. This is a particular problem for our purposes because the financial developments being addressed are relatively recent. Thus, for any given country, changes may have come about only during the last few years of a tabulated time period and thus may not yet have impacted the country's data series, or changes may have been so recent that the effects simply may not yet have been experienced at all.

The crudest measure of higher education financing is percent of gross national product (GNP) devoted to higher education. Although the information in Table A.1 is incomplete, dated, and comparable only in the crudest sense, it is a beginning. In Australia the percent of GNP provided to higher education institutions *by the commonwealth* in the early 1970s was 1.36 compared with 0.99 in the mid 1980s. In contrast, *considering all expenditures*, U.S. higher education had experienced an increase of from 2.10 to 2.33 over the same time period. The Australian data are more pertinent to our thesis, however, because government support is the reference point, the point of departure, upon which our thesis is based. The *total expenditure* data for the United States would contain any declines in government support *plus* any compensatory revenue gains.

Nevertheless, that total resources for public higher education were beginning to decline toward the end of the period covered in Table A.1 is apparent in Table A.2, which shows that in the United States the 3.57 annual growth rate of institutional expenditures in the 1970s had dropped a full percentage point in the first half of the 1980s. (We use the terms *resources* and *expenditures* interchangeably here because government mandates for balanced university budgets

247

Table A.1   Percentage of GNP Devoted to Higher Education

Country[a]	Year	Early 1970s	Mid 1980s
Australia	1975–88	1.36	0.99
Finland	1970–88	0.60	0.71
France	1975–84	0.68	0.67
Germany	1970–86	1.02	1.18
Greece	1974–88	0.54	0.83
Japan	1970–85	0.66	0.88
Netherlands	1970–84	1.87	1.97
Norway	1975–87	1.08	1.04
Spain	1972–86	0.22	0.51
United Kingdom	1984		0.80
United States	1970–85	2.10	2.33

Source: *Financing Higher Education: Current Patterns*, Organization for Economic Cooperation and Development, 1990.

[a] Australia: total commonwealth government grants to higher education as percentage of GDP. Finland: total expenditure on higher education as percentage of GNP.

France: total public expenditure on higher education as percentage of GDP (excluding funds for research).

Germany: total expenditure on higher education as percentage of GNP.

Greece: total expenditure on higher education as percentage of GDP.

Japan: public and private expenditure on higher education as percentage of GNP.

Netherlands: total expenditure on higher education as percentage of GNP.

Norway: total higher education expenditure as percentage of GNP.

Spain: total expenditure on higher education as percentage of GNP.

United Kingdom: public current expenditure on higher education as percentage of GNP.

United States: total expenditure on higher education as percentage of GNP (includes purchases of land, buildings, and equipment).

in most states result in revenue approximately equaling expenditures.) A more consistent pattern was evident in Australia, where the 1.9 percent annual growth rate of the last half of the 1970s in commonwealth grants (*revenues from the federal government*) had become 1.2 percent during the first eight years of the 1980s. In the United Kingdom the annual *expenditures* growth rate of 1.30 percent in the 1970s actually increased, to 1.89 percent, in the first six years of the 1980s. A change in *revenue* mix was evident, however, as the annual rates for *university general grants + subsidized fees only*, which is a revenue category, declined dramatically from 1.28 percent to –1.46 percent. Perhaps the most important realization from these data is that where revenues *from government* are considered, declines are evident, whereas when *total* revenues are reflected (in the form of total expenditures), a pattern of growth emerges. This difference may suggest that institutions are increasing revenues from other sources, in a compensatory manner.

Table A.2 Annual Rate of Growth of Current Expenditures on Higher Education Institutions at Constant Prices

Country and period	Annual rate	Country and period	Annual rate
Australia		Netherlands	
Commonwealth government		All higher education	
grants only		1975–80	2.29
1975–80	1.90	1980–85	−3.63
1980–88	1.20	Spain	
Denmark		Universities, including	
1973–80	2.39	capital expenditure	
1980–85	−1.20	1975–80	10.91
France		1980–85	6.18
Total recurrent public expenditure		United Kingdom	
1975–80	2.64	Universities	
1980–83	5.40	1970–80	1.30
Germany		1980–86	1.89
Total recurrent expenditure		Polytechnics (England only)	
1970–80	2.63	1982–86	0.51
1980–86	1.53	University general grants +	
Greece		subsidized fees only	
All higher education		1970–80	1.28
1974–80	7.18	1980–86	−1.46
1980–88	5.30	United States	
Universities		Public institutions	
1974–80	5.84	1970–80	3.57
1980–88	4.39	1981–85	2.57
Japan		Private institutions	
Public institutions		1970–80	2.20
1970–80	13.83	1981–85	3.92
1980–87	2.64		
Private institutions			
1971–80	19.84		
1980–85	7.39		

Source: Financing Higher Education: Current Patterns, Organization for Economic Cooperation and Development, 1990.

When considerations of the changing scale of the task and inflation (reflected in the *constant prices* column) are addded, the aforementioned patterns are reinforced, and additional information is gained (Table A.3). Again, in all categories where government support is considered separately, declines are evident. In Australia the most stable pattern of commonwealth grants to institutions between 1975 and 1980 becomes a decline of about 13 percent, from A$10,161 to A$8,754, in 1987 compared with 1980. In the United Kingdom

Table A.3   Average Current Institutional Expenditures per Student

Country and period[a]	In national currency	Exchange rate (in dollars)	In dollars (1990)	Constant prices
Australia				
All institutions				
1975				10,170
1980				10,161
1987	8,754	1.43	6,126	8,754
Denmark				
Universities				
1973				40,950
1980				46,660
1985	37,030	10.59	3,495	37,030
All institutions				
1973				52,235
1980				53,177
1985	40,068	10.59	3,784	40,068
France				
All institutions				
1975				6,528
1980				6,617
1988	17,513	5.96	2,915	6,227
Germany				
All institutions				
1985	11,700	2.94	3,976	
Greece				
All institutions				
1974	22,402	30.00	747	58,400
1980	70,800	42.64	1,660	70,800
1988	285,849	141.64	2,018	67,000
Universities				
1974	22,939	30.00	765	59,800
1980	79,600	42.64	1,867	79,600
1988	343,019	141.64	2,422	80,400
Other				
1974	18,720	30.00	624	48,800
1980	46,000	42.64	1,079	46,000
1988	182,175	141.64	1,286	42,700
Japan				
National institutions				
1971	468,000	348.94	1,341	468,000
1980	1,215,000	226.70	5,360	545,000
1985	1,424,000	238.62	5,968	558,000

Table A.3   *(Continued)*

Country and period[a]	In national currency	Exchange rate (in dollars)	In dollars (1990)	Constant prices
Japan				
Private institutions				
1971	165,000	348.94	473	165,000
1980	704,000	226.70	3,105	316,000
1985	1,062,000	238.62	4,451	416,000
Netherlands				
All institutions				
1975	15,400	2.53	6,087	21,000
1980	18,800	1.98	9,457	18,800
1985	18,000	3.32	5,608	16,800
Universities				
1985	23,665	3.32	7,126	
Other institutions				
1985	8,262	3.32	2,488	
Norway				
Universities				
1975	32,857	5.22	6,291	
1981	48,922	5.73	8,535	
1987	67,556	6.74	10,028	
Nonuniversity				
1981	26,733	5.73	4,664	
1987	43,137	6.74	6,403	
Portugal				
Laboratory subjects				
1987	371,200	140.79	2,637	
Other subjects				
1987	129,500	140.79	920	
Spain				
All institutions				
1975	33,268	57.40	580	33,268
1981	99,525	92.26	1,079	38,816
1985	154,070	170.06	906	39,273
United Kingdom				
Universities (all recurrent income)				
1970–71	1,333	0.41	3,259	5,787
1980–81	5,010	0.50	10,060	5,010
1986–87	7,926	0.61	12,950	5,581
Universities (grants + fees)				
1970–71	1,033	0.41	2,526	4,485
1980–81	3,998	0.50	8,028	3,998
1986–87	5,445	0.61	8,897	3,836

(Continued on next page)

Table A.3   *(Continued)*

Country and period[a]	In national currency	Exchange rate (in dollars)	In dollars (1990)	Constant prices
Polytechnics				
1982–83	3,429	0.66	5,196	3,041
1986–87	3,770	0.61	6,160	2,655
Polytechnics (grants + fees)				
1982–83	3,330	0.66	5,045	2,608
1986–87	3,555	0.61	5,808	2,352
United States				
All institutions				
1969–70	2,452	1.00	3,349	7,526
1980–81	7,263	1.00	7,263	7,263
1984–85	10,049	1.00	10,049	8,065
1986	11,049	1.00	11,049	
Public institutions				
1967–70	2,908	1.00	2,908	6,536
1980–81	6,365	1.00	6,365	6,365
1984–85	8,724	1.00	8,724	7,001
Private institutions				
1969–70	4,510	1.00	4,510	10,135
1980–81	10,003	1.00	10,003	10,003
1984–85	13,955	1.00	13,955	11,200

Source: Financing Higher Education: Current Patterns, Organization for Economic Cooperation and Development, 1990.

[a] Australia: Commonwealth grants to institutions (1987 prices).

Denmark: Ministry of Education appropriations (1985 prices).

France: Budget of Ministry responsible for Higher Education (1974 prices) excludes expenditures specifically for research.

Germany: All institutional expenditures except hospitals attached to universities.

Greece: Ministry of Education budget (1980 prices).

Japan: All institutional expenditure (1971 prices).

Netherlands: All recurrent expenditures (1980 prices). If research is excluded, the university figure for1985 is about Gld 12,000 or $3,000.

Norway: Net current expenditure in public institutions.

Portugal: Institutional expenditure.

Spain: Institutional budgets (1975 prices).

United Kingdom: Institutional expenditures (1980–81 prices). If research is excluded, the universities' grants-plus-fees figure for 1986–87 falls to about $6,600. Polytechnics figures are for England only.

United States: Current-fund expenditures, all sources of income (1980–81 prices).

government support (grants + fees) declines for both the universities and the (English) polytechnics. Where total revenues are reflected (data actually are for total expenditures), a pattern of increases is apparent during the most recent and pertinent years. In the United States total public institution expenditures, ergo revenues, increase by about 10 percent ($7,001 versus $6,365), and in the *universities* category in the United Kingdom the increase is about 11 percent ($5,010 versus $5,581). The only category that at first glance seems inconsistent with the patterns and our theme is *English polytechnics*, where total income declines. Two hypotheses are offered on the basis of the above data: (1) government support has declined and, overall, public institutions have compensated by increasing revenues from other sources; (2) nonuniversities, such as polytechnics, are less able (or successful) than universities in attracting compensating revenues as government support declines.

These postulates are only partially testable using OECD data (see Table A.4). In 1970–71 *general public funds* comprised 71.20 percent of British university income compared with 55.00 percent in 1986–87. For the universities, *fees* made up more than twice as large a share in 1986–87 than they had in 1970–71, 13.70 versus 6.30 percent, although roughly half of the fees came from public funds, rendering these data problematic. A better test is represented by *other income*, which shows an increase from 22.40 to 31.30 percent over the time period. In the United States *general public funds* shares for all public institutions combined declined from 61.10 to 59.30 percent; *fees* declined by 0.60 percent; and *other income* shares increased from 23.70 to 26.30 percent over a similar time period. These data would seem to support the first hypothesis of shifting reliance toward nongovernmental revenue sources. However, the data are not adequate to test for differences between universities and nonuniversities. We know for example that U.S. community colleges, on the whole, have become more dependent on state governments and less dependent on local governments. In this data set the lack of university versus nonuniversity data for the United States and of financial data for polytechnics for the baseline year makes analysis for this sector impossible. For better insights, we will have to turn to data from individual countries.

Table A.4   Sources of Income of Higher Education Institutions

Country and period[a]	General public funds	Fees	Other income
Australia			
1987	87.96	2.11	9.93
Finland			
Public institutions			
1987	85.00	n.a.[b]	15.00
France			
All institutions			
1975	93.00	2.90	4.20
1984	89.50	4.70	5.80
Germany			
All higher education			
1986	68.50	0.00	31.50
Japan			
Private four-year institutions			
1971	9.00	75.80	51.10
1985	15.00	65.80	19.10
Public institutions			
1970	83.10	2.00	14.90
1987	63.10	8.80	28.00
All institutions			
1971	53.06	31.69	15.20
1985	41.99	35.78	22.20
Netherlands			
All institutions			
1985	80.00	12.00	8.00
Norway			
Public institutions			
1975	95.00	n.a.	5.00
1987	90.00		10.00
Spain			
Universities			
Mid 1980s	80.00	20.00	n.a.
United Kingdom			
Universities			
1970–71	71.20	6.30	22.40
1986–87	55.00	13.70	31.30
Polytechnics (England only)			
1986–87	72.40	16.20	11.40

Table A.4   *(Continued)*

Country and period[a]	General public funds	Fees	Other income
United States			
Private institutions			
1969–70	20.70	38.60	40.60
1984–85	18.40	38.70	42.90
Public institutions			
1969–70	61.10	15.10	23.70
1984–85	59.30	14.50	26.30
All institutions			
1969–70	46.50	20.50	29.90
1986	44.80	22.40	32.80

Source: Financing Higher Education: Current Patterns, Organization for Economic Cooperation and Development, 1990.

[a] Finland: Figures for fees not available but very small.

France: Expenditure of National Ministry of Education.

Japan: 73 percent of other income is revenue of hospitals attached to universities.

Norway: Figures for fees not available but very small.

United Kingdom: Almost all the fees of undergraduate students are paid out of public funds. This amounts to about half the fee income of universities and probably a greater proportion of the fee income of polytechnics.

United States: Figures include all government expenditure at all levels. Loans and grants to students amounted to about 80 percent of fees in 1969–70 and 95 percent in 1984–85

[b] n.a. not available.

REFERENCES

Abbott, Andrew D. 1988. *The System of Professions: An Essay on the Division of Expert Labor.* Chicago: University of Chicago Press.

American Association of University Professors. 1915. General report on the committee on academic freedom and tenure: General declaration on principles and practical proposals. *Bulletin of the American Association of University Professors* 1:17–18.

Anderson, Richard E., and Barry Sugarman. 1989. Options for technology transfer. *Capital Ideas* 4:1–15.

Aronowitz, Stanley, and William DiFazio. 1994. *The Jobless Future: Sci-Tech and the Dogma of Work.* Minneapolis: University of Minnesota Press.

Atkinson, Anthony, Lee Rainwater, and Timothy M. Smeeding. 1995. *Income Distribution in OECD Countries: Evidence from the Luxembourg Income Study.* Paris: Organization for Economic Cooperation and Development.

Barnet, Richard J., and John Cavanagh. 1994. *Global Dreams: Imperial Corporations and the New World Order.* New York: Simon and Schuster.

Barnett, Ronald, and Robin Middlehurst. 1993. The lost profession. *Higher Education in Europe* 18:110–28.

Bell, Daniel. 1973. *The Coming of Post-industrial Society: A Venture in Social Forecasting.* New York: Basic Books.

Bell, Stephen, and Jan Sadlak. 1992. Technology transfer in Canada: Research parks and centers of excellence. *Higher Education Management* 4:227–44.

Ben-David, Joseph. 1965. The scientific role: The conditions of its establishment in Europe. *Minerva* 4:15–54.

Benjamin, Ernst. 1996. Review of *Strangers in Their Own Land: Part Time Faculty in American Community Colleges,* by J. E. Roueche, S. D. Roueche, and M. D. Milliron. *Academe* 82:71.

Berdahl, Robert O. 1959. *British Universities and the State.* Berkeley: University of California Press.

Berdahl, Robert O., Martha Levin, and John Ziegenhagen. 1978. *Statewide Coordination and Governance of Postsecondary Education: Quality, Costs and Accountability.* Wayzata, Minn.: Spring Hill Center.

Bledstein, Burton J. 1976. *The Culture of Professionalism: The Middle Class and the Development of Higher Education in America.* New York: Norton.

Blumenthal, David, Sherrie Epstein, and James Maxwell. 1986. Commercializing university research: Lessons from the experience of the Wisconsin Alumni Research Foundation. *New England Journal of Medicine* 31:1621–26.

Blumenthal, David, Michael Gluck, Karen Seashore Louis, Michael A. Stoto, and David

Wise. 1986a. University-industry research relationships in biotechnology: Implications for the university. *Science* 232:1361–66.

Blumenthal, David, Michael Gluck, Karen Seashore Louis, and David Wise. 1986b. Industrial support of university research in biotechnology. *Science* 231:242–46.

Bok, Derek. 1993. *The Cost of Talent: How Executives and Professionals Are Paid and How it Affects America.* New York: Free Press.

Bollag, Burton. 1994. Rectors of Europe's universities discuss economic forces reshaping their institutions. *Chronicle of Higher Education* September:A67.

Bonefeld, Werner. 1993. Crisis of theory: Bob Jessop's theory of capitalist reproduction. *Capital and Class* 50:25–47.

Bowles, Samuel. 1992. Post-Marxian economics: Labour, learning, and history. In *Interfaces in Economic and Social Analysis,* edited by Ulf Himmelstrand, 95–111. London: Routledge.

Braverman, Harry. 1975. *Labor and Monopoly Capital: The Degradation of Work in the Twentieth Century.* New York: Monthly Review Press.

Breneman, David W. 1993a. Guaranteed student loans: Great success or dismal failure? In *ASHE Reader on Finance in Higher Education,* edited by David W. Breneman, Larry L. Leslie, and Richard Anderson, 377–87. Needham Heights, Mass: Ginn.

———. 1993b. *Higher Education: On a Collision Course with New Realities.* Washington, D.C.: Association of Governing Boards of Universities and Colleges.

Brint, Steven G. 1994. *In an Age of Experts: The Changing Role of Professionals in Politics and Public Life.* Princeton: Princeton University Press.

Buchbinder, Howard, and Janice Newson. 1990. Corporate-university linkages in Canada: Transforming a public institution. *Higher Education* 20:355–79.

Buchbinder, Howard, and P. Rajagopal. 1993. Canadian universities and the politics of funding. In *The Funding of Higher Education: International Perspectives,* edited by Philip G. Altbach and D. Bruce Johnstone, 271–85. New York: Garland Publishing.

———. 1995. Canadian universities and the impact of austerity on the academic workplace. In *Academic Work: The Changing Labour Process in Higher Education,* edited by John Smyth, 60–73. London: Society for Research into Higher Education and Open University Press.

Business–Higher Education Forum. 1983. *America's Competitive Challenge: The Need for a National Response.* Washington, D.C.: Business–Higher Education Forum, April.

———. 1986a. *Export Controls: The Need to Balance National Objectives.* Washington, D.C.: Business–Higher Education Forum, January.

———. 1986b. *An Action Agenda for American Competitiveness.* Washington, D.C.: Business–Higher Education Forum, September.

Campbell, Teresa D. 1995. Protecting the public's trust: A search for balance among benefits and conflicts in university-industry relations. Ph.D. diss., University of Arizona, Tucson.

Caplow, Theodore, and Reece McGee. 1958. *The Academic Market Place.* New York: Basic Books.

Carnoy, Martin. 1993. Multinationals in a changing world economy: Whither the nation state? In *The New Global Economy in the Information Age: Reflections on Our Changing World,* edited by Martin Carnoy, M. Castells, S. S. Cohen, and F. H. Cardoso, 45–96. University Park, Pa.: Pennsylvania State University Press.

Castells, Manuel. 1993. The informational economy and the new international division of labor. In *The New Global Economy in the Information Age: Reflections on Our Changing World,* edited by Martin Carnoy, M. Castells, S. S. Cohen, and F. H. Cardoso, 1544. University Park, Pa.: Pennsylvania State University Press.

Castells, Manuel, and Laura D'Andrea Tyson. 1988. High technology choices ahead: Restructuring interdependence. In *Growth, Exports, and Jobs in a Changing World Economy,* edited by John Sewell and Stuart Tucker, 55–95. Washington, D.C.: Transaction Books.

Cheit, Earl F. 1971. *The New Depression in Higher Education.* New York: McGraw-Hill.

Chomsky, Noam. 1994. *World Orders Old and New.* New York: Columbia University Press.

Clark, Burton. 1993. The problem of complexity in modern higher eduction. In *The European and American University since 1880,* edited by S. Rothblatt and B. Wittrock, 263–79. Cambridge, U.K.: Cambridge University Press.

Clinton, Bill, and Al Gore. 1992. *Technology, the Engine of Economic Development: A National Technology Policy for America.* Little Rock, Ark.: National Campaign Headquarters.

Cohen, Stephen S. 1993. Geo-economics: Lessons from America's mistakes. In *The New Global Economy in the Information Age: Reflections on Our Changing World,* edited by Martin Carnoy, M. Castells, S. S. Cohen, and F. H. Cardoso, 97–148. University Park, Pa.: Pennsylvania State University Press.

Cohen, Stephen S., and John Zysman. 1987. *Manufacturing Matters: The Myth of the Post-industrial Economy.* New York: Basic Books.

Collins, Randall. 1979. *The Credential Society.* New York: Academic Press.

Committee on Science, Engineering, and Public Policy. 1992. *The Government Role in Civilian Technology: Building a New Alliance.* Washington, D.C.: National Academy Press.

———. 1993. *Science, Technology, and the Federal Government: National Goals for a New Era.* Washington, D.C.: National Academy Press.

Cooperative Institutional Research Program and American Council on Education. 1994. *The American Freshman: National Norms for Fall 1994.* Los Angeles: Cooperative Institutional Research Program.

Crean, Simon. 1990. Science policy. Paper presented at the Australian Tertiary Institutions Consulting Companies Association conference, Canberra, Australia, June 1990.

Dawkins, J. S. 1988. *Higher Education: A Policy Statement.* Canberra, Australia: Australian Government Publishing Service.

de la Mothe, John R. 1987. Educating for progress: Post-modernist images of the university-industry interface. *Quarterly Journal of Education* 11:89–95.

Denison, Edward F. 1962. *The Sources of Economic Growth in the United States and the Alternatives before Us.* New York: Committee for Economic Development.

Department of Employment, Education, and Training. 1993. *National Report on Australia's Higher Education Sector.* Canberra, Australia: Australian Government Publishing Service.

Dey, Eric L. 1994. Dimensions of faculty stress: A recent survey. *Review of Higher Education* 17:305–22.

Dickson, David. 1984. *The New Politics of Science.* New York: Pantheon.

Dimancescu, Dan, and James W. Botkin. 1986. *The New Alliance*. Cambridge, Mass.: Ballinger.

Dunn, L. 7. 1977. Quantifying nonpecuniary returns. *Journal of Human Resources* 12:347–59.

Durkheim, Emile. 1951. *Suicide: A Study in Sociology*. New York: Free Press.

Eicher, Jean-Claude, and Thierry Chevaillier. 1992. Rethinking the financing of post-compulsory education. *Higher Education in Europe* 17:6–32.

Elliott, James F. 1995. Provincial expenditures for postsecondary education in Canada, 1977–1991. Ph.D. diss., University of Arizona, Tucson.

Etzkowitz, Henry. 1983. Entrepreneurial scientists and entrepreneurial universities in American academic science. *Minerva* 21:198–233.

———. 1989. Entrepreneurial science in the academy: A case of the transformation of norms. *Social Problems* 36:14–29.

———. 1992. Individual investigators and their research groups. *Minerva* 30:29–50.

———. 1994. Academic-industry relations: A sociological paradigm for economic development. In *Evolutionary Economics and Chaos Theory: New Directions in Technology Studies?* edited by Loet Leydesdorff and Peter Van den Besselaar, 139–51. London: Pinter.

Etzkowitz, Henry, and Loet Leydesdorff. 1996. The triple helix: University-industry-government relations. A laboratory for knowledge-based economic development. Paper presented at the Triple Helix Conference, Amsterdam, April.

Etzkowitz, Henry, and Loet Leydesdorff, eds. 1997. *Universities in the Global Knowledge Economy: A Triple Helix of Academic-Industry-Government Relations*. London: Cassell.

Fairweather, James S. 1988. *Entrepreneurship and Higher Education*. Washington, D.C.: Association for the Study of Higher Education.

———. 1989. Academic research and instruction: The industrial connection. *Journal of Higher Education* 60:388–407.

Feller, Irwin. 1988a. Evaluating state advanced technology programs. *Evaluation Review* 12:232–52.

———. 1988b. Universities as engines of R&D-based economic growth: They think they can. Paper prepared for the Association for Public Policy Analysis and Management's Annual Research Conference, October.

Feller, Irwin, and S. Seshadri. 1989. The impacts of state technology programs on American research universities. Paper prepared for the Anglo-American Conference on Research Universities. University of York, September.

———. 1990. The evolving market for university patent rights. Pennsylvania State University, mimeographed.

Finegold, Kenneth, and Theda Skocpol. 1995. *State and Parity in America's New Deal*. Madison: University of Wisconsin Press.

Fligstein, Neil. 1990. *The Transformation of Corporate Control*. Cambridge, Mass.: Harvard University Press.

Forman, Paul. 1987. Beyond quantum electronics: National security as basis for physical research in the U.S. 1940–1960. Part 1. *Historical Studies in the Physical and Biological Sciences* 18:149–229.

————. 1994. Recent science: Late modern and post modern. Paper prepared for conference on the historiography of recent science, Goteborg University.

Freidson, Eliot. 1986. *Professional Powers: A Study of the Institutionalization of Formal Knowledge.* Chicago: University of Chicago Press.

Friedman, Milton. 1981. *The Invisible Hand in Economics and Politics.* Pasir Panjang, Singapore: Institute of Southeast Asian Studies.

————. 1991. *Monetarist Economics.* Cambridge, Mass.: Blackwell.

Friedman, Milton, and Kurt R. Leube. 1987. *Essence of Friedman.* Stanford: Hoover Institution Press.

Frobel, Folker, Jurgen Heinrichs, and Otto Kreye. 1980. *The New International Division of Labor.* Cambridge, U.K.: Cambridge University Press.

Fulton, Oliver. 1991. Slouching towards a mass system: Society, government, and institutions in the United Kingdom. *Higher Education* 21:589–605.

Furner, Mary O. 1975. *Advocacy and Objectivity: A Crisis in the Professionalization of American Social Science, 1865–1905.* Lexington, Ky.: University of Kentucky Press.

Furstenbach, John. 1993. University strategies for the third stream of income. In *The Funding of Higher Education: International Perspectives,* edited by Philip G. Altbach and D. Bruce Johnstone, 45–61. New York: Garland Publishing.

Gamble, Andrew. 1989. Privatization, Thatcherism, and the British state. *Journal of Law and Society* 16:1–20.

Geiger, Roger L. 1989. Milking the sacred cow: Research and the quest for useful knowledge in the American university since 1920. *Science, Technology, and Human Values* 13:322–48.

Geiger, Roger, and Irwin Feller. 1993. The dispersion of academic research during the 1980s. *Journal of Higher Education* 63:336–60.

Gellert, Claudius, ed. 1993. *Higher Education in Europe.* London: Jessica Kingsley.

Gering, Thomas, and Helwig Schmied. 1993. Intellectual property issues: Technology licensing. Costs versus benefits. *Higher Education Management* 5:100–110.

Gibbons, Michael, et al. 1994. *The New Production of Knowledge: The Dynamics of Science and Research in Contemporary Societies.* Thousand Oaks, Calif.: Sage.

Gilley, Wade. 1986. Higher education and economic development: A symbiotic relationship. *Issues in Higher Education and Economic Development.* Washington D.C.: American Association of State Colleges and Universities.

Goggin, Malcolm, and William Blanpied. 1986. *Governing Science and Technology in a Democracy.* Knoxville, Tenn.: University of Tennessee Press.

Government-University-Industry Research Roundtable. 1992. *Fateful Choices: The Future of the U.S. Academic Research Enterprise.* Washington, D.C.: National Academy Press.

Griliches, Zvi. 1980. R&D and the productivity slowdown. *American Economic Review* 70:343–48.

Grubb, W. Norton, and John Tuma. 1991. Who gets student aid? Variations in access to aid? *Review of Higher Education* 14:359–82.

Gummett, Philip. 1991. The evolution of science and technology policy: A U.K. perspective. *Science and Public Policy* 18:31–37.

Gumport, Patricia, and Brian Pusser. 1995. A case of bureaucratic accretion: Context and consequences. *Journal of Higher Education* 66:493–520.

Guthrie, James W., and Lawrence C. Pierce. 1990. The international economy and national education reform: A comparison of education reforms in the United States and Great Britain. *Oxford Review of Education* 16:179–205.

Hackett, E. J. 1990. Science as a vocation in the 1990s: The changing organizational culture of academic science. *Journal of Higher Education* 61:241–77.

Halliday, Jo. 1993. Maoist Britain? The ideological function of vocationalizing the higher education curriculum. *Curriculum Studies* 1:365–81.

Harrison, Bennett, and Barry Bluestone. 1990. *The Great U-turn: Corporate Restructuring and the Polarizing of America.* New York: Basic Books.

Haskell, Thomas L. 1977. *The Emergence of Professional Social Science: The American Social Science Association and the Nineteenth-Century Crisis of Authority.* Urbana, Ill.: University of Illinois Press.

Haveman, R. H., and B. L. Wolfe. 1984. Schooling and economic well-being: The role of nonmarket effects. *Journal of Human Resources* 19:377–407.

Hearn, James C., and David Longanecker. 1993. Enrollment effects of postsecondary pricing policies. In *ASHE Reader on Finance in Higher Education,* edited by David W. Breneman, Larry L. Leslie, and Richard Anderson, 275–90. Needham Heights, Mass.: Ginn.

Henderson, Jeffrey, and Manuel Castells. 1987. *Global Restructuring and Territorial Development.* London: Sage.

Herken, Gregg. 1992. *Cardinal Choices: Presidential Science Advising from the Atomic Bomb to SDI.* New York: Oxford University Press.

Hill, Stephen. 1993. Concentration of minds: Research centres in Australia. Paper presented to the Third International Conference on University-Industry Relations. State University of New York at Purchase, May 1.

Hill, Stephen, and Timothy Turpin. 1993. The clashing of academic symbols. *Science as Culture* 20:1–35.

Jaschik, Scott. 1987. States trying to assess the effectiveness of highly touted economic programs. *Chronicle of Higher Education* June 3:19.

Jellema, William W. 1971. *The Red and the Black.* Washington, D.C.: Association of American Colleges.

———. 1973. *Redder and Much Redder.* Washington, D.C.: Association of American Colleges.

Jencks, Christopher, and David Riesman. 1968. *The Academic Revolution.* Garden City, N.Y.: Doubleday.

Jessop, Robert. 1993. Towards a Schumpeterian workfare state? Preliminary remarks on post-Fordist political economy. *Studies in Political Economy* 40:7–39.

Johnes, Geraint. 1992. Bidding for students in Britain: Why the UFC auction failed. *Higher Education* 23:173–82.

Johnson, Lynn G. 1984. *The High Technology Connection: Academic/Industry Cooperation for Economic Growth.* ASHE-ERIC Higher Education Research Report 6. Washington, D.C.: Association for the Study of Higher Education.

Jones, Glen. 1991. Modest modifications and structural stability. *Higher Education* 21:573–87.

Jones, Glen, and Michael Skolnik. 1992. A comparative analysis of arrangements for state coordination of higher education in Canada and the United States. *Journal of Higher Education* 63:121–42.

Joseph, R. A. 1989a. Technology parks and their contribution to the development of technology-oriented complexes in Australia. *Government and Planning* 7:173–92.

———. 1989b. The politics of high technology in Australia. *Prometheus* 17:103–29.

Julien, Gilles. 1989. The funding of university research in Canada: Current trends. *Higher Education Management* 1:66–72.

Kennedy, Donald. 1984. Witness testimony at U.S. Congress, Senate Committee on Commerce, Science, and Transportation, Subcommittee on Science, Technology, and Space. *Congressional Record* 98th Cong., 1st sess., 81–85.

———. 1993. Making choices in the research university. *Daedalus* 122:127–55.

Kenney, M. 1986. *Biotechnology: The University-Industrial Complex.* New Haven: Yale University Press.

Kerr, Clark. 1994. Knowledge, ethics, and the new academic culture. *Change* January/February:9–15.

Kevles, Daniel J. 1978. *The Physicists.* New York: Knopf.

Kevles, Daniel J., and Leroy E. Hood. 1992. *The Code of Codes: Scientific and Social Issues in the Human Genome Project.* Cambridge, Mass.: Harvard University Press.

Kleinman, Daniel L. 1995. *Politics on the Endless Frontier: Postwar Research Policy in the United States.* Durham, N.C.: Duke University Press.

Kogan, Maurice, and David Kogan. 1983. *The Attack on Higher Education.* London: Kogan Page.

Krimsky, Sheldon. 1991. *Biotechnics and Society: The Rise of Industrial Genetics.* New York: Praeger.

Kuttner, Robert. 1991. *The End of Laissez-faire: National Purpose and the Global Economy after the Cold War.* New York: Knopf.

Lambright, W. Henry, and Dianne Rahm. 1991. Science, technology and the states. *Forum for Applied Research and Public Policy* 6:48–60.

Larson, Magali S. 1977. *The Rise of Professionalism: A Sociological Analysis.* Berkeley: University of California Press.

Latour, B., and S. Woolgar. 1979. *Laboratory Life: The Social Construction of Scientific Facts.* Thousand Oaks, Calif.: Sage.

Lederman, Leonard L. 1991. U.S. research and development policy and priorities and comparisons with selected countries: Canada, France, Germany, Japan, Sweden, United Kingdom, and United States. In *What Should Be Done? What Can Be Done? Science and Technology Policy Research: Proceedings of the NISTEP International Conference on Science and Technology Policy Research,* edited by H. Inose, M. Kawasaki, and F. Kodama, 343–66. Tokyo: Mita Press.

Lee, Y. 1997. Technology transfer and the research university: A search for the boundaries of university-industry collaboration. *Research Policy,* in press.

Leslie, Larry L. 1995. *Toward Privatization of Public Universities.* Tucson, Ariz.: Center for the Study of Higher Education.

———. 1996. What drives higher education management in the 1990s and beyond?: The new era in financial support. *Journal of Higher Education Management* 10: 5–16.

Leslie, Larry L., and Paul T. Brinkman. 1988. *The Economic Value of Higher Education.* New York: American Council on Education and Macmillan.

Leslie, Larry L., and Gary P. Johnson. 1974. The market model and higher education. *Journal of Higher Education* 15:1–20.

Leslie, Larry L., and Howard F. Miller, Jr. 1974. Higher education and the steady state. ERIC Research Report 4. Washington, D.C.: ERIC Clearinghouse on Higher Education.

Leslie, Larry L., and Gary Rhoades. 1995. Rising administrative costs: On seeking explanations. *Journal of Higher Education* 66:41–61.

Leslie, Stuart. 1993. *The Cold War and American Science: The Military-Industrial-Academic Complex at MIT and Stanford.* New York: Columbia University Press.

Levin, Richard C., Alvin K. Klevorick, Richard R. Nelson, and Sidney G. Winter. 1987. Appropriating the returns from industrial research and development. *Brookings Papers on Economic Activity* 3:783–831.

Lewington, Jennifer. 1994. Canada proposes major changes in financing. *Chronicle of Higher Education* October 19:60.

Leydesdorff, Loet. 1994. New models of technological change: New theories for technology studies? In *Evolutionary Economics and Chaos Theory: New Directions in Technology Studies?* edited by Loet Leydensdorff and Peter Van den Besselaar, 180–92. London: Pinter.

Louis, Karen S., Melissa Anderson, and Lenn Rosenberg. 1995. Academic misconduct and values: The department's influence. *Review of Higher Education* 18:393–422.

Louis, K. S., D. Blumenthal, M. E. Gluck, and M. A. Stoto. 1989. Entrepreneurs in academe: An exploration of behaviors among life scientists. *Administrative Science Quarterly* 34:110–31.

Lyotard, Jean-François. 1984. *The Postmodern Condition: A Report on Knowledge,* translated by Geoffrey Bennington and Brian Massumi. Minneapolis: University of Minnesota Press.

Mahony, David. 1994. Government and the universities: The "new mutuality" in Australian higher education. A national case study. *Journal of Higher Education* 65: 123–46

Mangan, Katherine S. 1994. Hahnemann U. angers faculty with threat to fire those who don't attract grant money. *Chronicle of Higher Education* October 5:A20.

Mansfield, Edwin. 1980. Basic research and productivity increase in manufacturing. *American Economic Review* 70:863–73.

———. 1989. The social rate of return to academic research. Paper presented at the Annual Meeting of the American Economic Association, December.

Marginson, Simon. 1993. *Education and Public Policy in Australia.* Cambridge, U.K.: Cambridge University Press.

———. 1995. Markets in higher education: Australia. *Academic Work* 17–39.

Marshall, Neil. 1995. Policy communities, issue networks, and the formulation of Australian higher education policy. *Higher Education* 30:273–93.

Martin, Ben R., and John Irvine. 1992. Government spending: Trends in government spending on academic and related research. An international comparison. *Science and Public Policy* 19:311–19.

Martin, Ben R., John Irvine, and Phoebe A. Isard. 1990. Input measures: Trends in U.K.

government spending on academic and related research. A comparison with Federal Republic of Germany, France, Japan, the Netherlands, and U.S.A. *Science and Public Policy* 17:3–13.

Martino, Joseph P. 1992. *Science Funding: Politics and Porkbarrel.* New Brunswick, N.J.: Transactions.

Marx, Karl. 1975. *Karl Marx, Frederick Engels: Collected Works,* translated by Richard Dixon. New York: International Publishers.

Massy, William F. 1994. *Resource Allocation Reform in Higher Education.* Washington, D.C.: National Association of College and University Business Officers.

Massy, William F., and Robert Zemsky. 1990. *The Dynamics of Academic Productivity.* Denver: State Higher Education Officers.

———. 1994. Faculty discretionary time: Departments and the academic ratchet. *Journal of Higher Education* 65:1–22.

Matkin, Gary W. 1990. Commercializing the university: The practical consequences of overturning university tradition. Paper presented at the Fifteenth Annual Meeting of the Association for the Study of Higher Education, Portland, November.

Maxwell, J., and S. Currie, 1984. *Partnership for Growth.* Montreal: Corporate–Higher Education Forum.

McFarland, Laurel. 1993. Top-up student loans: American models of student aid and British public policy. *Oxford Studies in Comparative Education* 3:49–67.

McMahon, Walter W. 1982. Externalities in education. Unpublished manuscript, University of Illinois, Urbana-Champaign.

MEGA Documents. 1971. Washington, D.C.: U.S. Department of Health, Education, and Welfare, mimeographed.

Melman, Seymour. 1982. *Profits without Production.* New York: Knopf.

Merton, Robert K. 1942. Science and technology in a democratic order. *Journal of Legal and Political Sociology* 1:115–26.

Michael, Steve O., and Edward A. Holdaway. 1992. Entrepreneurial activities in postsecondary education. *Canadian Journal of Higher Education* 22:15–40.

Miller, Henry. 1995. States, economies and the changing labour process of academics: Australia, Canada, and the United Kingdom. *Academic Work* 40–49.

Miller, Howard F., Jr. 1976. Institutional and departmental adaptations and the steady state. Ph.D. diss., Pennsylvania State University.

Minasian, Jora R. 1962. Economics of research and development. *The Rate and Direction of Inventive Activity.* National Bureau of Economic Research. Princeton: Princeton University Press.

———. 1969. Research and development, production functions, and rates of return. *American Economic Review* Proceedings Issue 2:80–85.

Mowery, David C. 1994. *Science and Technology Policy in Interdependent Economies.* Dordrecht: Kluwer Academic Publishers.

National Center for Education Statistics. 1993. *Digest of Education Statistics.* Washington, D.C.: U.S. Department of Education.

———. 1995. *The Condition of Education.* Washington, D.C.: U.S. Department of Education.

National Science Foundation. 1983. *Science and Engineering Indicators, 1993,* Appendix Table 4.12. Washington, D.C. U.S. Government Printing Office.

———. 1989. *Industrial Participation in NSF Programs and Activities.* Washington, D.C.: U.S. Government Printing Office.

———. 1993. *Federal Funds for Research and Development: Federal Obligations for Research by Agency and Detailed Field of Science and Engineering. Fiscal Years 1971–1993.* Washington, D.C.: National Science Foundation. Prepared by Quantum Research Corporation.

Neave, Guy. 1988. Education and social policy: Demise of an ethic or change of values? *Oxford Review of Education* 14:273–83.

Neave, Guy, and Frans A. Vught. 1991. *Prometheus Bound: The Changing Relationship between Government and Higher Education in Western Europe.* Elmsford, N.Y.: Pergamon Press.

Newson, Janice. 1994. Subordinating democracy: The effects of fiscal retrenchment and university-business partnerships on knowledge creation and knowledge dissemination in universities. *Higher Education* 27:141–61.

Noble, David. 1976. *America by Design: Science, Technology, and the Rise of Corporate Capitalism.* New York: Knopf.

O'Connor, James. 1973. *Fiscal Crisis of the State.* New York: St. Martin's.

Omenn, G. 1982. Taking university research into the marketplace. *New England Journal of Medicine* 307:694–700.

Organization for Economic Cooperation and Development. 1990a. *Financing Higher Education: Current Patterns.* Washington, D.C.: OECD.

———. 1990b. *Higher Education in California.* Washington, D.C.: OECD.

Oxley, Howard, and John P. Martin. 1991. Controlling government spending and deficits: Trends in the 1980s and prospects for the 1990s. *OECD Economic Studies* 17:145–201.

Perkin, Harold J. 1989. *The Rise of Professional Society in England since 1880.* London: Routledge.

Peters, Barbara H., and Jim L. Peters. 1991. *Total Quality Management.* New York: New York Conference Board.

Peters, Lois, and Herbert Fusfeld. 1982. Current U.S. university research connections. In *University-Industry Research Relationships,* edited by the National Science Board, 1–161, Washington, D.C.: Government Printing Office.

Peters, Michael. 1992. Performance and accountability in "post-industrial society": The crisis of British universities. *Studies in Higher Education* 17:123–39.

Peters, Thomas J., and Robert H. Waterman. 1982. *In Search of Excellence.* New York: Harper and Row.

Pfeffer, Jeffrey. 1992. *Managing with Power: Politics and Influence in Organizations.* Boston: Harvard Business School Press.

Pfeffer, Jeffrey, and Gerald R. Salancik. 1978. *External Control of Organizations: A Resource Dependence Perspective.* New York: Harper and Row.

Phillips, Kevin. 1993. *Boiling Point: Democrats, Republicans, and the Decline of Middle Class Prosperity.* New York: Random House.

Philpott, Rodger F. 1994. Commercializing the university: The costs and benefits of the entrepreneurial exchange of knowledge and skills. Ph.D. diss., University of Arizona, Tucson.

Porter, Michael. 1990. *The Comparative Advantage of Nations.* New York: Free Press.

Pratt, John. 1992. Unification of higher education in the United Kingdom. *European Journal of Education* 27:29–43.

President's Council of Advisors on Science and Technology (PCAST). 1992. *Renewing the Promise: Research Intensive Universities and the Nation.* Washington, D.C.: The White House.

Pusey, Michael. 1991. *Economic Rationalism in Canberra: A Nation Building Society Changes Its Mind.* Cambridge, U.K.: Cambridge University Press.

Rahm, D. 1994. U.S. universities and technology transfer: Perspectives of academic administrators and researchers. *Industry and Higher Education* June:72–78.

Reich, Robert B. 1991. *The Work of Nations: Preparing Ourselves for Twenty-first Century Capitalism.* New York: Knopf.

Rhoades, Gary. 1997. *Managed Professionals: Restructuring Academic Labor in Unionized Institutions.* Albany, N.Y.: State University of New York Press.

Rhoades, Gary, and Sheila Slaughter. 1991a. The public interest and professional labor: Research universities. In *Culture and Ideology in Higher Education: Advancing a Critical Agenda,* edited by William G. Tierney, 187–211. New York: Praeger.

———. 1991b. Professors, administrators, and patents: The negotiation of technology transfer. *Sociology of Education* 64:65–77.

———. 1996. From balance wheel to cogwheel: The National Science Foundation from 1970 to 1995. Unpublished manuscript, University of Arizona, Tucson.

Rhoades, Gary, and Donald Smart. 1996. The political economy of entrepreneurial culture in higher education: Policies towards foreign students in Australia and the United States. In *Comparative Perspectives on the Social Role of Higher Education,* edited by Ken Kempner and William Tierney, 125–60. New York: Garland Publishing.

Rifkin, Jeremy. 1995. *The End of Work: The Decline of the Global Labor Force and the Dawn of the Post-market Era.* New York: G. P. Putnam's Sons.

Robins, Kevin, and Frank Webster. 1985. Higher education, high tech, high rhetoric. *Radical Science Journal* 18:36–57.

Rosenthal, Kenneth, and Christine A. Fung. 1990. Technology survey of twenty universities. *Les Nouvelles* 25:133–37.

Sakakibara, Eisuke. 1993. *Beyond Capitalism: The Japanese Model of Market Economics.* Lanham, Md.: University Press of America.

Sassen, Saskia. 1991. *The Global City: New York, London, Tokyo.* Princeton: Princeton University Press.

Schumpeter, Joseph. 1934. *The Theory of Economic Development.* Cambridge, Mass.: Harvard University Press.

Science Council of Canada. 1987. *Winning in a World Economy: Canadian Universities and Economic Revival.* Ottawa: Science Council of Canada.

Secretary of State for Education and Science. 1987. *Higher Education: Meeting the Challenge.* London: HMSO, Cmnd. 114:iv.

Shattock, Michael. 1989. Thatcherism and British higher education: Universities and the enterprise culture. *Change* 21:31–39.

———. 1994. *The UGC and the Management of British Universities.* London: Society for Research into Higher Education and Open University Press.

Shattock, Michael, and Robert O. Berdahl. 1984. The British University Grants Committee 1919–83: Changing relationships with government and universities. *Higher Education* 13:471–99.

Silva, E. T., and S. Slaughter. 1984. *Serving Power: The Making of the American Social Science Expert.* Westport, Conn.: Greenwood.

Skolnik, Michael. 1983a. Will high technology save higher education from decline? *Canadian Journal of Higher Education* 13:71–77.

———. 1983b. The university and manpower planning: A reexamination of the issues in light of changing economic conditions and new developments in labour market information. *Canadian Journal of Higher Education* 13:77–95.

———. 1987. The shell game called system rationalization: The politics and economics of retrenchment in the Ontario university system. *Higher Education* 16:155–71.

———. 1990. Lipset's "continental divide" and the ideological basis for differences in higher education between Canada and the United States. *Canadian Journal of Higher Education* 20:81–93.

Slaughter, Sheila. 1987. New York State and the politics of public spending. *Higher Education* 16:173–97.

———. 1990. *Higher Learning and High Technology: Dynamics of Higher Education Policy Formation.* Albany, N.Y.: State University of New York Press.

———. 1993. Retrenchment in the 1980s: The politics of prestige and gender. *Journal of Higher Education* 64:250–82.

———. 1994. Dirty little cases?: Problems in academic freedom, governance, and professionalization. In *Academic Freedom: An Everyday Concern*, edited by Ernst Benjamin and Donald Wagner, 58–75. San Francisco: Jossey-Bass.

Slaughter, Sheila, and Gary Rhoades. 1990. Renorming the social relations of academic science: Technology transfer. *Educational Policy* 4:341–61.

———. 1993. Changes in intellectual property statutes and policies at a public university: Revising the terms of professional labor. *Higher Education* 26:287–312.

———. 1996. The emergence of a competitiveness research and development policy coalition and the commercialization of academic science and technology. *Science, Technology, and Human Values* 21:303–39.

Smith, Bruce L. R., and Joseph J. Karlesky, 1977. *The State of Academic Science: The Universities in the Nation's Research Effort.* New Rochelle, N.Y.: Change Magazine Press.

Smyth, John, ed. 1995. *Academic Work: The Changing Labour Process in Higher Education.* London: Society for Research into Higher Education and Open University Press.

Stahler, Gerald J., and William R. Tash. 1994. Centers and institutes in the research university. *Journal of Higher Education* 65:540–54.

Starr, Paul. 1982. *Social Transformation of American Medicine.* New York: Basic Books.

State Higher Education Executive Officers. 1994. Higher education delivery systems in the twenty-first century. *Redesign* 1:1–4.

Statistics Canada. 1992. CANSIM Cross-Classified Database, Table 00590207. Ontario, Canada: Department of Education, Culture, and Tourism.

Stauffer, Thomas. 1986. The responsibilities of public universities for economic development. In *Issues in Higher Education and Economic Development*, 73–79. Washington, D.C.: American Association of State Colleges and Universities.

Terleckyj, Nestor E. 1974. *Effects of R&D on the Productivity Growth of Industries: An Exploratory Study*. Washington, D.C.: National Planning Association.

Thompson, James D. 1967. *Organizations in Action*. New York: McGraw-Hill.

Thrift, Nigel. 1987. The fixers: The urban geography of international commercial capital. In *Global Restructuring and Territorial Development*, edited by J. Henderson and M. Castells. London: Sage.

Thurow, Lester. 1980. *The Zero Sum Society: Distribution and the Possibilities for Economic Change*. New York: Basic Books.

———. 1985. *The Zero Sum Solution: Building a World Class Economy*. New York: Simon and Schuster.

Touraine, Alain. 1974. *The Post-industrial Society: Tomorrow's Social History. Classes, Conflicts, and Culture in the Programmed Society*. London: Wildwood House.

Trow, Martin. 1992. Thoughts on the white paper of 1991. *Higher Education Quarterly* 46:213–26.

Turpin, T., and S. Hill. 1991. Boundaries of creation: Observations on the impact of the unified national system on higher education research cultures. *Higher Education Research and Development Society of Australasia: News* November:42–54.

Tyson, Laura D'Andrea. 1992. *Who's Bashing Whom: Trade Conflicts in High Technology Industries*. Washington, D.C.: Institute for International Economics.

Universities: Towers of gabble. *Economist* December 25, 1993–January 4, 1994:72–74.

U.S. Congress, Office of Technology Assessment. 1984. *Technology, Innovation, and Regional Economic Development*. Washington, D.C.: U.S. Government Printing Office.

———. 1991. *Biotechnology in a Global Economy*. BA-494. Washington, D.C.: U.S. Government Printing Office.

U.S. Department of Commerce, Technology Administration. 1995. *Delivering Results: A Progress Report from the National Institute of Standards and Technology*, revised ed. Gaithersburg, Md.: National Institute of Standards and Technology.

Useem, Michael. 1984. *The Inner Circle: Large Corporations and the Rise of Business Political Activity in the U.S. and U.K.* New York: Oxford University Press.

Varma, Roli. 1995. Restructuring corporate R&D: From autonomous to linkage model. *Technology Analysis and Strategic Management* 7:231–47.

Volk, Cynthia E. 1995. Assessing competing models of resource allocation at a public Research I University through multivariate analyses of state financing. Ph.D. diss., University of Arizona, Tucson.

Wasser, Henry. 1990. Changes in the European university: From traditional to entrepreneurial. *Higher Education Quarterly* 44:110–22.

Weber, Max. 1958. *The Protestant Ethic and the Spirit of Capitalism*. New York: Scribner.

Weiner, Charles. 1986. Universities, professors, and patents: A continuing controversy. *Technology Review* February/March:33–43.

———. 1987. Patenting and academic research: Historical case studies. *Science, Technology, and Human Values* 12:50–62.

White Paper. 1993. *Realizing our Potential: Strategy for Science, Engineering, and Technology*. London: HMSO.

Wilger, Andrea K., and William F. Massy. 1993. Prospects for restructuring: A sampling of the faculty climate. *Policy Perspectives* 5:1–4.

Williams, Gareth L. 1992. *Changing Patterns of Finance in Higher Education.* London: Society for Research into Higher Education and Open University Press.

―――. 1995. Reforms and potential reforms in higher education finance. In *Through a Glass Darkly,* edited by D. Dill and B. Sporn. Oxford, U.K.: Pergamon Press.

Winston, Gordon C. 1994. The decline in undergraduate teaching. *Change* 26:8–15.

Wolfle, Dael Lee. 1972. *The Home of Science: The Role of the University.* New York: McGraw-Hill.

Wood, Fiona Q. 1992. The commercialisation of university research in Australia: Issues and problems. *Comparative Education* 28:293–313.

Wood, Fiona Q., V. Lynn Meek, and Grant Harman. 1992. The research grant application process: Learning from failure? *Higher Education* 24:1–23.

World Bank. 1993. *The East Asian Miracle: Economic Growth and Public Policy.* Washington, D.C.: The World Bank.

Wyatt, Joe B. 1984. Witness testimony at U.S. Congress, House Committee on Science and Technology, Subcommittee on Investigations and Oversight. *Congressional Record* 98th Cong., 1st sess., 53–75.

INDEX

academic, defined, 9n
academic capitalism: defined, 8–12, 209–10, 217; and distribution of power within research universities, 226–33; epistemology of, 21; future implications of, 242–45; and undergraduate education in U.S. public research universities, 233–42
academic entrepreneurism, 9, 210
Academic Work (Smyth), 2
Advanced Technology Program (U.S.), 7, 35, 56, 188n, 207, 224, 228
Africa, and theories of globalization, 36
Alexander, Robert (head of CPR), 155–56, 160, 162, 192–93
Asia: and Australian higher education policy, 49; and Hearing Aid CRC, 156; and theories of globalization, 31, 32, 33, 34, 36
Australia: and convergence of higher education policies, 55–62 passim; entrepreneurial academic units in, 116–19; globalization and higher education in, 37, 210–13 passim; incidence of academic capitalism in universities in, 217–19; institutional financial policies influencing academic capitalism in, 134–37; and international changes that shape higher education, 13, 15; pace and timing of move toward academic capitalism in, 13; recognizing market potential of science, 184–86; research, basic and applied in, 182–84; research emphasis on, 12, 13, 209; resource dependence and changing patterns of national higher education finance in, 216; responses to political economic change and resource dependence, 16–21; scope of change in, 2, 7, 208; strategies of institutional leaders and center and department heads in, 219–22; and theories of globalization, 32, 33, 35. *See also* financing higher education, in Australia; national

higher education policies, Australian; technology transfer, strategies, at Australian centers
Australian Research Council (ARC), 107n, 150, 151–52, 167, 183, 216
Australian Vice-chancellors Committee (AVCC), 238
autonomy, 68–71

Baldwin, Michael (Australian junior minister of higher education), 196
Barnett, Ronald (and Middlehurst), 70
Bayh-Dole Act (U.S.), 45, 188n
Bell Laboratories, 223
benefits, 115–34 passim; consulting, 124; contributed services, 125–26; employment, of students, 124–25, 127; equipment gains, 126–27; external relations, 122; other benefits, 127–28; prestige, 122–23; recruitment: —faculty / staff, 127; — student, 125; spillovers: —to research, 123; — to teaching, 123–24. *See also* costs
block grant funding, 65, 68–71, 73–74, 76–111
Bollag, Burton, 225
Breneman, David, 1, 70, 208, 227, 233, 239
Brint, Steven, 141, 174, 175n. 10, 176, 218
Buchbinder, Howard (and Newson), 2, 208
Bush administration (U.S.), 47
Bush, Vannevar, 181
Business–Higher Education Forum (U.S.), 45, 52
Business / Higher Education Round Table (Australia), 51

Campbell, Teresa, 121n. 1, 131n, 233
Canada: and convergence of higher education policies, 55, 60; — exceptions, 24, 37, 54, 60, 61–62, 211; globalization and higher

271

The Library Of Congress has cataloged the hardcover edition of this book as follows:

Slaughter, Sheila.
    Academic capitalism : politics, policies, and the entrepreneurial
university / Sheila Slaughter and Larry L. Leslie.
    p.   cm.
    Includes bibliographical references (p.   ) and index.
    ISBN 0-8018-5549-7 (alk. paper)
    1. Education, Higher—Economic aspects. 2. College teachers—
Economic conditions. 3. Higher education and state. 4. Education,
Higher—Political aspects. 5. Technology transfer. I. Leslie,
Larry L. II. Title.
LC67.6.S53   1997
378.1′21—dc21   96-49956

ISBN 0-8018-6258-2 (pbk.)